S0-AWQ-617

CHASING THE DRAGON

CHASING THE

DRAGON

Into the Heart of the
Golden Triangle

CHRISTOPHER R. COX

A MARIAN WOOD / OWL BOOK

HENRY HOLT AND COMPANY

NEW YORK

Henry Holt and Company, Inc.
Publishers since 1866
115 West 18th Street
New York, New York 10011

Henry Holt® is a registered
trademark of Henry Holt and Company, Inc.

Copyright © 1996 by Christopher R. Cox
All rights reserved.
Published in Canada by Fitzhenry & Whiteside Ltd.,
195 Allstate Parkway, Markham, Ontario L3R 4T8.

Library of Congress Cataloging-in-Publication Data
Cox, Christopher R.
Chasing the dragon: into the heart of the Golden Triangle /
Christopher R. Cox.
p. cm.
1. Golden Triangle (Southeastern Asia)—Description and travel.
2. Opium trade—Golden Triangle (Southeastern Asia)   I. Title.
DS526.9.C69   1996   96-12398
959.1—dc20   CIP

ISBN 0-8050-5507-X

Henry Holt books are available for special promotions and
premiums. For details contact: Director, Special Markets.

First published in hardcover in 1996 by
Henry Holt and Company, Inc.

First Owl Book Edition—1997

A Marian Wood / Owl Book

Designed by Kate Nichols
Maps designed by Jeffery L. Ward

Printed in the United States of America
All first editions are printed on acid-free paper. ∞

1   3   5   7   9   10   8   6   4   2

"Who'll Stop the Rain," words and music by John C. Fogerty
of Creedence Clearwater Revival, © Jondora Music,
courtesy of Fantasy, Inc.

To my parents,
Gerald and Nancy,
for the gift of wanderlust
and to my wife, Maria,
for granting the visa

Come not between the dragon and his wrath.

—SHAKESPEARE, *KING LEAR*, I, i, 124

A great man's sword is never blunt.

—BURMESE PROVERB

CONTENTS

SOUTHEAST ASIA

BHUTAN

INDIA

CHINA

BANGLADESH

Salween River

Mekong River

KACHIN STATE

Irrawaddy River

Lashio

Mandalay

B U R M A

SHAN STATE

GOLDEN TRIANGLE

Red River

Dien Bien Phu

Hanoi

Keng Tung

Pagan

Taunggyi

Salween River

L A O S

Gulf of Tonkin

KARENNI STATE

Ho Mong

Mae Hong Son

THAI-BURMA BORDERLANDS

Chiang Mai

Vientiane

Mekong River

V I E T N A M

Sittang River

Rangoon

KAREN STATE

Ping River

T H A I L A N D

Andaman Sea

Chao Phraya River

CAMBODIA

Phan Rang

N

Bangkok

Phnom Penh

Saigon

Gulf of Thailand

Mekong River Delta

0   200 km

0   300 miles

South China Sea

MALAYSIA

SUMATRA (INDONESIA)

SINGAPORE

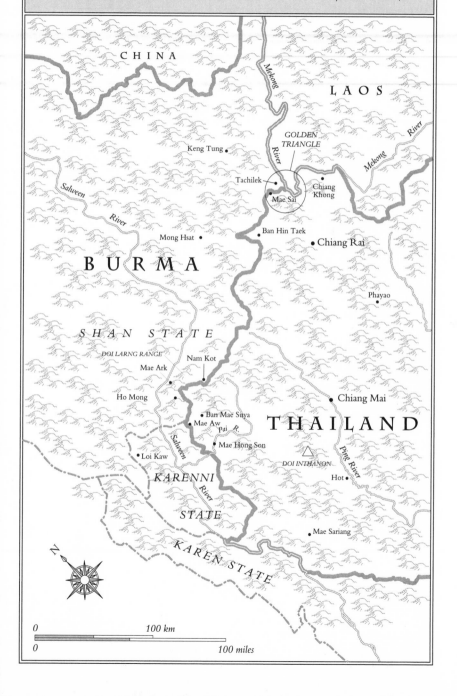

THAI-BURMA BORDERLANDS

CHINA

LAOS

Mekong River

Keng Tung

GOLDEN TRIANGLE

Mekong

Tachilek

Chiang Khong

Salween

Mae Sai

River

Mong Hsat

Ban Hin Taek

Chiang Rai

BURMA

Phayao

SHAN STATE

DOI LARNG RANGE

Nam Kot

Mae Ark

Ho Mong

Chiang Mai

Ban Mae Suya

Mae Aw

THAILAND

Pai R.

Saluween

Mae Hong Son

Loi Kaw

River

DOI INTHANON

Ping River

Hot

KARENNI

STATE

KAREN STATE

Mae Sariang

N

| 0 | | 100 km |

| 0 | | 100 miles |

CHASING THE DRAGON

PROLOGUE

The hilltribe women back slowly through the sloping fields. Bulbs the size of bird's eggs sway atop vein-thin, chest-high stalks, dancing in the soft highland breeze like tentacles of a poisonous sea anemone. In the late-morning glare, the women work carefully, mindful of their harvest's value. The earth is soft and warm beneath their feet, which rustle the dead ruby- and amethyst-colored petals blanketing the mountainside.

Wielding curved, tri-bladed knives as sharp as an eagle's talons, they gently pinch the poppy pods between thumbs and forefingers and make quick, vertical incisions. In the heat of a brass-brilliant winter sun, tears of chalk-white sap soon well in the shallow cuts. Opium. The latex will ooze during the day; the droplets will coagulate and darken overnight. The next morning, while it is still cool, the women will return to painstakingly scrape the henna-colored gum from the pods with semicircular blades, then deposit the treasure into metal cans hanging from their necks like amulets.

This year, the spirits have smiled upon their mountain village. The earth the menfolk ate the previous spring to test its quality had been sweet with alkaline. A good place to burn the forest for the mineral-rich ash. The summer monsoon watered the cover crop of maize; autumn, dry and cool, was perfect for the poppy seedlings. The women descend through the fields. Gradually, their metal cans grow heavy with the weight of the blackened beads that bring both dreams and despair. Beneath their burden, the women smile. There will be opium enough to barter for salt, sugar, tobacco, and cloth. They know not where the opium goes, only that it brings merchants to their distant huts, that the fruit of their fields is coveted by the powerful men whose soldiers walk the dragon-toothed mountains. They know their hard, simple life will endure another year. Their ancestors knew the same rituals, endured the same risks, kowtowed to the same unseen, omnipotent warlords. It has always been thus in a land as wild as the waves of a raging typhoon.

―――――

In January 1996, Khun Sa, the most powerful, most infamous warlord in this lawless region, announced he had peacefully relinquished his control of the opium trade to become a private citizen and legitimate businessman. The following account is of a series of journeys through the shadowlands of the Golden Triangle on the eve of Khun Sa's "retirement."

Boston, Massachusetts
June 1996

Objective, Burma!

The night brought no dreams. There was only an infuriating half-sleep, with the promise of relief dangling just beyond reach, like a precious jewel. Twelve thousand miles of air travel, one dozen time zones crammed into five flights over two days, had created a chasm of anxiety spanned only by a few frayed nerves.

Mae Hong Son, Thailand, at three o'clock in the morning of March 2, 1994—or was it three in the afternoon of March 1? A hotel candle glowed in an opalescent pool of its own warm, milt-colored wax. Its shrine-like light bathed the Baiyoke Chalet's teakwood paneling and the cheap nightstand heaped with cracker boxes and a trio of amber, empty Singha beer bottles, a small offering to the god of jet-lagged travelers.

Must sleep. A quarter tab of Xanax would help. A half tab had been good for eight drooling hours between Detroit and Tokyo. Was that technically yesterday? The word would come at four o'clock, the truck for the mule camp at five. We'd be saddled up and on the old smuggling trail before six. Any later and the Thai Border Patrol Police would have us. Tomorrow night the sleep would come. With effort, with luck, with a wad of Thai *baht*, tomorrow night would be spent in Burma, in the forbidden Shan State, inside the fortress of Khun Sa, the world's most powerful druglord. Can't miss the word. No Xanax, not even a bump. Not for the world. The King of Opium waited for no one.

I should have slept like a drugged Romantic poet. I had stumbled through the day, a somnambulist. The morning Thai Airways flight from Chiang Mai to Mae Hong Son had been canceled—poor visibility. It happened every spring in Mae Hong Son, this distant town in northwestern Thailand whose civic boosters had nicknamed "The City above the Clouds." A more truthful slogan would have been "The City Obscured by Clouds." The persistent mountain fogs were now compounded by smoke and ash as nomadic hilltribes—Lisu, Lahu, Akha, and Hmong—slashed and then burned the forest before planting crops of upland rice and maize, melons and gourds, barley and illegal opium poppies.

Finally, in the warm mid-afternoon, the ATR-72 turboprop was able to fly through the purplish haze. The 2,590-meter peak of Doi Inthanon, Thailand's highest mountain, jutted like a South Seas island from the foamy surf of cirrus clouds and smoke from freshly set hilltribe swidden fires. On the sweeping, final approach, the twin-engine plane skirted forested summits, banked hard to port a few hundred yards from a temple-topped mountain, then bounced down the runway on the edge of town. Mae Hong Son: the last outpost of order and lawful authority, the last stoplight until Taunggyi, Burma, nearly two hundred miles to the northwest. In between lay bad country, the rugged, anarchic mountains of Shan State, one of the least known regions of one of the world's most xenophobic nations. This was my ultimate destination: the land of opium dreams, where poppies bloomed on a thousand hillsides.

A one-stoplight town, Mae Hong Son was the drowsy seat of

Thailand's most remote province. Not until 1965 did a paved road connect Mae Hong Son with Chiang Mai. Even today, the two-hundred-mile drive over buckled, washed-out Highway 108, negotiating a thousand switchbacks while tempting head-on collisions around every blind curve, was not to be undertaken lightly. The forty-minute flight to get here had been bumpy, but less so than the poor roads would have been. And at 345 baht (less than $14) it had to rank among the world's cheapest airfares.

My sidekick, Jay F. Sullivan, a corporate employee–benefits broker with an unquenchable thirst for adventure, and I had alighted in a trekker's mecca. There were elephants to ride through pristine forest and around impossibly scenic karstic massifs that erupted out of emerald-green paddy fields. Motorized dugouts carried *farang*, the all-purpose Thai term for foreigners, down the tea-colored Pai River to gawk at the Padaung women whose elongated necks were wrapped in and supported by brass coils. However, we had a business agenda to pursue, not a packaged-adventure tour. But first we needed to eat. We carbo-loaded a mound of *pad thai* at the Fern Restaurant, where trees sprouted through the boards of the raised, open-air deck. Keep it simple. Never drink the water and avoid the house specialties: grilled fatty pork, grilled tough beef, and fish maw spicy salad. The trail to Burma was not lined with Portosans.

To walk off dinner we perambulated Jongkhum Lake, the centerpiece of Mae Hong Son. Thai lovers strolled along the shoreline while trekkers gathered in the lakeside restaurants. Along the southern edge of the pond, the ancient gilt-and-whitewashed *stupa* of Wat Chong Kham was strung with electric lights. Under the cheap effect, the dignified temple resembled a fantastic spacecraft in a low-budget science-fiction film. Sullivan and I stopped at a waterfront gazebo to watch children buy two-baht bags of fish food, then toss the gray pellets to tame perch. The lake's inky surface erupted into a roiling mass of flashing, tarnished silver. A diminutive Lisu girl with a sackful of textiles hovered near the cafes. Her flowery clothing was her best advertisement: magenta-colored pants and shirt trimmed in bands of yellow and blue, topped by a sleeveless, knee-length tunic of black, soft green, and royal blue, and an intricately embroidered sash.

The hilltribe girl approached and shyly displayed her handi-work, cloth bracelets and charm bags. She smiled, showing teeth blackened by betel juice, and spoke in a birdlike voice reeking of pungent *nam plaa* fish sauce.

"*Sip* baht."

Too tired to haggle, I gave her the small, quarter-sized coin worth about forty cents and took a tiny black embroidered bag that could hold only a small amulet. Somewhere, somehow, I'd fill it with the luck I'd need for tomorrow.

Back at the Baiyoke Chalet, as Sullivan dozed I mulled the advice I'd been given by a Western photographer, an Army veteran who had come down with malaria and typhoid fever during his brief visit to Shan State: "I highly advise you to keep your head up. There is a potential for a lot of misery in your life. You're going into a biological environment you can't even imagine. You're going to Burma, my friend. More Americans have been to the moon than where you're going. You're going into a war zone."

Like the ghostly mist clinging to the surrounding mountains, the discouraging words could not be shaken even now, in the still, predawn hours.

More Americans have been to the moon than where you're going.

Don't sleep. Wait for the word.

━━━━━

What little I knew about Burma I owed to the rainy, television-free days of my peripatetic, Navy-brat childhood. In distant military bases in the Aleutian Islands and the Panama Canal Zone, I pored through my father's old *National Geographic*s, four decades worth of African safaris, topless Amazon maidens, and Spam ads. For a boy weaned on the adventure tales of Rudyard Kipling and Arthur Ransome, Burma was a vision of crumbling temples, lazy rivers, timber elephants, and giraffe-necked women. Now, as I neared forty, *The Jungle Book* and *Missee Lee* were still my Baedeker's guide to the Orient.

When I determined to travel to Burma, I had combed the bookstores and academic libraries of Boston and Cambridge, Massachusetts. The shelves held few books about this enigmatic nation wedged between India, China, and Thailand. As for Shan State, wasn't that a mediocre college somewhere in the Midwest? If Burma was an exotic mystery to all but the most worldly, well-read American travelers, Shan State was a complete cipher. The few books and monographs about the region were musty and brittle, obscure and out of print. Even before 1962, when General Ne Win led a military coup that effectively sealed Burma from outside influence for the following quarter century, few foreigners, beyond a handful of British civil servants and a smattering of Italian and American missionaries, had lived or traveled extensively in the Shan hills.

The area's most recognizable feature was the Burma Road— a three-hundred-mile lifeline hacked out of the jungles and mountains in 1938 to connect Siakwan in China's Yunnan Province with the railhead at Lashio in the north of Shan State and used to carry supplies to the Chinese army after Japanese forces had captured the coastal ports. Thai and Japanese troops later occupied Shan State, but the brutal fighting that characterized the World War II Burma theater, portrayed so indelibly in Hollywood films such as *Objective, Burma!*, *Never So Few*, and *Merrill's Marauders*, occurred hundreds of miles away in Kachin

State, the fabled Land of Jade. Shan State hardly rated a mention in the histories of the campaign.

My armchair-traveler's Bible, *National Geographic*, provided little enlightenment. The most recent feature on the country, in a 1984 issue, barely mentioned Shan State. For two other stories, a 1974 feature on the leg-rowers of Inle Lake and a 1963 overview of Burma, the magazine's writers and photographers could visit only the western fringes of Shan State controlled by the military government. Even in prewar Burma, when the country was part of the British Raj, Shan State rated scant coverage. Two intrepid *Geographic* writers did drive the length of the serpentine Burma Road in 1940, but devoted just two pages of their article to Shan State. Lashio, they noted, was sprinkled with "adventurers and beachcombers of all nationalities" and rife with disease, while the chaotic mountains held brigands and truculent hilltribes. Perhaps the endemic riff-raff, disease, and fierce natives explained the magazine's circumspect coverage. The *Geographic*'s last exclusive look at the region, an eight-page pictorial entitled "Shan Tribes Make Burma's Hills Flash With Color," appeared in 1931.

The earlier historical record was also spotty. Neighboring Burmese and Yunnanese had given Shan State a wide berth because the mountain valleys were thought to contain a poisonous morning gas that caused a fatal "trembling disease." In 1863, an English expedition was dispatched to the Salween River to explore the region for an alternate route to western China. Although the British officers traveled by elephant, the expedition soon found the terrain nearly impassable and the local people clearly inhospitable. The party struggled for two and a half weeks to reach the great river—a distance, as the large-billed crow flew, of less than sixty miles from their starting point in the foothills east of the Sittang River. Once along the great Salween, the explorers were advised to hold to the western bank, as the land beyond was wild and full of dacoits, the organized robber bands that infested the hills of Burma and India. Following the Salween and its tributaries northward, the party slogged on for another one hundred miles to the southern fringes of Shan State. There, further exploration was blocked by Burmese soldiers. Objective denied.

Two of the giants of English literature in colonial Asia, Kipling and George Orwell, shed no light on Shan State. Kipling, immortalizing Mandalay, the dusty royal capital with the magical name, had made the nation synonymous with Eastern exotica. Quite a feat, since he had spent but a few days in the country, yet could cast words that felt like warm, wistful rain upon the Asian landscape I imagined:

> *By the old Moulmein Pagoda, lookin' eastward to the sea,*
> *There's a Burma girl a-settin', and I know she thinks o' me;*
> *For the wind is in the palm-trees, and the temple bells they say:*
> *"Come you back, you British soldier; come you back to*
> *   Mandalay!"*

Orwell had the advantage of in-country experience with the Indian Imperial Police, a stint that inspired his novel, *Burmese Days*. The semiautobiographical book was notable for its anti-imperialism and its keen eye for the details of local life in a Kachin timber town. But Orwell had almost nothing to say about Shan State.

The best travel book ever written about Burma, Norman Lewis' *The Golden Land* (1952), did include several chapters about the author's adventures along the Burma Road, but that was in extreme northern Shan State, far from my objective. The most thorough Western accounts of southern Shan State were to be found in a trio of prewar British travelogues: W. Somerset Maugham's *The Gentleman in the Parlour* (1930);

Sir James Gordon Scott's memoir, *Burma and Beyond* (1932); and Maurice Collis's 1938 record, *Lords of the Sunset.*

In 1922, Maugham undertook a three-month tour through Burma, Siam, and French Indochina. Armed with a letter of introduction from Winston Churchill, Maugham and his lover/secretary, Frederick Gerald Haxton, set off from the hill station of Taunggyi on a four-hundred-mile journey by horseback through the heart of Shan State. The pair rode east for the trading town of Keng Tung, making only twelve to fifteen miles a day on the rough trail, chancing encounters with a half-dozen species of poisonous serpents (Burma led the world in snakebite mortality), man-eating tigers, bandits, and headhunting Wa tribesmen. It took Maugham and Haxton four weeks to arrive in Keng Tung, and after a week of Shan urban life, they left for Siam. Maugham's account barely hinted at the arduous physical demands and very real danger of the journey through Shan State. The logistics of such an adventure apparently did not interest the author, who traveled with steamer trunks, porters, a cook, and Marcel Proust's *Le côte de Guermantes.* Reading *The Gentlemen in the Parlour*, I was mindful of the scant daily progress Maugham made on established trails, of the secluded, primeval character of the land he traversed, and of the fact that, despite all the trappings of creature comfort, the writer had still contracted a near-fatal case of malaria in Shan State.

Scott, part of the line of great scholar-administrators that Britain posted to its nineteenth-century empire, came out to Rangoon in the late 1870s and was immediately smitten with the country. Blessed with a keen eye for detail and a mind free of colonial condescension, Scott produced the definitive Western work about local customs and habits, *The Burman: His Life and Notions*, published in 1882 under a pseudonym, Shwe Yoe (Burmese for "Golden Honest"). Four years later, in the immediate aftermath of the third—and conclusive—Anglo-Burmese war, Scott was sent to the newly acquired Shan State, where he served with distinction until 1910. In 1932, fifty years after publication of *The Burman*, he summoned his Shan experience to write *Burma and Beyond*, describing the hill-dwelling minority races that encircled the lowland Burmese.

For the dreamy, neophyte traveler, *Burma and Beyond* made for sobering reading. Scott described a land of staggeringly inaccessible terrain afflicted with pestilence and parasites, a fractious countryside that held brigands, feuding *saopha* princes, and suspicious, violent tribesmen condemned to a permanent condition of "bewildering crossfighting." The Wa, whom the Burmese called "man-bears," held a particular fascination for Scott. Of the two main groups of Wa, the "wild" ones were animists who settled in the distant reaches of northern Shan State. They lined the approaches to their fortified settlements with "skull avenues"—rows of stout posts topped with human heads—in the belief that the ghosts of decapitated men would remain nearby and ward off the evil, trespassing spirits that brought sickness to the village and failure to the fields. The wild Wa preferred strangers as their victims, believing their ghosts, unfamiliar with the area, would be unlikely to stray from the village. (The nominally Buddhist "tame" Wa avoided the messy details of head-hunting and bought skulls from their incorrigible cousins.) As befitted a bellicose people who grew opium as a cash crop and cultivated rice exclusively for liquor consumption, the wild Wa were not in complete accord about skull-avenue aesthetics. The issue had split the sect into two philosophical factions: the "wet heads" and the "dry heads." The former preferred fresh—"wet"—heads when it came time for spring planting and fertility rites; the latter group opted for "dry," seasoned skulls.

In 1893, Scott served as political officer on the lone British expedition to head-hunting country, a trip that dovetailed with the planting/head-taking season in the watershed between the Salween and Mekong Rivers. Barely into the Wa hills, the party encountered an avenue of dozens of skull-topped posts. Scott soon discovered fresh handiwork of the wet-head wild Wa: "Full in the middle of the path . . . a headless body was found lying, apparently killed where it was, for the body lay askew across the track. There was nothing in the way of mutilation except the missing head." The head-taking activity of these hard-working, if hard-drinking, farmers was hardly wanton. Rather, explained Scott, it was community-minded behavior intended to ensure good harvests and to discourage outside settlers, who had already displaced the tribe from northern Thailand and the Keng Tung region. "No Wa makes a collection of skulls as some people do of postage stamps, match-box labels, or pressed ferns," wrote Scott. "The Wa does it for the common good." And the best Wa paddy land had always been watered with the blood of strangers.

The third Western account, which was also the most effusive in its praise of Shan State, came from the pen of Maurice Collis, an Orientalist and author of three dozen books, including biographies of Marco Polo and Sir Thomas Stamford Raffles, the colonial administrator of Singapore. Collis had served as a British magistrate in Rangoon and, like Scott, was fascinated by the local people. His superiors discouraged his fraternization and eventually posted him to Mergui, in the remotest southern reaches of the colony. On Collis's journey through Shan State, he avoided the Wa territory that Scott had found so difficult. He also had the advantage over Maugham of making the passage from Taunggyi to Keng Tung by automobile instead of pony, although he described the route beyond the Salween River as the most difficult motor road in Asia. To Collis, the very inaccessibility of the region seemed a virtue, and he proceeded to champion its unspoiled attractions and, on the eve of World War II, its strategic importance: "The Shan States are in the imperial attic. Not one Englishman in ten thousand has ever heard of them. They have become our frontier to the fighting east; they are China's back door. Moreover, they are delightful states, an Arcadia of sorts, romantically far, the farthest off of all our land possessions, clean beyond India, on the high road to the world's end."

———

In Mae Hong Son, I realized that conditions in these isolated hills had changed little since the colonial days. Travel by horse or mule was still recommended throughout the borderlands. The few roads were choked with dust in the spring dry season and became quagmires during the summer monsoon. Burma retained its dubious honor as the world's leader in snakebite death. Malaria remained endemic. The area, in fact, was a petri dish for disease. Yaws, polio, hepatitis, cholera, yellow fever, blackwater fever, dengue fever, leprosy, scabies, amoebic dysentery, Japanese encephalitis, meningitis, and typhoid were not uncommon, according to the tropical-disease specialist who had enthusiastically injected me with various vaccines before my departure. Nor, sadly, was AIDS, the plague of the late-twentieth century. There did, however, seem a glimmer of progress in Shan State. The wet heads and the dry heads were sects of the past; the Wa had finally sworn off head-hunting a generation before. Discreet, knowledgeable outsiders still gave them wide berth.

You're going into a war zone.

No amount of preparation could help the footloose foreigner who contemplated a Shan State vacation. Re-creating the rambles of Maugham, Scott, or Collis was impossible; only the western periphery of Shan State near Inle Lake and

Taunggyi was open to Westerners. The remainder of the 62,500-square-mile region, an area only slightly smaller than Washington State, had been off-limits ever since the 1962 coup d'etat. General Ne Win, a one-time postal clerk who harbored a deep suspicion of the West, had isolated Burma behind a "lacquer curtain" and ruled with an iron hand until 1988. Borders were sealed, private businesses confiscated. An internal madness descended upon the promising nation. Ethnic Indians, the heart of the British civil service, were deported. For years, foreign visitors had been limited to one-day visas. Ne Win's egocentric experiment, "The Burmese Way to Socialism," had transformed Burma from a prewar Asian breadbasket to an international basket case worthy of United Nations' "least-developed nation" status by 1987. His quarter-century reign was a muddled mix of Marxism and xenophobia, corruption and terror, numerology and superstition. Since 1970, when his oracles determined that the left side of the road—the English side— was unlucky for Ne Win, Burmese motorists have driven on the right side. In 1987, believing that his fortunes were in decline, Ne Win countered with *koe nawin chay*—the power of the number nine. He decreed that Burma's largest-denomination currencies, the 75-, 35-, and 25-*kyat* notes, were worthless and replaced them with currencies—the 45- and 90-kyat bills—that were multiples of nine. This move, which immediately eliminated more than half of the money in circulation, proved too much for millions of his long-suffering, newly destitute, subjects. In the face of popular unrest, the Pyithu Tatmadaw, the Army of the People, intervened in 1988. Shooting or imprisoning thousands of unarmed protestors, they organized an Orwellian-sounding ruling council of generals: the State Law and Order Restoration Council (SLORC). Ne Win "retired" to a guarded, lakeside compound in a fashionable Rangoon suburb, becoming the éminence grise, wielding power from the shadows.

Like their paternalistic mentor, SLORC regarded the military as the "very heart and soul" of Burma. As such, army leaders occupied senior-level government positions and held an interest in any business enterprise of importance. SLORC also constricted the people as methodically as a python strangles its prey, buying more than $1 billion in Chinese arms and doubling the number of Tatmadaw troops. Only vise-like force could hold together Burma, a diverse cultural and geographic landscape of overwhelming social and political problems. The country was a bewildering mix of more than one hundred different racial, tribal, and ethnic groups strewn across the central Irrawaddy River valley, the immense delta intruding upon the Andaman Sea, and the horseshoe-shaped ring of mountains that sealed Burma hermetically from its neighbors. To preserve this fragile union, both Ne Win and SLORC strove to crush dissent, especially in the rugged ethnic strongholds of the Shan, Karen, and Karenni States. And so for more than thirty years, the mountains beyond Mae Hong Son had been a battlefield pitting the Burmese army, local militias, ethnic Shan rebels, aggrieved hilltribes, Communists, narco-insurgents, exiled Nationalist Chinese soldiers, and dacoits against one another in a series of often brief, always confusing, alliances. During the day, these scattered groups all claimed nominal control. No one ruled the night.

The candle on the nightstand flickered, sizzled, faded. The word would come soon. I turned on the overhead light. Sullivan, who possessed a rare talent for deep sleep under impossible circumstances, did not stir. Under the chrome-colored fluorescence boiling from the ceiling, I reconfirmed the priceless contents of my daypack:

Passport	Camera
Airplane tickets	Color and black and white film
Thai phrasebook	Nelles map of Burma
Baht	Swiss Army knife
Traveler's checks	Flashlight
Zip-Loc bags	Water canteen
Notebooks	Power Bars
Pens	Shaving kit
Tape recorder	Compass
Microcassettes	Lisu amulet bag
AA batteries	

The navy-blue daypack, my "boogie bag," would cling to my back like a leech. It held the essentials I would require in an emergency. My larger, camouflaged backpack, which held extra clothes and spare shoes, freeze-dried beef stew and canned tuna, trinkets and cigarettes, would be loaded onto a mule. The animal and its load could be abandoned should we need to "boogie," to make a run from soldiers, smugglers, or thieves on our early-morning foray into Burma.

There was little peace of mind to be found in my pocket-size Lonely Planet Thai phrasebook. The booklet did not translate Tai Yai, the related language of the Shan, or any of the babble of hilltribe dialects. Sections entitled "Small Talk," "Shopping," and "Food" were filled with inane conversation, but there weren't any listings for "Interrogation" or "Robbery," for the words that might smooth over the complications of an illegal border-crossing. Under the harsh hotel light, I scoured the pages and dog-eared the few helpful Thai phrases I might need later:

> *Rao mai pen khon farangseht.*
> We're not French.

Phom mai mii taang.
I don't have any cash.

Pen maak mai.
Is it serious?

I was going to Burma, to a war zone, to the moon, with a full backpack, a bullshit phrasebook, and an empty charm bag.

2

Always an Eagle

"Let's strap it on, buddy."

It wasn't yet four o'clock. Sullivan, my groggy partner, rolled out of his hotel bed, looked at the alarm clock in disbelief, then slipped into the same clothes he had worn since we had left Boston. There was no one to impress in Mae Hong Son, and clean shirts and pants were not to be frivolously worn. Clothing had to be rationed as carefully as food and water, Xanax, and Absolut vodka. Sullivan, the leader of Boy Scout Troop One in Dover, Massachusetts, was, as ever, prepared.

This was not the first time we had found ourselves in the outback of Thailand, far from the scenic beaches of Phuket or the sinful temptations of Bangkok. Our road to Burma, in fact, had begun less than two hundred miles to the east of Mae Hong Son, with a September 1991 trip to the Golden Triangle town of Chiang Khong. Then, I had come with Sullivan to Southeast Asia in pursuit of a quarry even more elusive than opium warlords.

In his youth, Sullivan had known these places: Indian country, where intrigue, insecurity, and death stalked a man through elephant grass and triple-canopy jungle. He thought he had seen the last of these badlands in 1971, the year he left Vietnam. Back in the world he married a general's daughter, started a family, and began a lucrative business career. Yet he could not shake the persistent ghosts of Asia. These phantoms were to be found in the blurred, grainy photographs of middle-aged men he believed were American prisoners of war, men he swore had been left behind in the ignominious cut-and-run from Southeast Asia. At work, at play, in the sleep that came once he muffled his head with a pillow—a wartime habit acquired to shut out the crump of fire-base howitzers—he could not avoid their cryptic stares. So, like a Victorian explorer, he plunged headlong into the tropical unknown, driven by obsession, compelled by the necessity for action and stoic self-deprivation.

Sullivan had come to Thailand to continue the exorcism. But Bangkok, an odalisque grown flabby and familiar, would no longer satisfy. The tempting new mistress was Chiang Khong, less than thirty miles east of the infamous Golden Triangle, the nexus of Thailand, Laos, and Burma. And so, on that September 1991 trip, we had foresaken Bangkok, crammed into a Toyota van at Don Muang International Airport, and bored northward along Highway 1 through the hot night and hotter day that followed. Along the five hundred miles to the borderlands, we chased boredom and fatigue with lukewarm Absolut and Coca-Cola and the tape-deck twang of Merle Haggard and Willie Nelson crooning "Seashores of Old Mexico"—redneck counterpoint to the endless Asian vista of rice paddies, water buffalo, and Lampang cattle. In the late morning, at the provincial capital of Phayao, our route broke northeast of Highway 1 onto a secondary road that followed the meandering Ing River nearly one hundred miles to its confluence with the Mekong. Every few minutes, the varicose, two-lane roadway bisected a small village shaded by the feathery leaves and dagger-like seedpods of tamarind trees, and a Buddhist *wat* would appear like a fantastic castle surrounded by a lake of green paddy. The landscape was immutable, familiar, ominous.

In his futile search, Sullivan had exhausted his life savings, jeopardized his insurance business, alienated his ex-wife, taken foolhardy chances that could have left his two teenaged children without a father. The way Sullivan saw it, he had no choice. Not since he was a teenager and had donned the olive-drab sash festooned with twenty-one merit badges, raised three fingers in the familiar salute, and pledged fealty to the oath laid down by Lord Baden-Powell, founder of the Boy Scouts. Honor. Duty. God. Country. The lessons learned in adolescence had served Jay Sullivan, Eagle Scout, well as he slouched toward middle age.

"There are no former Eagle Scouts," he was fond of telling me, a man who had washed out of scouting while barely a Tenderfoot. "You carry a responsibility and a liability with you for the rest of your life."

Responsibility and liability: the twin-edged sword repeatedly prodded Sullivan and his longtime partner, Cal Bowden, a tall, taciturn CPA from Tampa, Florida, to the Mekong River bordering Laos, a landlocked, hardline Communist country that had long been the hotspot of POW hunters. Bowden, who wasn't a veteran, had met Sullivan through a mutual acquaintance involved in the MIA issue. The two men had diametrically opposed personalities—Bowden was as laconic and laid-back as Sullivan was loquacious and impulsive—but they had struck up a close friendship cemented by frequent travel to Third World hellholes in their search for missing American soldiers. The burden of morality had exacted a financial cost upon both men. Bowden, who had funded an American POW hunter living in Bangkok, had taken a half-dozen trips there himself. He had also invested heavily in commercial real estate and the economic downturn in Florida, coupled with his POW-hunting expenses, had left him flirting with bankruptcy. As for Sullivan, in five years he had made eight pilgrimages to Thailand, and the journeys did not come cheap.

"Every time you get on that damn plane," he groused, "you figure it's gonna cost five grand. Minimum. But I've been bitten on the ass by the dragon. I can't give up."

Their hunt, begun in 1986, had netted fascinating material—photographs, I.D. cards, letters, dogtags, even a jawbone—but irrefutable evidence of a live American prisoner had eluded them. Along the slippery red-clay banks of the Mekong, hard truth flitted like the hazy silhouette cast by a shadow-puppet god. By the autumn of 1991, their funds were dwindling, and this trip was to be the last hurrah. A few months earlier, Sullivan had collared Patrick J. Purcell, the publisher of my newspaper, the Boston *Herald*, and poured out his story. In short order, the *Herald*'s editor, Kenneth A. Chandler, had pulled me out of the feature department and assigned me along for the ride. I would take a break from my steady diet of oddball assignments—Elvis impersonators, female private investigators, llama farmers—and have a real, ripping adventure. At worst, reasoned Chandler, the *Herald* would have a series about private cloak-and-dagger operations to run as a "curtainraiser" to the November 1991 Senate committee hearings on the POW/MIA issue, which were to be chaired by the junior senator from Massachusetts, Democrat John F. Kerry. At best—well, at best my tabloid could trumpet a worldwide scoop in sixty-point type: AMERICAN POWs RESCUED FROM HELL.

At the heart of Chandler's gamble was U.S. Army Captain Donald G. Carr, MIA in Southeast Asia for twenty years. The Green Beret had disappeared July 6, 1971, while flying a covert, armed reconnaissance mission over Attapu Province in extreme southeastern Laos. In the summer of 1991, a flurry of pictures of alleged POWs appeared in the media. All but one were quickly debunked. All but the photograph of a smiling, jug-eared, middle-aged man who bore a striking resemblance to Carr. The photo had been released to the press by Jack Bailey, a controversial POW hunter who divided his time between Garden Grove, California, where his family lived, and Bangkok, where he had set up his Thai girlfriend. The picture had caused a sensation among POW activists, Washington politicians, and Department of Defense brass. A respected forensic anthropologist, Michael Charney of Fort Collins, Colorado, using high-tech computer superimposition to compare Bailey's photo with preshootdown pictures of Carr, had pronounced, "I don't think it's the same man; I know it's the same man." Two official photo analyses done by Los Alamos National Laboratory and Sandia National Laboratories could not debunk the picture. The Carr photo immediately topped the Pentagon's investigation list.

What intrigued Chandler was that Jay Sullivan also possessed the Carr photo, which he had obtained months before Bailey had it published. Sullivan also had the same intelligence that Bailey was providing to the Pentagon in secret briefings. The two POW hunters, who had never met, shared another thing: their primary source. For both searchers, the conduit to the sewer world of private POW/MIA operations was Phoumano Nosavan. A Lao expatriate who lived in a villa in suburban Bangkok, Phoumano was a witty, urbane man who loved country-and-western music, had waterskiied the Mekong in pre-Pathet Lao days, had flown combat missions as a Royal Lao Air Force pilot, and now commanded an anti-Communist resistance group, the majestically titled United Front of Lao People for the Liberation of Laos. His late father, Phoumi

Nosavan, had been a right-wing general who briefly ran Laos courtesy of a CIA-rigged election. General Phoumi had gone on to amass a small fortune monopolizing the vice rackets in Vientiane before fleeing into comfortable Thai exile in 1965.

Phoumano, depending on the point of view, was either a true patriot dedicated to the liberation of his homeland, a wily politician like Cambodia's Prince Norodom Sihanouk, or a situational ethicist on the order of Captain Louis Renault in *Casablanca*. Sullivan, always the trusting Eagle Scout, considered Phoumano a patriot. The portly freedom fighter, whose search efforts Sullivan and Bowden underwrote with monthly checks for hundreds of dollars, *had* produced the precious Carr photo, he noted. And Phoumano had promising news to relay during our sweltering ride northward. We would hold secret meetings in Chiang Khong with men who claimed to hold POWs in off-limits Phong Saly Province in the far north of Laos. The Lao wanted to deal, said Phoumano, and the deal could include Carr. According to Phoumano, the Green Beret was now mentally unbalanced and imprisoned in a border camp about thirty miles northwest of Dien Bien Phu, Vietnam. Chiang Khong was a logical meeting place; it offered the quickest egress from Phong Saly Province to Thailand.

This was it, Sullivan kept saying. This was no drill, no fool's errand. The Carr photo was the smoking gun. Doctor Charney said so. The Carr family said so. Even the doubters that staffed the Pentagon's POW/MIA office could not shoot down the picture. This was the undeniable proof that live Americans were being held against their will in Southeast Asia. And if the Lao were serious and had brought American prisoners with them to the border, he and Bowden would find a way to close the deal.

"There's more circumstantial evidence to prove there are MIAs alive than there is to prove the existence of God,"

Sullivan said in his dramatic manner. "And I believe there is a God."

Sullivan was buoyed by a faith his government did not share. The Pentagon had remained unswayed, had discounted the fifteen hundred live-sighting reports of POWs filed since 1975. Only one serviceman, Air Force Colonel Charles Shelton, shot down over northern Laos in 1965, was listed as a prisoner of war. Shelton's designation was purely symbolic, meant to convince activists that Washington had not forgotten the men it allegedly left behind. Since the spring of 1973, when 591 Americans were released by North Vietnam during Operation Homecoming, only one American POW, Marine Private Robert Garwood, an accused collaborator, had come out of Indochina. In cold, hard, official numbers, the Department of Defense listed more than two thousand Americans as MIA in Southeast Asia.

Official United States policy did not discount the possibility of live American prisoners. But activists viewed the government's "highest national priority" status as so much lip service. Some private groups even accused Washington of a giant cover-up. Darker conspiracy theories—often involving the CIA, covert operations, and the heroin trade—were also prevalent. And people other than POW activists were doubtful: in a *Wall Street Journal* poll conducted a month before we departed for Chiang Khong, 69 percent of respondents said they believed U.S. servicemen were still imprisoned in Southeast Asia. For true believers such as Sullivan, there was no question but to chase wraiths and shadows all the way to the banks of the Mekong River.

Laos, with its porous border and its shady history, was the perfect venue for POW intrigue. During a decade-long secret war conducted by the CIA, more than five hundred servicemen— Army long-range reconnaissance patrols, Air Force pilots and forward air controllers, Air America crewmen—went missing in its mountains and jungles. Only nine men captured in Laos by the North Vietnamese were repatriated during Operation Homecoming. No Americans captured by the Communist-backed Pathet Lao, which during the war had publicly claimed to hold "some tens of prisoners," were ever released.

Until now, thought Sullivan. Until Donald Carr.

But at what cost? Old Bangkok hands could attest that nothing, absolutely nothing, in Southeast Asia was free. That was rule number one. The second ironclad truth: Nothing was what it seemed. And rule number three held the key to maintaining sanity in Thailand: Nothing ever went as planned. In accordance with rule number one, Sullivan and Bowden had paid for the cramped van and all the expenses for our entourage: Phoumano, a pair of drivers, and our bodyguard—a former Royal Lao Army officer we called The Captain, whose dessicated looks belied a killer's mien. The outlay of millions of baht had worked a miracle for the searchers, who believed they now had the first shot at making a deal for Carr. But rules two and three clouded Sullivan's mind. This was a land of smiles, façades, and surprises.

As we neared Chiang Khong on a hot September afternoon that held the humid residue of the 1991 monsoon, Sullivan opened his wallet and pulled out a Roman Catholic prayer card he had carried for most of his adult life. The crinkled, laminated card was an invocation to Saint Jude, the patron saint of hopeless causes.

Dear Lord, Sullivan thought, just give me a sign.

Chiang Khong was a two-wat town, with a main street that looked to have been paved sometime before the French abdicated Indochina. The cafe au lait–colored Mekong, full of flotsam, ruddy and swift with the summer monsoon runoff, was the town's lifeblood. It provided sustenance—including *plaa buk*, the giant Mekong catfish (*Pangasianodon gigas*) that could exceed ten feet in length and weigh nearly half a ton—and gave smugglers easy access to its twin city in Laos, Ban Houei Sai, a centuries-old ferrying point for trading caravans. Very little had changed in the town since the arrival of the first Europeans, a doomed French river expedition that came through Chiang Khong in 1867. Then as now, Chiang Khong was the limit of the Thai king's suzerainty. Upriver lay petty, primitive, feudal states where political strife was a constant and the authority of any distant monarch carried little weight. The area's most recent notoriety had come in the early 1970s, when Ban Houei Sai was the hub of the Golden Triangle's heroin industry and Chiang Khong was the convenient port of entry.

Motorized pirogues, dubbed *reua hong yao* (long-tail boats) for their lengthy propeller shafts, buzzed across the river, ferrying local passengers and their day-trip purchases. Along the single business block, a few shops displayed tiger teeth, hilltribe pipes, and silken Lao sarongs known as *sin*. A column of solemn, saffron-robed monks, each clutching a black umbrella, walked through the late-afternoon rain. Dining was no problem in Chiang Khong—there was only one restaurant. On the restaurant's stage, a two-man band backed a local beauty warbling Thai songs, including a minor hit by Phoumano's younger brother, now a Bangkok nightclub entertainer. On a restaurant television, elephants kicked a soccer ball. On the menu, only *khao phat kai*, fried rice with chicken, looked safe. A Western-looking black man entered the room, gave us the once-over, and took a seat in a dim corner by the door, where he was soon greeted effusively by a local Thai man. There were no tourist attractions to lure farang to this part of Thailand. The only draws were drugs and other contraband from nearby Laos.

"Just talk of tourist things," Phoumano whispered.

After a hurried dinner, we headed for our riverside "resort" hotel, a prefab building with a view of Ban Houei Sai and its moldering French colonial garrison, Fort Carnot. In town only a few hours, we were already an item. Word of farang traveled fast here, and Sullivan and Bowden wondered if the black man in the restaurant was Drug Enforcement Administration or, worse, CIA. Sullivan amended the three laws of Southeast Asia. Rule number four: There was no such thing as coincidence. It was my first trip to the East and I didn't know if his reaction was paranoia or prudence. Fearing an after-hours visit to our hotel room, Bowden rigged a homemade alarm system: he placed a small, plywood table against the door, then balanced a glass ashtray on the table's edge.

"Not that I'd know what to do if the glass ever broke," he drawled, then turned out the lights.

———

The sounds floated like ghosts across the morning mist that blanketed the Mekong. The crowing of roosters. The barking of dogs. The sputtering of a reua hong yao. The noises were distant and disembodied, yet proof of life in a small town in Laos. Likewise, the circumstantial evidence compiled by Sullivan and Bowden—the grainy photos, the scrawled letters, the cryptic prison rosters—was enough to convince them that somewhere beyond that thick shroud of fog, American POWs like Donald Carr were very much alive. And given the diplomatic inertia and bureaucratic red tape of Washington, and the actuarial tables for men they believed to be languishing in primitive jungle camps for decades, any rescue effort was morally justified.

I already knew that Sullivan, a self-described "tenacious bastard," would go to any extreme. He had started ten Boston Marathons and finished them all. He'd stalked brown bears in the Alaskan wilderness, refusing to quit until he bagged one. I was only surprised that he had never before infiltrated Laos on a covert operation with retired Army Lieutenant Colonel

James G. "Bo" Gritz, the old Green Beret who had mounted several cross-border forays during the early 1980s. (The exploits of Gritz's team would inspire an entire Hollywood subgenre—the Vietnam POW film—that included Chuck Norris's *Missing in Action* series.) But Sullivan and Bowden had chosen the businesslike, not the bellicose, approach. Rambo was not their m.o. They had spent nearly $300,000 of their own money and refused to work with the lone wolves, Army vets such as Vinnie Arnone and Mark Smith, who got the headlines and the on-camera face time with journalists covering the issue.

"It's easy to see why private efforts like ours haven't worked," sighed Bowden. We sat in the hotel's riverside pavilion, staring at a breakfast of canned Vienna sausages and runny fried eggs. "It's just been a comedy of errors."

There was no united front among the various private POW/MIA groups. Constant feuds erupted over conflicting motives and methods. There was little communication, less cooperation. The climate of self-interest bred deceit, and there were enough two-timing rogues to pack a bar in the Patpong, Bangkok's notorious red-light district. Con men passed off animal bones as human remains. Charlatans bilked families out of thousands of dollars for POW "rescue attempts." Activists such as Jack Bailey conducted emotionally charged fund-raising campaigns. Sullivan and Bowden had purchased their share of fakes, yet their steady, dogged approach had brought them, they were now sure, to the edge of success. Who could doubt the Carr photo? Say the right words, pay the proper people, and a POW might really come floating across the Mekong.

Our meeting with the Lao officials would take place in our twelve-dollar-a-night hotel room, where geckos clung to the walls and worms flowed from the faucet along with the discolored, unpotable water. There was one glitch, however. We had been followed. The Thai man who had greeted the black man so warmly in the restaurant last night strolled through the veranda, eyed us warily, then left.

"Rule number four," said Sullivan. No coincidences.

He had been tailed before in small Thai border towns. We laid out a stack of baht to cover the breakfast bill and retreated to our room. Our life insurance policy, The Captain, began walking the perimeter of the hotel's ragged grounds. Sporting a smartly pressed jumpsuit, aviator sunglasses, and ivory cigarette holder, the small, wiry soldier was a welcome vision of malevolence. Over the next two days, the Thai man would return periodically to the hotel to spy, hovering on a cheap motor scooter like an agitated dragonfly. He would not breach The Captain's defense.

Inside our stark room, Sullivan and Bowden probed the story of the two wary Lao men. They had surreptitiously paddled across the Mekong in a pirogue, then beached the dugout on the banks of a small stream behind the hotel. It soon became apparent that these men were not senior officials but merely go-betweens, the Rosencrantz and Guildenstern of this dark, uncertain deal. Still, their conversation piqued the searchers' interest. One of the men claimed to have viewed American POWs in a camp just a few months before, and to have seen one prisoner from a distance of just three meters. He offered no proof. No photos, no letters, no prison rosters. But he had come to this border before, he said, armed with documentation of POWs and under orders from a Vietnamese colonel to look for "interested parties." He had returned empty-handed. This time, he said, he was so sorry, he had no papers. Very coy.

"There was difficulty on the other side," Phoumano translated. "Before, he come for ten days. Sit like a bird. Nothing. He came back and was almost thrown in the river. Now they say, 'Bring me something that shows you come from these people that are interested.' "

Sullivan and Bowden produced a letter that described their deal: two POWs for $1 million. Money was no problem, they assured the Lao men. After Vietnam, Sullivan had spent four years employed by Electronic Data Systems, the Dallas-based firm owned by H. Ross Perot, a staunch POW activist. Sullivan remained in telephone contact with a trusted Perot executive who served as the Texas billionaire's point man on the POW issue. One phone call. One million dollars. No problem.

The senior Lao man sounded hopeful. He would return to Phong Saly. If his superiors wanted to deal, he would come back to Chiang Khong and alert Phoumano within thirty days. Phoumano could contact Mister Jay and Mister Cal in America, and we could all return to Chiang Khong. Agreed. Everyone posed for group Polaroid pictures, allegedly to be delivered to the Vietnamese officer as proof of a meeting with "interested parties." The snapshots and the letter were sealed in a Zip-Loc bag. Sullivan also gave each man one thousand baht, about forty dollars, to cover travel expenses. After farang handshakes, traditional *wai* bows, and a vow to contact Phoumano as soon as they had received authorization from their superiors, the two men left. Perhaps they paddled back to Laos immediately. Perhaps they went uptown to admire the relative wealth of the small Thai shops, wads of baht burning holes in the pockets of their cheap pants.

A brief, hard rain of the waning monsoon swept across the Mekong, flushing the clogged ditches, cleansing the cracked streets, chasing the brutal heat. The smell of ozone, fresh mud, and jungle flora hung in the air. It was time to saddle up. There was nothing more to do but wait and, in Sullivan's case, read the prayer card to Saint Jude and the Book of Job, reciting the lessons of hope and patience.

On the long drive from Chiang Khong back to Bangkok, the mood in our van was weary, yet optimistic. This last hurrah had brought the team to the brink. Ahead lay Laos and, they hoped, final resolution. In one month they would experience either unimagined success or yet another depressing scam. Enshackled by hope, obsessed with the Carr photo, Sullivan and Bowden would have to find the resources to prolong their search. This was not the time to give up. All a good hunter required was a slight sign, a furtive movement or a faint footprint, and the pursuit was joined again. The thrill of this chase, the hint of ultimate reward, was as intoxicating as the sweet smell of opium being put to the flame.

Indian country faded behind us. The driver ejected the Haggard-Nelson cassette from the stereo and loaded a pirated tape by Creedence Clearwater Revival, a band that had provided a virtual soundtrack to the Vietnam War. "Fortunate Son." "Run Through the Jungle." "Bad Moon Rising." The opening chords of "Who'll Stop the Rain" resonated through the van. The song had burst across the airwaves like an illumination round the year that Lieutenant Sullivan, fresh from Boston College ROTC, went off to basic training in Fort Belvoir, Virginia:

> *Long as I remember, the rain been comin' down.*
> *Clouds of myster pourin' confusion on the ground.*

Sullivan looked out the tinted windows at the fertile plains of central Thailand, cut into neat, geometric paddies, and the green, rolling hills, once stripped of their timber, now covered with second-growth forest. Time could be the great healer. "It's twenty years later," he sighed, his eyes misting. "And I'm still fighting the damn war."

3

In Like Flynn

We never endured another trip to Chiang Khong. The thirty days came and went without a call from Phoumano Nosavan. The Lao contacts had melted into the misty far shore of the Mekong, never to be heard from again. Rule number two: Nothing was what it seemed. Not even the indisputable Carr photo, which turned out to be a world-class hoax perpetrated by unknown parties, although Bailey and Phoumano topped the Pentagon's list of suspects. The startling picture was not of Donald Carr, the MIA Green Beret, but of his doppelgänger, Gunther Dittrich, an East German expatriate who lived the low life in Bangkok as a smuggler of exotic birds.

In late October 1991, as the Senate Select Committee on POW/MIA Affairs was to begin its fifteen-month, two-million-dollar inquiry (it would eventually come down conclusively on the side of inconclusiveness), my "curtainraiser" series on Jay Sullivan's travels, "On the POW Trail," ran for three days and for over two hundred column inches in the Boston *Herald*. The stories generated scores of telephone calls. A haunted Special Forces veteran claimed to have been part of a 1969 search to "terminate" two MIAs in Cambodia. From a pay phone, a nervous Lao refugee said he had a friend back home, a prison-camp guard, who knew where dozens of American POWs were held in caves. A Bayonne, New Jersey, conspiracy theorist argued that a CIA hit team had killed Elvis Presley: the King, an Army vet, was about to throw his considerable weight and prestige behind the POW/MIA cause.

And then there was the call from Bernard J. "Barry" Flynn, III.

"Vinnie Arnone is a fat tub of shit!" Flynn blurted by way of introduction. Arnone, an Army veteran and former Boston-area private eye who had resettled in Ubon Ratchathani in northeastern Thailand and now worked as a "security consultant," had merited a single, innocuous paragraph in my POW series. Arnone had had a small role in Operation Lazarus, a 1982 cross-border raid into Laos organized by Bo Gritz.

"Vinnie Arnone is a liar and a thief!" Flynn continued. "He never crossed the Mekong. He can barely cross the Patpong!"

It wasn't the first time I had heard disparaging words about the balding, bespectacled Arnone. As if to back his charges, Flynn offered his bona fides. His father had been the Massachusetts State Police detective who had investigated the Chappaquiddick accident involving Senator Edward M. Kennedy and campaign aide Mary Jo Kopechne. Flynn went on to describe a vitae as colorful as it was farfetched: minor Hollywood actor in television dramas such as "Room 222" and "Medical Center"; aide to billionaire Saudi arms dealer Adnan Khashoggi and his son, Mohamed; Bangkok station chief for Bo Gritz. Flynn said he now lived in northern Thailand, where he was persona non grata for his association with Khun Sa, the Shan rebel commander–cum–druglord, and tried to pay the bills by brokering rubies smuggled from the famed gem mines of northern Burma. "I'm charged by the Thai with crimes from drug running to murder to arms smuggling," Flynn said. "They're all lies."

He was passing through his hometown, New Bedford, a depressed fishing port with a burgeoning heroin problem, when he read my story. Flynn promised to call again before he returned to Thailand and his home in the ancient city of Chiang Mai, four hundred miles north of Bangkok. He never did. And when I tried the New Bedford number he had left me, it was no longer in service. Flynn had disappeared into Southeast Asia, I imagined, to dodge Thai immigration and cook deals with Burmese insurgents. Here was a character born of a collaboration between Joseph Conrad and Hunter S. Thompson: the mysterious farang who lived in the last house on the river, who got by on brash charm and clever guile, who consorted with billionaires, soldiers of fortune, and opium war-lords. I wanted more. I was hooked.

Nine fallow months would follow before my next fix.

Then, in July 1992, a handwritten letter landed on my desk. Faxed by Flynn, who was still at large in Chiang Mai, the scroll contained the words any reporter would love to read: "Any-time you want to visit the General you are welcomed." Here was a chance to interview one of the world's most-wanted men, to tramp again through lush jungles, as I had done for hours as a child in Panama, imagining myself a conquistador, a buccaneer, an archeologist. From the tone of Flynn's commu-nication, scheduling an interview with Khun Sa would be a breeze, no more difficult than arranging a sit-down Q & A with a TV personality on a promotional tour. Over the next eighteen months, I would learn just how lengthy, costly, and maddening a process "anytime" could be.

It seemed a good idea to check up on Flynn, whose résumé sounded too good, too surreal, to be true. I didn't know any

Thai or Shan nationals in Boston who could vouchsafe for his character, but Flynn's father, now retired from the state police and living on Cape Cod, backed his son's story.

"He's telling you the truth when he talks about these people and what he's done," marveled Flynn *père*. "I went out to Hollywood in 1982 and he introduced me to well-known actresses and they all knew him, which amazed me. I'm talking about people you've seen in the movies in the last ten years. It's absolutely incredible, and I've been around. I shake my head in bewilderment."

In her neat, wood-frame house on the west side of New Bedford, Debbie Flynn, a local junior-high teacher, showed me snapshots of her fancy-free brother. Her mother, she said, had similar pictures of Barry in a scrapbook entitled "I Can't Believe It." There were pictures of Barry in the French Riviera aboard the *Nabila*, the yacht Adnan Khashoggi had named after his daughter, and aloft in the billionaire's private jet over Utah. Pictures of Barry with 1979 Playmate of the Year Monique St. Pierre. Of Barry in a scene from "Columbo." Of Barry in the jungles of Burma with General Khun Sa.

"He's not a nine-to-five person," said Debbie Flynn of her brother.

"I've been around," said actor Paul Cavonis, a friend of Flynn's since the early 1970s. "I've known a lot of people and the most interesting madman I ever met was Barry Flynn. No one surprises me more, time after time, than Barry. His survival skills are incredible."

In *A Nation Betrayed*, his self-published screed alleging a massive cover-up by the federal government about evidence of live POWs in Southeast Asia and the involvement of U.S. officials in the heroin trade, Bo Gritz described Flynn as his Bangkok station chief. But Lance E. Trimmer, a former Green Beret who served as a member of Gritz's Operation Lazarus missions to Laos, offered a less-than-ringing character reference of his former cohort.

"Barry Flynn?"

The incredulity came through all the way from Great Falls, Montana, where Trimmer hung his shingle as a private investigator and bounty hunter.

"Jesus Christ! He's working with Khun Sa, selling gems. He's a fucking wacko. I don't know how he's lived so long."

The secret to survival, it seemed, was constant movement. Flynn was out of touch with me until September 1992, when he called collect from Chiang Mai International Airport. Because of fighting in Burma, he said, Thai troops were positioned all along the border, effectively sealing the smuggling trails to Khun Sa's camp. We could still go to Shan State, he offered, but we would have to ride horseback through China and Burma. That meant somehow getting to the outer limits of Yunnan Province, buying horses, hiring guides, then dodging armed rebels, dacoits, and Chinese and Burmese soldiers for several hundred miles. I declined.

Flynn did have a spot of good news. He would be passing through New Bedford before the end of the year, but first he had to chase potential business in England, where an auction house and a nobleman, Lord Brocket, Member of Parliament, had expressed interest in top-quality Burmese gemstones. My entrepreneurial contact had also arranged meetings with war-memorabilia collectors about a possible expedition to salvage two Japanese Zero fighter planes from an overgrown airstrip in the hinterlands of Burma.

"It's in northern Shan State, Wa territory," Flynn said over the din of the Thai public-address system that was announcing his departing flight. "It was the last Japanese airbase, put there just before the end of World War II. Six Zeroes were just left on the airfield. The jungle has grown back and Wa blacksmiths have taken metal off four planes and made farming utensils. But two planes are basically intact. They're worth a fortune to collectors or museums." His solution for salvaging rusting, priceless planes from a trackless wilderness inhabited by lapsed headhunters turned Iron Age farmers? Disassemble the Zeroes, then float them aloft on hot-air balloons. I wanted to ask how the vigilant Thai military massed along the Burmese border might react when those airborne relics hovered into view, but this long-distance call was on my mounting account. The question, and a hundred others, would just have to wait.

═══════

He opened his black address book to the letter G. There, among the scrawled names and numbers, was a sketch of a bearded man. I didn't understand. Goatee, he said, for John Goatee. I still didn't understand. Goatee, he said, as in Gotti, as in John Gotti. Now I understood. He flourished an American passport. Although he had flown from England to Boston, there was no U.S. entry stamp. Was he using another, false passport? He grinned, evasive, self-confident.

"I'm not here," said Barry Flynn, sitting in the offices of an old high-school friend who owned a Boston-area software company. Flynn arched his eyebrows and, in his best British accent, he pronounced, "I'm in England, old boy. Who said I'm over here as Barry Flynn? Barry Flynn is in the U.K."

He laughed. But then, I was to find that Flynn often laughed. It was constant, natural punctuation to his swashbuckling life story, which seemed a series of serendipitous, free-association events. After graduating from high school in 1968, he left New Bedford for Los Angeles to study engineering. His bad asthma kept him out of the military, and before the school semester began, he was introduced to an agent and became a male model. Soon he was walking the runways with a designer name: Richard Lawrence Harlow.

"For Jean Harlow's illegitimate son," he said, then laughed. His agent's idea of mystery and glamour.

After several months, he said, he quit modeling and enrolled in acting school. He landed actress Tyne Daly's sister Glynis as his manager and began to get steady work. In old head shots where he posed in a torn sweatshirt, a jumpsuit, and a turtleneck, Flynn looked like actor James Brolin, but with a harder, more worldly edge. In Hollywood, Flynn changed stage names the way Imelda Marcos changed shoes, from Harlow to Seth Granger to Bernie Flynn to Bernard Flynn to Barry Flynn. A member of the Screen Actors Guild, he still received residual checks made out to his many pseudonyms. His biggest credit came in "Room 222," the ABC schoolroom drama that aired from 1969 to 1974. Flynn had a recurring role as the cocksure high-school quarterback and boyfriend of Helen Loomis, "the class problem girl."

When other parts were slow in coming, he did "The Dating Game," trying to lose, not to win. You lost, you got money or lovely parting gifts and could reappear in three months. You won, well, you had to go on the date. Worse, you couldn't go on the show again for two years. "The Dating Game" was "survival money," a sure thing every three months—until the day that Flynn's luck, or rather Seth Granger's luck, ran out. The homely girl picked Seth, bachelor number one. Shit, an all-expenses-paid date, and not to Waikiki, not to Acapulco, not to Aspen, but a forgettable night in a chauffeur-driven Chevy Impala to the opening of the annex of the Beverly Hills Hotel. That was entertainment for you.

The Beverly Hills Hotel, however, would prove lucky to Flynn. It was there that he met Dodi Al Fayed, whose father, Mohamed, would later purchase Harrods, the English department store. Fayed wanted to get into the film business; Flynn was in the film business. Flynn was soon employed by Fayed's company, Allied Stars, which would produce the Oscar-winning film *Chariots of Fire*. Flynn eventually gravitated to Fayed's uncle, the billionaire Adnan Khashoggi, for whom he worked as an aide de camp. Among his duties was riding herd on Khashoggi's son, Mohamed. According to Flynn, that meant doing Mohamed's coursework at the University of Utah, even taking the young playboy's tests. With seed money from Mohamed, Flynn got back in the movie business, forming Nexus Productions with Cavonis, Tyne Daly and her husband, Georg Stanford Brown.

But the wanderlust soon struck Flynn. He began tagging along on surveillance and repossession jobs with a new acquaintance, David Scott Weekly, a former Navy SEAL nicknamed "Doctor Death" for his demolition expertise. It was like being a kid and going along on stakeouts and drug busts with his father back in New Bedford. It was through Weekly that Flynn found his passport to full-time adventure: Bo Gritz.

The articulate, telegenic Gritz, who was mounting private, illegal missions into Laos in search of American POWs, seemed a perfect subject for a Nexus Productions documentary. And Gritz, a forceful, persuasive man, had an irresistible proposal for the adventure-minded Flynn: why not sneak across the Mekong with the Lazarus team and film a POW rescue attempt? Flynn had a lifelong fascination with the Far East, believing he might have been Asian in a past life. He jumped at the chance to go to the Orient and never looked back. After the failed mission—the Lazarus team spent six fruitless days in the Lao panhandle near the provincial capital of Savannakhet—Flynn decided to resettle in Bangkok. He became Gritz's Bangkok station chief, living in the Lazarus "safe house" near the airport.

Flynn followed up reports sent by Gritz, working with Loh Tharaphant, a lawyer who lived in Nakhon Phanom, a Thai town along the Mekong River where the search for MIAs had spawned a cottage industry in bogus documentation. Flynn said he also served as a "cut-off" for William J. Gadoury, Jr., a Rhode Island native working out of the U.S. Embassy for the Joint Casualty Resolution Center, which investigated MIA cases in Southeast Asia. When the information seemed too far-fetched, explained Flynn, or the sources too unsavory, the government relied on cut-offs—men at home in the world of shadows who were willing to do the thankless spadework and take the fall unflinchingly should something go awry.

From his black briefcase, Flynn produced a 1988 letter sent from a Vietnamese refugee to Gadoury, then routed to him. "Why would Barry Flynn get mail from the U.S. Embassy?" He smiled. "It's a cut-off. In any operation, you have a cut-off, where they can deny any kind of existence. I was Bill's cut-off for Mister Loh; I was Bill's cut-off for Phoumano. Anybody that had questionable character, I was the cut-off."

In this capacity, said Flynn, he checked out the claims of POW hunters like Jack Bailey, Vinnie Arnone, and Al Shinkle, U.S. veterans who lived in Thailand and solicited money for their private "rescue" operations along the Laotian border. "Bill would give me the information they gave him," he said. "I'd send a report back. One hundred percent of it was not true."

Flynn had nothing but contempt for the over-the-hill *Soldier of Fortune* types that congregated at Lucy's Tiger Den, a raucous expat bar on Surawong Road located just a few staggering steps from the licentious Patpong. "All these bums hang around the same bars and try to fuck the same pussy," Flynn said.

Thailand was a wonderful life. Gritz's activities were the stuff of legend among MIA activists. And to be single, handsome, and farang in Bangkok, which produced beautiful women the way a greenhouse nurtured orchids, was to live like a conquering hero, particularly for a man like Flynn, who had a singular talent for connecting with powerful people. "Bo would tell people: Barry has his incapabilities and he has his whiskey, but one thing about Barry—you can parachute him into any country in the world without two nickels to rub together and by that evening he'll be having dinner with the president," Flynn recounted.

That life changed abruptly in November 1986 when Gritz heard a rumor that Khun Sa might have access to live American POWs purportedly held in western Laos. Gritz and Weekly flew to Bangkok, met up with Flynn and headed north, bound for Khun Sa's camp. With few roads in Mae Hong Son Province, the team rode mules through thick jungles and across razorback mountains for three days and two nights to arrive at Khun Sa's headquarters in Ho Mong, Burma. Their effort proved futile. The warlord had no POWs, but offered to send his men into Laos to search. He did, however, have opium, tons of it, and was only too happy to tell Gritz, on the record, that he had done business with American government officials.

The trip was a watershed experience for Flynn. Here was a stronger personality than Khashoggi, a more charismatic leader than even Gritz. Here was a man vilified by all but his own people, a man who would use any means necessary, even narcodollars, to carry on the fight against the reviled Burmese, a man who played all the angles. To Flynn, it seemed downright romantic: guerrillas who trained in an armed camp deep in the forest, who lived in simple huts and subsisted on what they could shoot, trap, or gain in trade, and who nurtured the long-held dream of liberating Shan State from the yoke of Burmese oppression. This was paradise. Flynn left Gritz and cast his lot with Khun Sa.

"He's attracted to the players," said Cavonis, his old friend. "A lot of people are sycophants and get a different kind of sustenance. For Barry, it's about the game, it's about the play."

Flynn did earn money guiding a few Western journalists, including ABC's Tom Jarriel, into Shan State to interview the warlord. He also brokered Burmese gems, some from the fabled Mogok mines north of Mandalay. There was more, he said, to Shan State than just heroin. "I'm their door to the West," said Flynn of his efforts in the Shan gem trade and warlord public relations. "I'm the only white man they trust."

By early 1990, Flynn's freewheeling activities had landed him in trouble with Thai authorities. Among the charges, he said, were weapons smuggling and escorting newsmen into Burma to interview Khun Sa, whom the U.S. Drug Enforcement Administration had labeled a major heroin trafficker. There was also a murder warrant in Burma, he added. The Burmese apparently considered Flynn a killer because he had videotaped a 1990 battle between Khun Sa's Mong Tai Army and soldiers of a rival opium force, the United Wa State Army, including footage of dead Wa troops. The reformed headhunters had allied with the Rangoon junta against Khun Sa in hopes of taking control of the lucrative cross-border trade in contraband. Flynn recounted all these accusations as if describing unwarranted parking tickets. A Chiang Mai neighbor, Colonel Vichit Vechasart of the Thai Border Patrol Police, had jokingly told him, "Barry, with all these charges you shouldn't be persona non grata—you should be a Thai general!"

Flynn lived openly in Chiang Mai with his wife, Malee, a Shan he said was a niece of Khun Sa, and their two children, daughter Ploipailin (whose name, which meant "precious stone," was conferred by the General), and son, Kevin Shan (whose initials matched those of Khun Sa). "They're both godchildren to Khun Sa," Flynn said. He reached into his briefcase and proudly produced a picture of himself and his daughter posed with Khun Sa's pet Bengal tiger. "I want to take a picture of her and Khun Sa with ten thousand of his troops behind them. I want to put it on the wall in my house so when she's sixteen and boys come by to take her on dates, I can point to the picture and say: Be home by ten o'clock, right?"

He laughed. His whereabouts in Chiang Mai were no secret. He rented a house in a quiet, upper-middle-class suburb off Changklan Road. He got drunk on Maekhong rice whiskey with Colonel Vichit. His friends included an exiled Wa leader, Mahasang, the son of the last saopha prince of Vingngun, a remote fiefdom along the Sino-Burmese border. Flynn's "office" was a bamboo table at a neighborhood restaurant along the western bank of the Ping River. Of course the Thai knew where he lived. "It's a game," he said, striking his best matinee grin.

As part of the game, Flynn entered Thailand in discreet, roundabout fashion. He flew from Los Angeles to Singapore, then on to Penang Island, a resort off the western coast of Malaysia. He then took the ferry to the mainland town of Butterworth and caught the Singapore-to-Bangkok train for a rail journey up the Malaysian Peninsula. At the border crossing, Flynn hopped the train, walked into Thailand, hailed a *song thaew*—the pickups that function as jitney buses (the name means "two rows," for the facing, lengthwise benches in the truck bed) in every corner of the country—and rode to Hat Yai airport. A few hours later, he was back in Chiang Mai, drinking Singha along the banks of the slow-moving Ping River.

———

On his next back-door trip to Thailand, Flynn carried my request for an interview with Khun Sa. I wrote that I would be accompanied by Sullivan, who was only too happy to put his business aside for two weeks of high adventure. Sullivan, like Gritz before him, wanted to hear if Khun Sa might have any MIA information. Maybe Gritz hadn't asked the right questions of this man whose influence extended deep into Laos, Sullivan reasoned. The rationale seemed hopeless, but I didn't criticize his motives. I was thrilled to have him along. With his firearms knowledge and Eagle Scout survival skills, he could be a life-saver should matters go awry, and on the road to Burma, that seemed a very real possibility.

Protocol dictated that my letter of request be sent to the External Affairs Department of the Shan State Restoration Council, the administrative body of the rebel-held territory. Two months later, in March 1993, a reply came, written on SSRC stationery, from liaison officer Khernsai Jaiyen. The news was bad, wrote Khernsai. Because of skirmishing between Thai and Burmese forces in Mae Hong Son Province, Thailand had sealed the border. Relations had been strained since the previous October, when SLORC soldiers seized Mae Hong Son officials in Burma. The functionaries were investigating the disappearance of Thai villagers and elephants involved in illegal logging; the woodcutters had not paid protection money to the Burmese soldiers and had been kidnapped. Now security promised to remain tight for several months, since King Bhumibol Adulyadej was expected to leave Bangkok and spend the upcoming hot season in the cooler north. One of His Majesty's royal summer palaces was located in Pang Tong, just a few miles northwest of Mae Hong Son, the staging area for any trip to see Khun Sa.

"Best to let things as they are so as not to complicate mat-ters," Khernsai advised.

Rule number three: "Anytime" seemed to slip from my grasp with maddening, quicksilver frequency. There was a small chance for entry, Khernsai continued. Contact the Thai Border Patrol Police. I contacted Flynn instead.

"Calling the border police is the last thing you want to do," said Flynn. "They'll say, 'You want to do *what*? Go visit *Khun Sa*?' They'll take your passport, flag your name in the immigration computer, tip off the DEA. I don't trust Khernsai, that little snake. I'll take you in."

There was no chance of entering Shan State during the summer rains, the "slide time" when the smuggling trails were either muddy morasses or slick as slate. My mood worsened when Reuters ran a story by a Thai reporter who had wangled, through Khernsai, a brief interview with Khun Sa. The story bore the dateline of Ho Mong, Burma—my magic, fugitive target. But at last, a brief phone message from Flynn awaited me in early September: "Everything is set. Meet me in Chiang Mai on October 20. The trip is a go."

Five days later, a two-week-old letter arrived from Khernsai. After several deliberations, he wrote, it was decided my visit should be delayed "until the return of a more suitable climate, both political and seasonal." He blamed the brief Reuters report for renewed border tensions. But perhaps, he added, by mid December "the clouds will be cleared enough to invite you again." The man did know how to run with a metaphor, and how to artfully sabotage Flynn's efforts. Khernsai, who was not part of Khun Sa's original band of brothers, held the foreign-relations job that Flynn coveted. Flynn loathed him; the feeling seemed mutual. Khernsai was determined to put off, however politely, any reporter associated with Flynn, the farang from Hollywood who had earned the general's confidence.

Protocol be damned. I wrote another interview request, far stronger in tone and addressed directly to the general. Flynn then prevailed upon Mook Keaw Kam, a Khun Sa confidant who supervised mining operations in resource-rich Shan State, to read the back-channel letter directly to the warlord. In late September, a terse letter arrived from Khernsai. This time, there was no talk of the weather, literal or symbolic. There was only one sentence: "This is to inform you that your request to visit the free Shan Territory has been accepted, subject to conditions prevailing at the time of your entry."

I called Sullivan, told him to reserve early November for a journey to Burma. We were in, in with Flynn. It was all a game, and the first round was ours.

4

Prince of Prosperity, Prince of Death

Like so many public buildings of the late twentieth century, the U.S. Federal Court of the Eastern District of New York reeks of diminished expectations. There are no granite pediments or fluted Doric columns, no marble steps or bronze statues, just a bland, concrete box, and across the street, a shabby, empty park. The only intrusions on the courthouse's anonymity are the concrete planters fronting its entrance—arranged to foil any drive-through car-bombing—and those ubiquitous symptoms of modern social dysfunction: guards, metal detectors, and X-ray machines.

My objective was just beyond the security phalanx: the ground-floor office of the Clerk of Court where paperwork went to die. I was looking for the federal indictment against Chang Chi-fu, alias Khun Sa. It took a few false starts on the office computer database. The search term "Sa" brought no hits; "Chang" resulted in forty irrelevant cases. "Khun" was a dead-center strike: one case. The lone line glowed in green, throbbing letters on the dark monitor, like a poisonous krait waiting to strike: *1:89cr00911 USA v. Chi-fu (072 dft)*.

In a few minutes, a pleasant court clerk retrieved a corresponding, curry-yellow legal folder. Inside were the contents of *United States of America v. Chang Chi-fu*, a.k.a. Khun Sa. Eighteen dog-eared pages represented the United States government's attempt to put Chang, the alleged sovereign of the Southeast Asian heroin trade, permanently out of business. His better known alias, Khun Sa, was a Shan honorific meaning "Prince of Prosperity." The ten-count federal indictment, written in unemotional legalese that muted the astounding scope of the purported crimes, concluded with this charge:

In or about February 1988, within the Eastern District of New York and elsewhere, the defendant CHANG CHI-FU, a/k/a/ "Khun Sa," and others did knowingly and intentionally attempt to import into the United States from a place outside thereof an amount in excess of one (1) kilogram of heroin, to wit, approximately one thousand and eighty-six (1,086) kilograms of heroin, a Schedule I narcotic drug controlled substance.

One thousand and eighty-six kilograms. Over one ton of heroin. A load to dwarf the giant, bottom-feeding plaa buk catfish. A bounty to feed millions of junkie dreams.

For all the notoriety of the accused and his federally designated "kingpin" status, however, this legal-sized folder seemed meager. Other sleeves bulged as thick as accordions from the reams of records generated by flurries of hearings, trials, and appeals but USA v. Chi-fu was less than one-quarter of an inch thick. The file had not grown since March 15, 1990, when then–U.S. Attorney General Richard Thornburgh announced the warlord's federal indictment and his new, less-than-honorable Drug Enforcement Administration moniker. "As the largest dope pusher in the Golden Triangle, the title 'Prince of Death'. . . might be more apt," Thornburgh remarked.

Four years later, the dark prince was still powerful and prosperous, with a drug kingdom spanning thousands of square miles over the nebulous borders of eastern Burma, western Laos, and northern Thailand. And file 89cr00911, the handiwork of U.S. Assistant District Attorney Catherine E. Palmer, gathered dust in a federal court house in Brooklyn.

The diminutive Palmer, described by one defense attorney as an awesome, "seventy pounds dripping wet" force after she had won a conviction and twenty-seven-year sentence against his heroin-dealing client, was the legal weight behind Group 41, one of the government's most successful counter-narcotics units. Organized in 1986 and operating out of the DEA's Chelsea offices, Group 41 targeted the secretive world of Southeast Asian heroin traffickers who controlled 60 percent of the junk used by New York City's estimated three to five hundred thousand addicts.

Along the cubicle partitions of its office, color photographs of Group 41 seizures were displayed in the proud yet casual manner of bowling- or softball-league trophies. Bags of heroin placed inside picture frames. Bags of heroin stuffed inside the hollowed braces of a crate packed with porcelain vases. Bags of heroin even tucked inside mah-jong tiles. And one pelt Palmer clearly wanted to hang alongside the seizure photos belonged to Khun Sa. She termed her nemesis "probably the most significant" single heroin trafficker in Southeast Asia. Through longevity, ruthlessness, and iron-clad control of his private armed force, the Mong Tai Army, Khun Sa commanded at least one-half of Burma's huge opium crop, which had annually topped two thousand metric tons since 1989. As Burma dominated the global market, producing 70 percent of the world's illicit opium, according to annual reports by the State

Department's Bureau of International Narcotics Matters (BINM), the at-large warlord was, by the DEA's estimation, ultimately responsible for at least one-third of the world's heroin. Even the hard-core junkies on the streets of America knew his name.

"He's God, man," fifty-year-old Tom "The Sailor" Williams had told me when I met him at a Boston drop-in program for junkie veterans. "He's so powerful. When I used to live in San Francisco, the people in Chinatown would not say anything against him. They say something against him, they're dead, automatically dead. He reaches everywhere. I think he's one of the Illuminati who run the world. There's a group of people who run the world. I think he's part of that group."

The object of The Sailor's desire, the bane of Catherine Palmer's efforts, was "China White," the popular appellation for No. 4 heroin. The numerical term refers to the four-stage refining process of the opiate that arrives in New York and other American cities clean as new-fallen snow. The lowest purity of Southeast Asian heroin that Palmer said she had ever seen in New York was 85 percent. Most of the loads were 95 percent pure, she said, or higher. Ingeniously smuggled into America, as Group 41's photo gallery attested, and barely "stepped on" with diluents such as lactose and mannitol to increase its bulk, the heroin was then distributed through a network of criminal organizations.

No monolithic group, however, controlled the local heroin market, said Palmer. Group 41 tracked the ancient, ethnic Chinese Triads, such as the 14 K Society, the Wo Shing Wo, and the Sun Yee On, which were all based in Hong Kong. Sun Yee On, which centered in Kowloon's Walled City, reportedly had links to Khun Sa. The society was founded by natives of China's coastal Swatow region, the seafaring Chiu Chao, who had established ethnic enclaves throughout Southeast Asia from which they displayed a remarkable acumen for legitimate trading and for contraband smuggling. These Triads, with criminal cores directed by *lung tao*—"dragon heads"—raked in millions of dollars through narcotics, prostitution, gambling, loan sharking, smuggling, and extortion. Unlike the Colombian cartels or the Italian Mafia, the Asian criminals did not operate in clean, hierarchical structures. They functioned without central administrations, communicated via elaborate codes, spoke in obscure dialects. In America, said Palmer, these Asian traffickers favored joint ventures and marriages of convenience, with different organizations fulfilling compartmentalized functions.

"That makes this a much more amorphous and difficult target to deal with effectively," Palmer explained. "It's not a vertically integrated, top-to-bottom distribution network. You have a lot of different people coming in at various levels: financial backing, initial importation, distribution. The heroin will go through several levels here in New York City before it ultimately gets to the street."

The damning charges against Khun Sa illustrated the complexity of the smuggling schemes. In three cases where the Shan druglord was alleged to have been "the ultimate source of supply," seven-hundred-gram bricks of heroin—a smuggling standard unit of measure known as a *jin*—were hidden in bales of rubber and shipped to a Thai-controlled warehouse in Queens, New York. According to Palmer, a total of 486 kilos were sent to this warehouse in March and June 1987. The heroin, accompanied by a Thai, had been shipped from Klong Toey, the bustling port of Bangkok, to Hong Kong. There, Palmer charged, control was turned over to a Taiwanese, and the load was then transshipped to New York and to another level of Chinese distributors. The first two multimillion-dollar shipments had been successfully delivered, but the massive third load had been discovered and seized on the docks of Klong Toey. Heavy rains delayed loading operations at the port, Southeast Asia's third busiest, and rainwater soaked through two hundred bales of rubber strips waiting for loading aboard a container ship. Workers saw white sap oozing from the bundles and alerted the Royal Thai Police. Ripping through the bales with chainsaws, they uncovered the 1,086-kilo shipment that now represented count ten of *USA v. Chang Chi-fu*.

———

Palmer, raised in the small, working-class town of Leicester, Massachusetts—less than an hour's drive north of New Bedford, Barry Flynn's hometown—was the first in her Irish-Catholic family to attend college. After graduating from the Jesuit-affiliated Boston College and from Catholic University Law School, she took a job with the high-powered New York corporate-law firm of Mudge Rose Guthrie Alexander & Ferdon. But after five years, she took a 50-percent pay cut, became a prosecutor, and immersed herself in the narcotics netherworld. Not unlike Sullivan, she had been compelled by service and sacrifice, selfless lessons inculcated by her parents. "I worked in a great law firm with good people," said Palmer, who served as the inspiration for the character of Shannon O'Shea, the female FBI agent in *China White*, Peter Maas' 1994 novel about heroin trafficking. "But at the end of the day there was just something missing . . . the ability to feel like you could do something that makes a difference."

In her work with Group 41, Palmer soon caught the attention of Asian smugglers, who gave her a street name: The Dragon Lady. The appellation was one of grudging respect, for the sky dragon, or *lung*, was one of the most important symbols in Chinese culture. The dragon, the strongest animal of the Chinese zodiac, was never the malevolent beast of Western mythology. The dragon did have the capacity to terrify, but it also represented good fortune, vigor, and beneficence. In Chinese cosmology, it occupied the eastern sky, the domain of sunrise, rain, and fertility. The Dragon Lady, therefore, was a powerful woman, not be trifled with or intimidated. In early 1990, Palmer received a parcel at work. Inside was a briefcase, which Palmer had been expecting as a present from her mother and father. Before she could open the case, two wary DEA agents intervened. They found a .22-caliber pistol rigged to fire when the top of the briefcase was opened. The message was clear: Palmer and Group 41 had made damaging progress.

"We've targeted and prosecuted some very significant heroin traffickers," she said. "We've closed off their world to a certain degree because we've made it more difficult for them to operate in various spheres. We've made an initial difference. As a result of the efforts DEA has undertaken, people are starting to pay more attention to the real problems that heroin poses."

She also hoped that some day, some way, the sphere of operations surrounding Chang Chi-fu would shrink to the size of a Brooklyn federal courtroom. And who was more qualified to vanquish the prosperous Prince of Death than a self-described "eternal optimist"? Who better than a diehard fan of the star-crossed Boston Red Sox, a woman who kept a framed picture of outfielder Carl Yastrzemski in her office? By almost the sheer force of his will, the steady, reliable Yaz had carried the Sox to the World Series in 1967, the year of the Impossible Dream. If Yaz could achieve a near-miracle, it would never be beyond the realm of possibility that the dogged, methodical prosecutor would not get her chance to fatten file 89cr00911.

"I certainly don't think [the indictment] was a waste of time," said Palmer. "Someone has to hold him accountable."

Last night it had been Bomber. Next week it could be Hard to Kill, Mambo, or Top Gun. Who knew? The Sailor didn't worry. The fix was in. Boston's bountiful heroin market was as glutted as a car dealership's lot on President's Day. Pushers loitered near the Veterans Administration outpatient clinic, just a few hundred yards from Boston Garden, confident that a few addicts would want to splurge and run a touch of scag on top of their prescribed methadone. They cruised the financial district, supplying the yuppies grown jaded or burned-out by the high-wire life of cocaine. They waited in the tenements of Mission Hill, where hard-core junkies like The Sailor went to score.

"Years ago, if you had a good connection you were lucky," said Jon Stuen-Parker, a former addict who now directs the National AIDS Brigade, a nonprofit group that operates needle-exchange programs in Boston, New York, and Bangkok. Years ago, the teen-aged Stuen-Parker and his junk partners mustered every morning at Leo's Pool Room in East Boston's Maverick Square to see who had a good thing going. Today, there's no need to network. "Now," said Stuen-Parker, "there are good things everywhere."

This was the Golden Age of heroin addiction. The fixes were plentiful, potent, and, best of all, cheap. Addicts who paid from twenty to twenty-five dollars per bag for heroin in 1992 could, just two years later, buy killer doses for as little as seven dollars, about the price of a six-pack of imported beer. Stuen-Parker articulated what The Sailor, what pushers, what law-enforcement officials knew all too well: "It is a drug addict's dream come true that there can be that much availability at that cheap a price with quality that high."

This downpour of despair formed half a world away, in the hills of northeastern Burma. Beyond the long reach of the

United States, beyond even the thuggish grip of SLORC, the thunderhead of another immense opium crop gathered, barely acknowledged by the West. For despite its critical importance to the global drug trade, Burma had managed to remain an obscure, eccentric tyranny until 1988, the year that Daw Aung San Suu Kyi came home.

The daughter of the late Aung San, the revered founder of independent Burma, she had returned to Rangoon from Oxford, England, to care for her invalid mother. Daw Suu Kyi found her homeland in turmoil. In the wake of Ne Win's crazed demonetization scheme, his docile, Buddhist subjects had finally soured on the old general and taken to the streets in protest. When Ne Win finally resigned in July, the autocrat tapped Sein Lwin, an old army crony, as his successor. The move backfired. The public loathed Lwin, whom they called "The Butcher of Rangoon," for his long history of savage suppression. Planets and auspicious numbers determine every undertaking in Burma, so a general strike began at exactly 8:08 a.m. on August 8, 1988, when Rangoon dockworkers walked off the job. Tatmadaw soldiers responded by machine-gunning hundreds of protestors in the streets. Daw Suu Kyi could not stomach the sorry state of the nation her father, assassinated in 1947 by a political rival, had fought so hard to establish. In an emotional August 26 speech to several hundred thousand people crowded at the base of Shwedagon Pagoda, Burma's most venerated site, Daw Suu Kyi emerged as the leader of the prodemocracy opposition. The dutiful daughter had become The Lady.

"The present crisis is the concern of the entire nation," she told the multitude. "I could not, as my father's daughter, remain indifferent to all that was going on. This national crisis could, in fact, be called the second struggle for independence."

Emboldened, citizens throughout Burma began daily mass

demonstrations. The Tatmadaw interceded on September 18, shooting thousands of protestors. Nearly ten thousand students and prodemocracy activists fled the violent crackdown, heading for Thailand. The army's chief of staff, General Saw Maung, announced the formation of SLORC, the abolition of the 1974 constitution, and the abandonment of "The Burmese Way to Socialism" in favor of a limited free-market economy. The Tatmadaw would govern until sufficient order allowed for general elections.

Suddenly, The Lady appeared everywhere—Shan State and Kachin State, Mandalay and Mergui—carrying the banner of the National League for Democracy (NLD) and pointedly criticizing the disastrous policies of Ne Win. Supported by peasants and professionals, Burmans and minorities alike, The Lady became the greatest unifying force in Burmese politics since her late father. In a panic, SLORC arrested her on July 20, 1989—the day after Martyrs' Day, the anniversary of Aung San's death—and confined Daw Suu Kyi to house arrest in the family home near Rangoon University.

The Lady's detention did not deter voters when elections were held the following May. In a stunning showing, NLD candidates captured 392 of 485 seats in the Assembly. But SLORC, whose National Unity Party won a paltry ten seats, simply ignored the mandate. NLD candidates were disqualified, pressured to resign, detained, or imprisoned. The junta packed a 1993 convention to draft a new constitution; hundreds of handpicked delegates then produced a document that guaranteed the military a "leading role" in government, granted the army sweeping "emergency" powers, and banned anyone married to a foreigner—i.e., Daw Suu Kyi, who had married an Englishman, Michael Aris—from holding elected office.

Nothing could shame SLORC, not the fact that The Lady

was the daughter of Burma's greatest national hero, not the moral prestige of her 1991 Nobel Peace Prize, not even condemnation by diplomats and nongovernmental organizations such as Human Rights Watch, which labeled Burma a "human-rights pariah." The U.S. State Department's *Country Reports on Human Rights Practices for 1993* criticized Burma's "pervasive security apparatus" and its unchecked military dictatorship that ruled "with an unyielding grip." The last American ambassador to Burma, Burton Levin, called SLORC a collection of "thugs and dopes." No matter. The Lady remained behind the green metal gates of 54 University Avenue, uncharged with any crime.

The bloody subjugation of unarmed protestors, the trumped-up detention of Daw Suu Kyi, and the subsequent nullification of legitimate elections briefly caught the attention of the international media. The United States downgraded diplomatic relations in 1990 and eliminated all direct aid to Burma, including funding of counter-narcotics efforts. American antidrug assistance was already being questioned in the wake of Shan allegations that the Burmese had indiscriminately sprayed a toxic, U.S.-supplied herbicide, 2,4-D, on hundreds of fields and villages near Lashio and Keng Tung between November 1986 and January 1987.

The crackdown on prodemocracy activists slowed international aid to a trickle. Undeterred, SLORC ignored drug eradication and counter-narcotics measures and moved to consolidate internal control. Since the junta's ascension in 1988, opium production in Burma had more than doubled. The country was "far and away" the world's leading producer of illicit opium, according to a 1994 BINM report, which determined that SLORC had "not undertaken serious or sustained narcotics control efforts" since taking power. Burma dominated the global heroin market, growing two-thirds of the world's supply of the illegal poppy and producing an equal share of its illicit opium. An estimated 60 percent of America's heroin flowed from Burma. The junkie's dream had become a national nightmare, used by more people than at any time since the end of the Vietnam War.

A generation before, tens of thousands of G.I. junkies had returned from Vietnam, strung out on dope allegedly grown by Hmong tribesman, the mercenary force employed by the CIA in neighboring Laos. Then, however, when Lou Reed or William S. Burroughs described the junkie life, it still held the aura of doomed, artistic romanticism. Even trafficking could seem a rogueish, existential enterprise, particularly the pure Saigon scag hustled by Nietzche-reading Marine vets in Robert Stone's 1973 novel, *Dog Soldiers*.

Stuen-Parker had seen his share of these lost characters on the street, had tracked the soldiers who passed through his Boston drop-in center, Veterans with AIDS. But hollow, haunted men like The Sailor, who had shot dope for forty years, were not the only abusers. As the 1994 BINM report noted ominously: "The drug, which cocaine displaced in the 1980s, is making a comeback everywhere." According to the report, heroin ran "a close second" to cocaine as the top choice of American drug users. The sinister comeback was a natural, if chilling, consequence of America's decade-long, abusive affair with cocaine. A stimulant such as cocaine will usually burn out users within a few years, the BINM report noted, while a depressant like heroin "can hold its prey for decades." Seeking addict diversification, the savvy South American cocaine cartels "appear to be looking to heroin as the drug of the '90s," observed BINM. The narcotraffickers had planted thousands of acres of poppies in the mountains of Colombia to guarantee opium market share. In a span of just a few years, Colombia had come from nowhere to rank third globally in illicit poppy cultivation, behind only Burma and Afghanistan. By the fall of 1993, DEA agents noted that the Cali cartel had devised an aggressive sales campaign for the American drug market: free samples of heroin No. 4 to its crack and cocaine customers.

If the State Department was correct, Burma—and especially the region of Shan State—had attained the notoriety of the Huallaga Valley of Peru, cocaine's mythic wellspring. The opium-poppy plant, *Papaver somniferum*, grew best in a relatively dry, mild climate at altitudes between three and seven thousand feet—making Shan State, with its temperate weather and mountain ranges, the perfect poppy hothouse. The State Department produced a map of major opium-producing nations, with cultivation densities indicated by color shadings of tan (low density), orange (medium), and red (high). Shan State was almost completely overlaid in tan, with huge splotches of orange and red sprouting like chancres the length and breadth of the region.

For decades, Shan State's coming of age in the international drug trade had gone virtually unnoticed among Western law-enforcement officials. During the 1970s, the FBI and the DEA targeted the so-called French Connection—the Istanbul-Marseilles–New York corridor—and Sicilian criminal organizations. The drug syndicates soon looked elsewhere, to Mexico and the Far East, for sources. Reagan-era counter-narcotics efforts were consumed with South American cocaine, particularly the purified, virulent form known as crack. Meanwhile, Triad members had left Hong Kong and settled overseas, extending the tentacles of their insular crime families. Local and federal lawmen, with few Chinese officers to penetrate the walls of culture, dialect, and ethnicity, found themselves overmatched and outmaneuvered by the dragon heads. Soon, the volume of heroin the Triads moved dwarfed the loads of the French Connection. The largest American bust on the old

Marseilles route had been one hundred kilos. That was less than 10 percent of the 1,086-kilo heroin shipment seized in Bangkok and allegedly traced to Khun Sa. A smuggler couldn't hide a load like that in the floorboards of a car; the load was the size of a car.

University of Wisconsin professor Alfred W. McCoy, the author of the seminal book, *The Politics of Heroin in Southeast Asia*, labeled Shan State a "natural outlaw zone." Not unlike the Huallaga Valley, noted McCoy, it was an area that lay at the intersection of national boundaries and ethnic frontiers, of trade and terrain. Shan State had chafed against Burmese rule for centuries. Armed insurgents now trafficked in the fruit of the poppy with a piercing logic: in these mountains, only opium had the buying power to deliver the weapons they desired.

The men who nurtured the misery that now grew so color-fully in Shan State were not bad men. Like their fathers and their fathers' fathers, they were simple, practical farmers who measured out their lives in late-summer monsoons. In the fall, after the rains, they broadcast poppy seeds across small plots, usually no more than an acre or two, cut in the weak laterite soil of the mountains. The farmers had little recourse but to grow poppies. Shanland's vast distances and few roads meant that price-weight ratio was critical for any product, and no cash crop was as compact, portable, or nonperishable as opium. Every spring in their beautiful, abject land, they sold their opium for a pittance to roving Chinese merchants. Brought to malarial trading towns in the valleys, the bulky opium cargoes were frequently converted to morphine, a relatively simple refining process that reduced drug weight by 90 percent and required only water, lime fertilizer, and ammonia.

The morphine bricks were then transported under armed guard by mule caravans to clandestine jungle refineries along the Thai border, where black-market "chemists" used a complicated, four-step method to transform morphine into heroin. The chemists first boiled morphine and acetic anhydride to bond as diacetylmorphine. In the second stage, water and chloroform were added to precipitate impurities; the introduction of sodium carbonate then formed heroin particles. In the third step, these clumps were filtered from the liquid, added to a solution of alcohol and activated charcoal, then heated until the alcohol evaporated. The result: brownish, smokable heroin No. 3. In the ultimate step, the heroin was again dissolved in alcohol; the addition of ether and hydrochloric acid caused white flakes of nearly pure heroin to crystalize. After final filtration and drying, only heroin No. 4, the Cadillac of catatonic highs, remained.

By the hot, dry season of April and May, this China White swept southward, virtually unchecked by Burmese, Thai, or American antidrug efforts. Like a rising tide, it inundated jungle hamlets and mining camps, seeped into border towns, crested in the braying sprawl of Bangkok, then receded in a dozen major rivulets across the globe. International outrage was reserved for the powerful few who fought to control the wellhead of this heroin pipeline. Some, like the wild Wa, had been headhunters a generation ago. Others, like the Kuomintang (or KMT), the remnants of Chiang Kai-shek's Nationalist Chinese army that fled from Yunnan Province to Burma in the late 1940s, were a lost, exiled band that now cared only for drug profits. But the most powerful, most cunning, most resilient among this collection of warlords, bandits, and lapsed patriots was Khun Sa, who had used the opium industry to enhance his power, prestige, and personal fortune for more than thirty years.

Through a maze of overseas smuggling routes controlled by the Triads, Khun Sa allegedly funneled tons of heroin No. 4 to the waiting, willing veins of addicts in Europe and the United States. At street level, this heroin was a far cry from the dime-bag ghetto smack of the 1970s. As Palmer knew all too well, purity levels had soared. Fifteen, twenty years ago, said DEA agents, a typical bag contained only 3 or 4 percent heroin. In the spring of 1993, when DEA made random street buys in twenty cities, the average, nationwide purity levels had leapt to 36 percent. The increase was even greater in the northeast: 80 percent pure in Philadelphia; 66 percent in New York City–Newark, N.J.; and 62 percent in Boston.

Whether grown and processed in Burma, Afghanistan, or Colombia, this heroin wrought health-care havoc. Even grizzled users such as The Sailor, who had mainlined nearly everything, had rarely tried anything as strong, or as deadly. There was more than bravado in the "brand" names—DOA, Murder One, TKO—there was truth in advertising. With rising street-level potency, more users overdosed. According to the Drug Abuse Warning Network (DAWN), a national survey of hospital emergency rooms, heroin-related ER visits climbed from 38,100 in 1988 to 63,000 in 1993—an increase of 65 percent. Over the same period, heroin-related ER visits in New York and Boston were even higher: 109 percent and 85 percent, respectively. Bad shit, this good thing.

"You gotta be careful," The Sailor had told me. "You can get killed walking across the street; you can get killed with an overdose. About a month ago, I got some heroin and the dealer chased me down. He knew where I was getting high. He fucked up. He didn't cut it right. It was pure. I missed my vein; I skin-popped it, and I almost died from that, it was so fucking strong." The Sailor smiled, nearly nostalgic for the great hit that almost put him away. Then laughed his dry, chain-smoker's laugh. "But that's the chance you take. It's the way life is. Don't stop you from doing it. It don't. That's what you do. You do what you do."

Overdoses weren't the only health issue. While the public

was being harangued with the safe-sex mes
quietly become the major culprit in the spread
was transmitted when an infected addict sha
1994, intravenous (IV) drug use was blamed fo
reported AIDS cases in Massachusetts. Among
use had supplanted homosexual sex as the prim   , mode for
HIV transmission by 1992. Among women, IV drug use was
the primary method of infection in two-thirds of the common-
wealth's cases. The cold numbers were equally troubling in
New York: 47 percent of male AIDS cases were attributed to
IV drug use, which had overtaken homosexual sex as the primary mode of HIV infection in 1987. Among women, IV drug
use caused HIV infection in six of ten AIDS patients.

The Sailor sounded detached, almost resigned, as he spoke of
a former lover he said died of AIDS several years ago. Junkie
fatalism: "I shot dope with her. I had sex with her. We never
used any precautions. . . . I won't be surprised if I do come up
positive. It ain't gonna put me on no death trip. I'm ready for it
if it comes up, all right? It's hard, man, when you know you're
gonna die sooner than everyone else. But sometimes it really
doesn't matter when you die."

The Sailor still held onto a dream: he was in Southeast Asia,
beyond the Annamese Cordillera, the saw-toothed mountains
he once saw from the deck of his destroyer. He was permanently AWOL, beyond the reach of his chief petty officer, of
any goddamn officer. He was beyond the reach of his government, of any goddamn government. He was in Burma, nodding on a sun-bathed hillside. It was heaven on earth.

"Sit in a poppy field, scrape some opium off a plant, and just
smoke it," he said with a cackle. "Right there. Right in its
environment." No more connections. No more rip-off paranoia. No more hot shots. The Sailor laughed a parched Marlboro laugh. His lifelong habit, begun when he was eleven years

had stolen his health, his wealth, his common-law wife, his lover. He drifted between cheap apartments, homeless shelters, veterans centers. The Sailor was on methadone now, but still danced with his harsh mistress, chipping smack about once a week. China White called the shots; The Sailor could not resist. Methadone promised no dreams. Sure, he was a needle freak. Sticking a spike in his arm, drawing blood, he got off on the whole vindictive scene, just oozing life.

"I miss that," he croaked. "I like that. It's crazy, but I like that. Heroin takes all the guilt, all the feelings away from you. That's why I use. If I get to feeling bad, feeling depressed, get the poor-me's, I see a bag of dope, it takes all that shit away. Automatic."

Many younger, more affluent users, however, were disturbed by the prospect of a mainline-induced death sentence. But concerns about AIDS hadn't deterred them from heroin— not when street-level purity often exceeded 50 percent. When heroin was that strong, dirty or stigmatizing needles could be avoided. Users could snort or smoke the drug (a practice dubbed "chasing the dragon" for the roiling fumes that resulted when heroin was heated on a piece of aluminum foil), drastically altering the demographics of smack. The DAWN reports had tracked an astounding shift in ingestion patterns from 1988 to 1993. In that five-year span, emergency-room visits attributed to sniffing or snorting heroin leapt 470 percent; episodes caused by IV injection rose 31 percent.

Users still lived in the ghetto, but they had also moved uptown and out to the suburbs. For sure, the usual suspects, The Sailor, the haunted Vietnam vets, the Times Square hookers, still used the shit. But college kids, fashion models, grunge musicians, and film stars had joined the swelling crowd. Of course, the long, depressing list of celebrity users stretched back to Billie Holiday, Charlie "Bird" Parker, and Lenny Bruce.

"It always comes back," said Carlo A. Boccia, the special agent in charge of DEA's New York field division who has waged counter-narcotics warfare for more than two decades. It has been a bloody, costly campaign, the law-enforcement equivalent of World War I stalemates at the Somme and Gallipoli. "Heroin is always here. We push it in a corner—boom—it's back."

5

Pussy Business

Loaded with enough baggage to give a Sherpa porter a double hernia, Sullivan and I left Boston on a bleak morning in November 1993 and flew to Bangkok. Our bulging backpacks held clothing, food, sleeping bags, medicine, water-purification equipment, first-aid stores, and three liters of Absolut vodka.

"We've gotta be prepared for any old thing," reasoned Sullivan.

My sidekick had also packed a large plastic jar of orange-flavored, Vitamin C-rich Tang, the logical mixer in our critical daily screwdrivers. The cocktails were the perfect prophylactic against the three Ys: scurvy, dysentery, and sobriety.

Somewhere over the Pacific, Sullivan recounted a caution-ary parable. Years before, he had traveled to Central America with Cal Bowden to scout a clandestine Bangkok-to-Boston route. (The pair wanted to be able to smuggle a POW into the United States.) In a Guatemala City bar, Sullivan had blithely ordered a screwdriver on the rocks. The vodka was top-shelf, the orange juice fresh-squeezed. The ice, made from unfiltered water, nearly killed him.

"I thought I was dying," said Sullivan. "Cal didn't know what to do with me. The bottom line is: We have to be careful. If one of us goes down, it's a big problem."

So we would have to drink Sullivan-style screwdrivers—Tang, filtered water, and Absolut—while inside Burma, served neat, at room temperature. Never, ever, over ice. In addition to our wet bar, we had also packed enough barter to buy Manhattan at current market prices. Flynn had told me that huge, gorgeous rubies could be had dirt-cheap in Burma. Pigeon's-blood stones for a pair of Levi's, even a couple of T-shirts. Why, the General even had a 43,000-carat rock the size of a basketball. Asian business protocol also demanded that we present gifts to the Shan functionaries and officials we would meet. Sullivan purchased several Swiss Army knives; I ransacked my closet for neckties. Khun Sa's henchmen would be smartly outfitted for jungle warfare and for back-room deals.

We had sweated a vexing etiquette problem: What do you bring the world's biggest druglord, a man with a private fiefdom, a personal army, and a multimillion-dollar fortune? Forget fine wine or liquor, Flynn advised. The General would give it away, thinking it might be poisoned. Flynn suggested a coffee-table book about horses, since the General was especially proud of his thoroughbred stallions, and X-rated videotapes, since he also enjoyed viewing pornography in the privacy of his jungle fortress.

"No Asians," Flynn said. "The General likes to watch white girls. Blondes."

I bought a 1994 horse-theme calendar at Barnes & Noble. Sullivan had just the X-rated tape: *The Chameleon*, a slick classic by porn standards that featured Tori Welles, a brunette, and several surgically enhanced blondes in ceaseless, complicated forms of hard-core coitus.

A profile of Khun Sa in an old issue of *Soldier of Fortune* noted that the warlord chain-smoked, so during the layover in Narita, Japan, Sullivan bought a duty-free carton of 555 State Express Filter King cigarettes, the cancer stick of choice in Anglophile Burma. As we boarded the connecting flight to Bangkok, Sullivan grinned conspiratorially. He had also purchased another bottle of Absolut. Be prepared for any old thing.

In spite of our exhaustive planning, the detailed pack lists we had checked and rechecked, the day-by-day itineraries, the swelling hogshead of vodka, I could not relax on the final leg to Bangkok. Too much doubt and unease, particularly about our man in Chiang Mai. To check out Flynn, I'd called in a favor with a Boston-area private investigator, Michael Szpuk, asking him to do a thorough workup, including a search of the National Crime Information Center database. No nothing. "I ran this guy every which way," my P.I. had said. "There are no identifiable records on this guy. He has no felonies in this country. He's clean up to this point. He could be like fucking Manson. Either he's clean or he's very, very slick."

I hoped for clean—and very, very slick. Given Flynn's abysmal relationship with Khun Sa's liaison officer, Khernsai Jaiyen, our stay in Burma would be strained, and might even degenerate into a power struggle. Had we backed the winner? I didn't want to contemplate the thought of failure. The Boston *Herald*, although intrigued by the chance for an exclusive interview with Khun Sa, had been unwilling to underwrite the story. To do so would mean covering my airfare and travel expenses, which I had estimated at three thousand dollars, and allowing me at least one month to report and write the stories for a lengthy series. A heavy commitment for a tabloid where long-term planning often went no further than a take-out order from the Chinatown Cafe. The story would also put me in *Herald* no-man's land. The news department wanted to take the proposed series, but I worked in features. My section would be short-staffed in my absence.

I considered the trip to the Far East, an interview with Khun Sa, and a chance to spend nearly a week in off-limits Shan State to be a golden opportunity. Dropping this story, particularly over turf distinctions or job-description semantics, was unthinkable. I would go to Burma on my own dime, my own time, I told the editors, then free-lance the story to the *Herald*. News would be happy. Features would be happy. There would be no interdepartmental problems. I had myself a deal. Now I just had to get the story, or I would be very, very unhappy.

In my last conversation with Flynn, a day before my departure, he had sounded supremely confident about our prospects. "The trip is 100 percent," he said. "I personally guarantee it."

He had also mentioned that an armed bodyguard, an ethnic Chinese mercenary by the name of Au Cheng, would ride shotgun on our cross-border foray. It seemed that Au Cheng was conversant in nearly a dozen local dialects and equally fluent with an assortment of automatic weapons.

"He's a killer," said Flynn. "When he gets angry, he means it. He's the only guy I apologize to."

Now, on the Bangkok-bound flight, Sullivan nudged me, then pointed to a passage from Bo Gritz's book, *A Nation Betrayed*. Sullivan had been studying the former Green Beret's account of his travels into Shan State, hoping to glean further intelligence about Burma. Sullivan hated surprises. "At Mae Hong Son," Gritz wrote, "we met one of Khun Sa's lieutenants who is in charge of opium trafficking by the name of Au Cheng, which means 'The Wall' in Chinese."

Terrific. It seemed our one-man security force also swam with drug smugglers. Not exactly the shy, retiring type. Why hadn't I packed that Kevlar vest? Before leaving for Thailand, I had gone to Empire Loan, a Boston pawnshop owned by a friend, Michael Goldstein, who had offered to let me borrow a bulletproof waistcoat. I had tried on the vest, found it too bulky and too hot. Besides, Goldstein only had one vest. John Wayne protocol dictated that everyone or no one should be armored in Indian country. Now if we got caught in a world of shit entering Shan State, we would have to count on Au Cheng's fighting spirit and Sullivan's connections to Saint Jude.

The suitcase also concerned me. Two weeks before my departure, Flynn had landed suddenly in Boston to sell more rubies and, apparently, to do some Christmas shopping. A few days before his return to Chiang Mai, I met him for dinner at the Chao Phraya, a Thai restaurant located in a shopping mall in Brockton, an old shoe-manufacturing town between Boston and New Bedford. In the mall's parking lot, Flynn handed over a large suitcase that he wanted me to deliver to him in Chiang Mai. Heavy luggage would be an unwieldy liability on his byzantine, illegal, roundabout route into southern Thailand, he explained. I hefted the bag, feeling like a cheap hood in a bad movie.

"Jesus Christ, Barry. This feels like a shot-put collection, not clothing. There wouldn't be any contraband, would there?"

"Yes," Flynn said with a chuckle. "I'm the first man to smuggle heroin No. 4 *into* Shan State."

I didn't want to be set up or surprised in Bangkok. I opened the suitcase. Inside was a compact Kmart: three quilted jackets, two new pairs of Levi's, new belts and socks, children's sweaters and sweatsuits, Play-Doh, blank videocassette tapes, cold medicine, and a large-scale toy train, a present for the second birthday of Flynn's son.

"The train's made out of C4," Flynn said. We both laughed. In 1986, David Scott Weekly had carried two hundred pounds of C4 plastic explosive aboard a commercial flight from

Oklahoma City to Las Vegas, where he was training Afghan *mujahedeen* with Gritz. Weekly plead guilty and received a five-year prison sentence at Lompoc, California.

Flynn asked another favor: he needed $250 so he could buy a one-way discount air-courier ticket to Singapore. The travel agent wouldn't accept his maxed-out Thai credit card. He was reluctant to ask his family for money. If he couldn't get out of New Bedford, how could he take me into Burma? In the face of this eleventh-hour hurdle, I agreed to advance the cash. As collateral, Flynn gave me seven cabochon-cut Burmese rubies. When I arrived in Chiang Mai, he would refund the loan of $250 and take back the rubies. I went to an automatic-teller machine at the Brockton mall and withdrew the money. Now, I thought, I'm smuggling Burmese rubies *back* into Thailand.

Flynn slipped me the gems, then smiled. "If you forget to bring the rubies to Chiang Mai, you'll have to explain to Khun Sa where his samples went."

═══════

It all came back, the aromas of Asia run amok, the smells of alluvial Bangkok, the low-tide stench of a shining city built on mud flats and rice paddies—olfactory overload the moment we left Northwest Airlines' quiet, filtered, air-conditioned comfort and lurched, half-Xanaxed, down the stairway to the oil-slickened tarmac of Don Muang International Airport. Around midnight, nearly 90 enervating degrees Fahrenheit, our lungs gasping thick, humid air laced with the acrid scents of jet fuel and car exhaust, wood smoke and peanut oil, stagnant water and rotting vegetation.

Nearly as soon as an unsmiling Thai immigration official cleared us through passport control, the hotel touts pounced. First time Bangkok? they sang. Here to shop? Where you stay? We ignored the rapacious, jostling mob and pushed through the scrum to grab the first available cab, agreed to the four-hundred-baht price to a cheap downtown hotel without even a half-hearted attempt to negotiate the fare. For sixteen dollars, our driver was only too happy to sit in gridlock. Inside his Toyota sedan, figurines of the Buddha, postcards of beatific monks, and cologne bottles rested on a saffron-colored swatch of shag carpet covering the dashboard. We could curse King Chulalongkorn, whose picture was taped to a window visor, for the abominable traffic. The turn-of-the-century monarch, the great modernizer of Thailand, had built the first paved roads and spawned his country's great love affair with internal combustion. Even at this late hour, the traffic still crept along Wiphawadirangsit Road, the superhighway from the airport into the city, some fifteen miles to the south.

Then again, traffic crawled at almost every hour of every day in Bangkok, home to 90 percent of Thailand's motor vehicles. Nearly six million people in the capital, most of them sitting in unmoving, overheated vehicles unequipped with catalytic converters. An astounding assortment of transport—scooters and motorcycles with multiple pillion riders, overcrowded *tuk-tuks* and song thaews, standing-room only two-baht buses and diesel lorries—jockeyed for position in the cacophony, revving engines, honking horns, farting blue fumes into the fecund night. Helpless policemen marched through the haze, dressed for the plague years: brown uniforms, sunglasses, helmets, and surgical masks. There was no salvation in this innermost ring of traffic hell. From 1984 to 1991, the number of vehicles in Bangkok had more than doubled, from 1.1 million to 2.5 million, yet road surface had increased just 1 percent. During the same period, traffic speed on the city's main streets had slowed from nine to five miles per hour, barely faster than a slow jog on a sultry day.

Our driver turned down the shrill Thai pop music on his car

radio, cranked up the air conditioning, and handed us a large scrapbook. Inside were brochures for hotels, restaurants, tourist attractions, and massage parlors catering to farang. "You want shopping tomorrow?" he asked. "I know good place for gem."

No thanks. No shopping. No gems.

"You want crocodile farm? Floating market? Bridge on River Kwai?" He whistled the familiar opening bars of "Colonel Bogey March."

No crocs. No markets. No bridges.

"You want Thai lady massage?"

No thanks. No Thai lady. The driver pointed to a small flyer taped to a page of his scrapbook. Known in the local trade as a "pussy-tricks" card, the typewritten handouts were brandished by Patpong touts to steer clients toward their bar's sex show. In broken English, the card promised acts that would make even Tori Welles blush:

> Boy & Girl Make Love Show
> Girl & Girl Lesbian Show
> Pussy Shooting Balloon Show
> Pussy Ping-Pong Show
> Pussy Smoking Cigarettes Show
> Pussy Write Letter Show
> Pussy Open the Bottle Show
> Pussy Candle Fire Show
> Pussy Chop Sticks Show
> Pussy Drink Beer Show
> Girl & Snake Show
> Sexy Dance Show

In his rearview mirror, the driver saw me making notes about the pussy-tricks bill of fare.

"You professor?"

No, I demurred.

"I think you professor, come to Thailand, write article," he continued. "I had professor last week. He fifty-four. He take two girl. Sandwich! Fifty-four, but strong!"

It was only logical the driver wanted to steer us toward a fuck-show bar or a massage parlor, for which he would receive a small commission. Every year, hundreds of thousands of male tourists, primarily from Japan, Germany, Australia, and the United States, fly to The Land of Smiles—not for the white-sand beaches, not for the jungle trekking, but for the cheap, available sex. Various estimates put the number of male and female sex workers from eight hundred thousand to almost two million, out of a total population of fifty-six million.

Bangkok cemented its fleshpot reputation during the Vietnam War. In 1965, the kingdom allowed the United States to use air bases in the northeast cities of Khorat, Ta Khli, Udon Thani, Nakhon Phanom, and Ubon Ratchathani; two years later, American soldiers stationed in Vietnam were permitted to visit Thailand for R & R, the bleary rest and recreation granted during a one-year tour of duty. In short order, GIs were raving about Thai bars, Thai beer, Thai beaches, but most of all about Thai boom-boom girls: Number One, better than Saigon whores. By 1970, the amount of money spent by U.S. service-men on R & R (also known as I & I, for Intercourse and Intoxication, or B & B, for booze and broads) approached twenty million dollars.

The sex trade, however, was not a sin foisted by the depraved West upon a chaste Asian nation. Prostitution had flourished in Thailand, entirely legal and completely accept-able, for centuries. British civil engineer Holt S. Hallett, who traveled extensively through northern Thailand in the 1870s to explore possible rail routes to Burma and China, noted that "many of the princes and nobles treat the brothel-keepers, some of whom wear his Majesty's uniform, as bosom friends and are seen riding in the same carriage with them." Hallet continued: "The prostitutes are all slaves, having been sold by their nearest relations in order to pay their gambling debts, or to aid their parents who are in the clutches of the law, the parents promising to buy them back as soon as they can. As a rule, they are said to be more modest and particular than the same class of women in Europe."

Slavery prospered in Thailand until 1905, when it was abolished by King Chulalongkorn. Before the king's action, prostitutes were acquired at slave markets to work in brothels and even in private homes. The Law of Three Seals, written in 1805, allowed for "slave wives." The law, now defunct, also codified another spousal role bound to offend Christian morals: the *mia noi*, or "minor wife." By his wife, minor wives, and consorts, King Chulalongkorn fathered seventy-six children. Monogamy, in the form of the "parental-consent wife," did not become the sole legal form of marriage until 1935. There was still no penalty in Thailand for polygamy and many men retained "minor" wives.

Prostitution was legal until 1960, when it was outlawed by Field Marshal Sarit Thanarat, who had taken control of the kingdom in 1957 in the time-honored Thai fashion of a bloodless coup d'etat. Although he repudiated whores, Sarit supported more than one hundred mia noi. He could afford to. When he died in 1963, the supremely corrupt prime minister left an estate worth a reported $150 million.

A flourishing cross-border trade now sentenced tens of thousands of rural Burmese women to Thai whorehouses. A 1993 Asia Watch report, *A Modern Form of Slavery*, painted their short, grim future: debt bondage, illegal confinement, sexual and physical abuse, inevitable HIV infection. The Thai Parliament had yet to ratify the Convention for the Suppression of the Traffic in Persons and of the Exploitation of the Prostitution of Others, which was approved by the United Nations General Assembly in 1949. Thai border guards and police had full knowledge and complicity in the racket—in fact, they were often the brothels' best customers, receiving complimentary sex for turning a blind eye to the slave trade.

No one, not the prime minister, not the members of parliament, not even revered King Bhumibol, could eliminate a practice ingrained deeply in a gracious culture that was alternately prim and profane. In Thailand, courting was almost puritanical; public displays of affection rarely heated up beyond hand-holding. Yet one Thai study reported that 75 percent of Thai men have had sex with a prostitute and that nearly half (48 percent) had their first sexual experience with a whore. Anthropologist Cleo Odzer, who lived in Thailand for three years to research *Patpong Sisters*, her 1994 book about sex workers, explained that this whoremongering was not considered adulterous behavior in Thailand; according to Buddhist precepts for laymen, there was no sin in having sex with a woman as long as she was unmarried.

Our disappointed driver was only too happy to dump us at our downtown hotel. A functional place frequented by mid-level Asian businessmen, the Sathorn Inn stood next to a decrepit Chinese Christian cemetery on a quiet lane, or *soi*, between Sathorn Road, which was dotted with embassies, banks, and hospitals, and Silom Road, where jewelry stores did land-rush business during the day and transient merchants turned bigger profits along the buckled brick sidewalks at night. After checking in and making a few phone calls, we decided to hit the town—a no-brainer decision. We were too keyed up by the time-zone differential, the adventure ahead, and by the news Sullivan had just received when he checked his answering machine. There'd been a message from an old acquaintance, Tim Williams, a Vietnam veteran from St. Cloud, Florida, who had made a half-dozen trips to Southeast Asia looking for POWs.

"You never call me," Williams had drawled. "I ought to keep you in suspense, but I won't. Phoumano has a two-hour video of a POW. Call Phoumano as soon as possible."

"Unbelievable timing!" said Sullivan. "He calls and I'm already heading over to Bangkok. I've got to see this video!"

I was dubious, given the quality of Phoumano's previous "evidence," his role in the scam surrounding the alleged Carr photo, and his links to Thai military and American intelligence officials. It would be imprudent to tip our hand, I argued, to let Phoumano know we were in-country and heading for Burma. Although Sullivan could barely contain his excitement, he agreed not to contact Phoumano until after our Shan State excursion. But the timing couldn't be better, Sullivan observed, as we headed out for a few hours on the still lively town. Talk about a daily double: an audience with Khun Sa *and* a video of a live POW.

We walked east along Silom Road, heading for the Patpong, wending our way through the good citizens of Bangkok who insisted on living every aspect of their lives out of doors on the teeming sidewalks. A woman stood engulfed in the flumes of her steaming wok, stir-frying chicken, mushrooms, and bamboo shoots for the late-night Saturday diners who waited to dine al fresco—or more accurately, *al olio*—in a Venusian atmosphere dense as grease and reeking of the *klongs*, the postcard-exotic, sewage-clogged canals. A few feet away, a seamstress stitched a trouser hem with an ancient, pedal-powered Singer machine that rocked on broken pavement mottled with bird droppings. Mongrel bitches, ears shredded and scarred from fights, black teats distended from unending litters, dozed in doorways. Amputees and cripples moved through the crowd, begging for a few baht.

Sullivan knew the terrain. Lucy's Tiger Den, a crossroads for the knaves, barstool commandos, and true believers involved in the search for POWs, had operated just north of the Patpong district, the three-block wide entertainment strip named for the family that owned the land between Silom and Surawong Roads. This night, as always, bulged with adventures in the skin trade: live-sex shows, no-holds-barred massage parlors, salacious go-go girls, and coy bar boys. The westernmost streets, Patpong 1 and Patpong 2, were connected by two narrow lanes, Soi Superstar and Soi Crazy Horse, and lined with clubs—Butterfly, Queen's Castle, Rififi—catering to heterosexual men. Patpong 3, or Soi Jaruwan, a parallel, dead-end alley known as Soi Katoey (Transsexual Lane) ran off Silom and was packed with homosexual bars like the Apollo Inn, Genesis, and Rome Discotheque. Thaniya Road, just east of Patpong 3 and lit up like the Ginza, catered exclusively to Japanese sex tourists. During the day, this area was home to legitimate enterprise. At night, however, the Patpong's storefronts became a souk of the senses, while its streets were jammed with booths selling pirated music cassettes, bogus Louis Vuitton luggage, fake Hermes scarves, imitation Ralph Lauren Polo shirts, laughable knockoffs of Moschino belts. Three tape? For you, one hundred baht. Best quality. Sandals better than Teva, 150 baht. You make offer. One hundred baht? Oh, my Buddha. For you, 140 baht. Best price. Have look-see.

Buttressing this carnival like surreal bookends were two American roadside icons, Kentucky Fried Chicken and McDonald's. Occidental tourists could order a Big Mac, fries, and a shake and still have enough money to buy out that red-light special on Patpong 2 for short-time love. A massage-parlor barker approached. Like a waiter presenting a menu, he casually opened a photo album, flipped through pictures of beautiful, sullen women.

"You want Thai lady?"

"Not interested."

We kept walking through the milling night bazaar crowd of bargain shoppers, appalled package tourists, self-righteous trekkers, drunken punters, and off-duty bar girls. The barker followed, persistent.

"You want Thai boy?"

A Patpong 3 pimp overhead the question, sidled up.

"You look for something special?" he whispered.

How about a titty-bar beer for 25 baht? That would be special. We turned into Patpong 1. The claims grew bolder. Best girl in Bangkok. Best gay in Bangkok. Outside Super Girl, an audacious hand-printed sign: "This bar is so good that it is only bar in Patpong that is mentioned by the Rolling Stone magazine." Any publicity, even in an article entitled "Death in the Candy Store," about the looming AIDS problem partly fueled by Bangkok's bar scene, was judged good for business.

Touts buzzed like horseflies, slapping backs, flashing pussy-tricks cards. Dull, wet thuds floated from Blue Sky Bar where two kickboxers traded bored, balletic blows. The air rippled with the manic energy of a stock-exchange trading pit, the unctuous sleaze of a state-fair midway.

"You like?" asked the tout. He nodded upward. "No cover. No rip-off."

The sex shows took place in second-floor bars, behind closed doors. This allowed the owners ample warning in the remote case that the Bangkok police decided to raid the premises. It also allowed management to charge hyperinflated prices for drinks, as it was very difficult for fleeced customers to leave without paying the tab. We climbed the stairs to Pussy

Galore, where the smoky, cooled air pulsed with the beat of "One Night in Bangkok"—the song from the London musical *Chess* in heavy rotation at every Patpong club—and what sounded like the honking of a flock of geese. Inside the club, four naked women lay on their backs on a raised, spotlit stage in the center of the bar, flexing powerful diaphragm muscles to force air through plastic horns inserted into their vaginas.

Pussy Blow Horn Show.

According to Cleo Odzer, there is a strict hierarchy among Patpong women; this would-be wind section ranked somewhere in the middle. The lowest employment was in blow-job bars, fellating strangers beneath tables, followed by work in a fuck show. (Rumor had it, however, that one married Thai couple made a lucrative income screwing onstage, a performance they repeated at a half-dozen Patpong clubs a night.) The next rung up the Patpong employment ladder was dancing nude or performing pussy-trick shows in a rip-off bar; the same job in a non–rip-off bar was considered better. A classy act was bikini dancing in a ground-floor bar. The prostitute's pantheon was occupied by women who wore evening clothes, who sat in dark booths in ground-floor bars and never shed their clothes to dance.

We grabbed stools at the bar and ordered Singhas. In a nearby booth, a thin bar girl dressed in shorts and a kimono with a numbered button pinned to her lapel, for convenient farang identification, was closing a deal. She refilled her sunburned, half-sodden customer's glass with beer, laughed at his profane gibberish, indulged his furtive groping beneath the folds of her kimono as she massaged his tumescent trousers. Tonight he would buy her out, pay Pussy Galore 350 baht to take her off-premises. He would slap down another 200 baht to rent a short-time room at one of the nearby "love hotels," such as Patpong's MMM Apartments, if his own hotel frowned on drunken guests parading garishly costumed prostitutes through the lobby. He would pay her at least a Purple King, the lilac-colored five-hundred-baht note adorned with King Bhumibol's portrait, worth about twenty dollars. A Purple King was the going farang rate for sex with a second-floor pussy-tricks girl—it looked cheap for a trick to have to make change. He would not think that there was at least a one-in-five chance that the delicate woman was HIV-positive.

A teenaged girl, barely five feet tall, with skin the hue of sesame oil and an ebony waterfall of hair cascading down her bare back, slid up and grabbed my thigh. It was time for Twenty Questions, Patpong style. She smiled, then proffered her magic fingers for that strange farang custom, the handshake.

"Hello whatyourname?" she sang in bar-girl English.

"Franz Kafka."

"Howlongstay Bangkok?"

"One night in Bangkok."

"Youmarry?"

"Yes."

She pouted.

"Youlikeme?"

"Yes, but . . ."

She beamed.

"Mister Franz, whatyoudo Bangkok?"

"Business."

Her Buddha eyes danced. Like many of the women in Pussy Galore, on Patpong in general, she was ethnic Lao and hailed from Isan, the poor, rural area of northeast Thailand. Isan bar girls were the dark, exotic fantasy favored by farang men. The "flowers of the north," the fair-skinned women from Chiang Rai and Chiang Mai provinces, were more prone to work in

Thai or Chinese brothels, where the color-conscious clients preferred lighter-complected prostitutes. On stage, the women positioned smoldering Krong Thips.

Pussy Smoking Cigarettes Show.

In the prewar era, street touts often presented male tourists in Bangkok with calling cards, but the ancient come-ons were veiled, seductive as sandalwood incense: "Oh, gentleman, sir, Miss Pretty Girl welcome you Sultan Turkish Bath, gentle polite massage, put you in dreamland with perfume soap. Latest gramophone music. Oh, such service. You come now! Miss Pretty Girl want you, massage you from tippy-toe to head-top, nice, clean, to enter Gates of Heaven."

Ah, but we lived in diminished times. I drained my Singha.

"Mister Franz, buy me lady drink?"

"Yes."

She smiled again. A commission. The girl waved for another beer and a fifty-baht glass of sweetened water. When the drinks came, she checked to ensure her bar-girl number was on the receipt, then stuffed the bill into a bamboo cup.

It was time for the farang's Twenty Questions.

"What's your name?"

"Bin," she said.

In Thai, the same word also meant "the bill." Among the first words a cash-flush visitor learns: *bin*. I pantomimed signing a receipt. Bin laughed and spoke in Thai to a girlfriend who was grilling and hellowhatyournaming Sullivan without success, aside from cadging a two-dollar lady drink.

"Bin, what do you do in Bangkok?"

"Business."

I arched my eyebrows, dubious.

"Business, Bin?"

She pouted and wiggled her pert, bare breasts. The stage

was a roiling mass of cigarette fumes, high heels, and honey-hued flesh.

"Pussy business, Mister Franz."

=====

We had reached Interzone, William S. Burroughs' unbridled bazaar. Entropic Bangkok was the epicenter of Thailand's hell-bent pursuit of baht. The country was an economic tiger, exploding at 9-percent annual growth. Anything could be plundered, nearly everyone had a price tag: endangered wildlife, tropical hardwood, Isan women, government officials. In Bangkok, even the dead were a commodity. Enterprising private ambulance companies were known to arrive at the scene of fatal accidents, take possession of the bodies, and then ransom the corpses to bereaved relatives of the dearly departed.

Official corruption seemed pandemic. "Squeeze" and "tea money" greased the skids for illegal logging, slapdash construction projects, unsafe working conditions. Profits rolled in, periodically interrupted by the disasters of business rapacity: In early 1989, scores of Thais died in flooding and landslides blamed on the illegal cutting of trees. Just three months before our trip, at least one hundred people were killed in Khorat when the Royal Plaza Hotel, considered the best in town, collapsed under the weight of a poorly built three-story addition. In May, fire had raged through a toy factory in Bangkok; substandard construction and locked emergency-exit doors pushed the death toll to nearly two hundred. After these disasters, there were brief bursts of indignation and outrage, then the inevitable return of chronic, collective amnesia.

And hovering over everything in the blithe, gentle kingdom was the specter of AIDS. In 1992, the Population and Community Development Association (PDA), the largest nongovernmental organization in Thailand, estimated two to four hundred thousand HIV-positive cases nationwide. Although intravenous drug use was the initial culprit in the spread of AIDS, most infections now occurred through heterosexual sex in brothels. Whorehouses were technically illegal but had flourished since the Entertainment Places Act of 1966 had transferred the licensing of nightclubs, bars, and massage parlors to the jurisdiction of local law-enforcement authorities. In short order, licensing and operating arrangements became steeped in tea money. A study by Chulalongkorn University estimated that Bangkok's one thousand "entertainment" houses paid out six hundred thousand dollars a month in bribes to local police.

While the police and brothel operators profited by the unholy alliance, the virus raged through the Thai populace. By the twenty-first century, predicted the PDA, Thailand would be decimated if nothing was done to halt the spread of AIDS. The gloomy forecast: approximately one hundred and eighty thousand deaths annually, two to four million HIV-positive men and women, a 10- to 20-percent loss in gross domestic product.

The Thai solution? Smile, profess wonderment and doubt, play "One Night in Bangkok" a little louder, utter the all-purpose Thai phrase: *Mai pen rai*. It was all right, it didn't matter. AIDS killed farang, not Thai. Any crackdown meant bad publicity, with farang men fleeing Bangkok and Pattaya for the girls and boys of Manila or Colombo, Hong Kong or Macau. Very bad for business.

We stumbled down Patpong 1, fatigue, Singha, and post-Xanax blues sparring with vestigal consciousness and the wary arousal that came from watching a naked woman extract razor blades from her vagina. The street scene resembled the French Quarter of New Orleans in the early, post-bacchanal hours of Ash Wednesday: crumpled plastic bags, discarded food wrappers, last-call drunks. Sweepers scratched straw brooms along the greasy road. Inside Blue Sky Bar, a dozen dateless *katoey* gathered glumly to watch an American boxing movie, *Gladiator*, and stare at male passersby. A lithe bar girl drifted out of the shadows, smelling of desperation and night-blooming jasmine.

"Hello, whereyougo?" she purred.

"We go to hotel, go to sleep. Alone."

The night-bazaar merchants dismantled scaffolding and loaded unsold bootleg goods into wheeled packing cases. Tuk-tuks lined up three-deep at curbside along Silom Road, hoping for cross-town fares. At 4 a.m., street vendors still hawked high heels, pulp fiction, skewers of sausage. Prepubescent girls walked toward the Patpong balancing food-stall plates of sticky rice and stir-fried vegetables. For whom? Mothers? Sisters? Pimps? Touts? Bangkok policemen stood by an empty paddy wagon, smoking Krong Thips, unimpressed with the illegal counterfeit merchandise, disinterested in the outlawed sex trade. Sullivan chuckled.

"The King has gotta know," he said. "I mean, look at this. Don't you think he sits in his castle, shakes his head, and says: This is one corrupt place?"

A warm breeze off the turbid Chao Phraya River caressed the *tabebuia* and *pradu* shade trees lining Silom Road. Through the rasping, grit-caked leaves, the gleaming, sinking skyscrapers built on former paddy land seemed to shudder. "The whole country's on the take," Sullivan pronounced.

6

The Gilded Triangle

We could only smile, shake our heads, and repeat rule number three: Nothing ever went as planned. We stood stewing at the ticket counter in the domestic terminal of the airport, tired, irritable, trying to process the disturbing, irrefutable fact that we were not listed on the manifest for Thai Airways 104, the 9:50 a.m. flight to Chiang Mai. Without a mention on the list, there was no way we were getting boarding passes. Some pathfinders we were, dead in the water, still inside Bangkok city limits. The worst-case scenario unraveled like a tire sloughing its retread. We would miss this flight and our connecting flight to Mae Hong Son, upsetting the tight choreography of our border crossing. That could scrub the entire trip, strand us in Bangkok, sentenced to a cheap hotel to stare at cinderblock walls and empty notebooks.

Our egregious sin: we had not reconfirmed the flight to Chiang Mai at least seventy-two hours in advance of travel. I waved our tickets, purchased the day before we left Boston. We couldn't reconfirm the flight seventy-two hours in advance—hell, we didn't even *buy* the tickets until forty-eight hours in advance. And we couldn't call to reconfirm after purchasing the tickets because we had been thirty-five thousand feet above sea level, in transit from America. Anyway, wasn't the fact we had already paid $147 apiece for the tickets evidence of our good faith and sincere commitment to fly Thai Airways?

No. Domestic tickets must be reconfirmed, in Bangkok, three days before flight. A rule was a rule.

Remain calm, refuse to leave, retell the story. Revert to ugly American form. Speak simply, slowly, loudly. Then they'll understand, right? We don't *have* tickets *three* days ago. We *buy* tickets just *two* days ago. Then we fly. *No* telephone on airplane. In the next queue, a distraught, newlywed Australian couple had learned their tickets to Phuket were no good. So sorry, the flight was overbooked. They had not reconfirmed. Perhaps there was room on the afternoon flight. Please to have a seat. The husband spoke quickly, loudly. *"Bloody hell . . ."*

"Smile," Sullivan said through clenched teeth. "And don't move. We ain't leaving this counter."

Behind us, travelers in our lengthening line craned their necks to see what the dumb, childish farang had done. We smiled and recited the woeful litany. We have tickets only two days ago. Then we fly. No way to call, to confirm. The ticket agent finally sighed and tapped her computer. A printer spat out two precious boarding passes: Chiang Mai. Have a pleasant flight.

We strutted through security, ebullient with our small victory. A sign advised passengers that it was forbidden to carry blowpipe darts, sickles, swords, tridents, and spears aboard the plane. Sidearms were allowed, so long as they were not loaded. The airport had thoughtfully provided sand-filled "pistol bullet clearing boots" for travelers to fire their gun magazines into. By the time we arrived at the gate, Thai Airways had already called for the monks. In Thailand, there were two aircraft boarding sequences: monks, then everybody else. Once the holy men were seated, the remaining passengers surged down the jetway and onto the sold-out Airbus.

"Now you know what I go through every time I come over," Sullivan said. "It's a wonder I don't blow my brains out."

The hour-long flight to Chiang Mai was uneventful—a slow, whining climb through the smothering smog of Bang-kok, a smooth, straight cruise over the green, gridded rice pad-dies and crocodile farms of the fertile central plains, a soft descent into the northern hill country—and enlivened only by the striking Thai bar girl sitting across the aisle. A sleeveless black top and fashionable black bell-bottom pants worked to great effect against her dark Isan arms and lithe legs. She was no pussy-tricks girl. Her farang companion would have paid a small fortune to buy her out of her club for several days, not to mention the fee—at least fifteen hundred baht a day, judg-ing by her sophisticated looks—it would cost to enjoy her company.

Sullivan and I declined the in-flight meal, a cold pastry stuffed with curried chicken, to discuss the day's nearly scuttled itinerary. We would meet Flynn at the airport in Chiang Mai, where I would turn over his gift-laden suitcase and his prob-lematic rubies. I had no intention of disappointing his children, or of crossing his favorite druglord. Khun Sa's gems were sequestered in my boogie bag, wrapped in a small, cotton-filled box snuggled inside a pair of soiled socks. The Thai considered the feet to be the lowest part of the body; in the remote case of a search of my baggage, I hoped this aversion also applied to foul-smelling hosiery.

After a forty-minute layover, we would connect on Thai Airways 192 to Mae Hong Son, arriving just after noon. We were to check in at the Baiyoke Chalet, across the street from the town's post office, and wait until 5 p.m. for Flynn and Au Cheng, who had been able to buy tickets only for Thai Airways 198, the last flight of the day to Mae Hong Son. A little dinner, a few local sights, a couple of Absolut-and-Tang cocktails, then lights out. At 5 a.m., we would move out for Burma. Easy, in theory.

In Chiang Mai less than five minutes, however, we could only smile, shake our heads, and sing two-part harmony: rule number three. After Flynn's Shan wife, Malee, had greeted us with a wai, a delicate prayer-like curtsey of respect, and fresh *malai* garlands, he gave us the bad news. The sharp, heady scent of marigolds, white-jasmine buds, tuber roses, and orchids cushioned Flynn's incredible Thai Airways tale. He had called and reserved tickets for himself and Au Cheng aboard flight 198, and even reconfirmed the flight by telephone. But when they arrived at the airport to meet us, Flynn was stunned to learn that he and Au Cheng didn't have tickets. So sorry, Mister Barry. The flight was sold out. His reservation was useless. Instead, he and Au Cheng had been waitlisted, along with twenty other irate passengers who had also reconfirmed the flight. Judging by the scene at the ticket counter, earlier flights had been canceled, causing a ripple effect on subsequent planes. It looked like the chaos on the U.S. Embassy roof just before the last American chopper flew out of Saigon.

"Lie-land," Flynn said, with tired derision.

A Thai man who owned the riverfront restaurant where Flynn was a fixture would drive him and Au Cheng to Mae Hong Son that afternoon. I made a quick decision: Sullivan and I would not fly on ahead to the border town—to do so seemed selfish. We were all in this foray together, and would share their miserable, two-hundred-mile passage across bad mountain roads. There was no need to worry about making it to Mae

Hong Son that night, Flynn assured me. His friend, Keutsada Panyatipaya, whom everyone called "Noi," was a pedal-to-the-metal wheelman who could shave plenty of time off the nine-hour drive. Until departure, there was nothing to do but curse Thai Airways and enjoy Flynn's haunts.

———

He had come a long way from New Bedford, Massachusetts. Chiang Mai, with less than two hundred thousand people and a mere fraction of Bangkok's vile tuk-tuks to foul its temperate breezes, was quite literally a breath of fresh air after the miasmal vapors of the capital. Bangkok had been built in desperation, after the Burmese had sacked the royal capital of Ayutthaya in 1767. Chiang Mai, on the other hand, had been built upon an inspiration. In 1296, King Mengrai, the monarch of Lanna Thai, The Land of One Million Rice Fields, elected to build his empire's new capital on an auspicious spot where he had seen two white sambar deer, two white barking deer, and five white mice near a scared Bo tree, *Ficus religiosa*.

For nearly seven hundred years, Chiang Mai had preserved its scale, intimacy, and cultural identity. Aggressive and fiercely independent, Lanna Thai waged an ongoing battle with Ayutthaya, the Siamese kingdom to its south, for most of the first half of the sixteenth century. In 1556, Chiang Mai fell to the expansionist Burmese, who also rolled through Ayutthaya and Laos. It would be thirty years before the Burmese were driven out, and two centuries until sporadic warfare ceased. It was not until 1796, during the reign of King Chakri, the founder of the dynasty that still held the Thai throne, that Chiang Mai was annexed by Siam. Well after World War I, a journey from Bangkok meant a month-long ordeal by boat and elephant. In this splendid isolation, "The Rose of the North" enjoyed a degree of semi-autonomy until 1939, when the last

Prince of Chiang Mai died. Since World War II it had risen from the status of distant backwater to become, after Bangkok, the most important city in Thailand.

Inside its silting moat, behind the crumbling, crenalated orange-red fortifications of the Old City, lay more than one square mile of an older, more traditional urban Asia, the kind that was rapidly being razed in Bangkok to make way for high-rise office buildings. Walled, shaded compounds held Lanna-style teak homes decorated with *kalae*, V-shaped carvings resembling buffalo horns that jutted from roof beams. Shop-keepers sold lacquerware, ceramics, and wood figurines from narrow storefronts that also served as living rooms and sleeping areas. Well-kept wats, many dating to the mid-fifteenth century when the city hosted a major synod of Thereveda Buddhism, dotted the city. Few dilapidated temples tainted devout Thailand, since contributing to monastery construction or *stupa* repair was considered one of the highest forms of *tam boon*, or making merit. (There were other, cheaper ways to build merit. Enterprising boys lurked outside many *bots*, the main temple prayer buildings, clutching small, bamboo birdcages. For twenty baht, sinners could buy two caged plain-back sparrows, then open the purse-shaped contraption, thus freeing the birds and accruing tam boon for the kind act.)

On every light post, telephone pole, and shop window, banners and posters announced Loi Krathong, and impending Festival of the Floating Leaf Cups. For centuries, the Thai had celebrated the retreat of the summer monsoon with offerings to Pra Mae Kong Kha, the river goddess. Every November, on the full moon, tiny lotus-shaped boats were cast into the Ping River. Fashioned from folded banana leaves and loaded with fresh gardenias, smoldering *joss* sticks, and lit candles, the kra-thong floats served a dual purpose—a gift of gratitude to the waters that nourished the rich earth of the valley, and an act of contrition for fouling Pra Mae Kong Kha's once-pristine rivers. At the same time, sky lanterns were released to the heavens. As one's sins were washed away by gifts to the river, so bad luck and sorrow were borne away by the wind.

The last decade had seen the tendrils of Western popular culture penetrate the aesthetic mortar of Chiang Mai. The walls of the Old City were crumbling fast. Formerly a trekker's secret, the region had been discovered by package tourists. In just an hour they could be transported from hellish Bangkok to a leisurely paradise where travel agencies offered elephant rides, river rafting, snake shows, and orchid-farm tours. Inevitably, these tourists had carried with them the spores of the "progress" they intended to flee. Resort homes dotted the hills. New hotels and guest houses sprouted along the banks of the Ping. Along nearby Changklan Road, where Asia's most famous commercial night bazaar was held, franchise restaurants— Burger King, KFC, Mister Donut, and Baskin-Robbins—had taken root. And for every merchant selling dried cuttlefish or hilltribe textiles at the market there was a knockoff artist peddling counterfeit Calvin Klein underwear or Lacoste shirts.

"Baby Bangkok," sniffed Flynn.

═══════

The young Akha mother shuffled down the street, clad in a filthy, faded indigo jacket, frayed halter, and dirt-caked leggings. Her hair lay uncovered, dull black and matted. Her appearance was shocking. Although her tribe was one of the poorest in Thailand, Akha women were renowned for their colorful everyday clothing and for their ornate, silver-encrusted headdresses. The fallen woman carried a cheap, tattered Chinese parasol to shade the infant son tied to her back. The smiling boy wore an incongruously jaunty cap. She greeted me with a wai, stared with thousand-yard eyes, and offered her open palm. No words, just a moan that sounded like total defeat.

She had lost The Way. For her ancestor-worshiping people, who had no term for religion, there was only "the Akha Way." Inside the close-knit Akha villages, The Way governed every aspect of life, from planting to home construction, from courting to death. The Way even dictated the site of a new village, which was determined through an "egg-drop test." The *nyi pa*, or shaman, dropped a chicken egg from shoulder height into a shallow hole. If the egg did not break, the locale was considered propitious. Construction could begin. If the egg did break, well, there were endless hills and plenty of eggs. In its own way, the egg-drop method was more practical than waiting for the auspicious appearance of white deer and albino mice.

This desperate woman had strayed from the righteous path and received her tribe's sternest sentence: banishment. Perhaps she had come to the city to search for work and to marvel at strange lowland ways and wondrous consumer goods brought by the *gala pyu*, the "white Indians" who trekked through her poor village. Perhaps she had been sold by her impoverished parents for a few thousand baht to a smooth-talking broker. Throughout the rural north, thousands of women annually quit school after *prathom* six, the last mandatory grade, to earn money for their families. The women of Chiang Rai, Phayao, and Lampang provinces were famous for their pale beauty, and brothel agents scoured the countryside looking for underage, virgin girls who would bring a premium in the whorehouses of Sampeng District, Bangkok's Chinatown. In the age of AIDS, the brokers cast their nets wider, seeking younger, disease-free children. The evil now broke over the mountains like dirty waves.

The brokers usually promised a city job in an office or factory; the girl would work off the agent's fee advanced to the parents, who would try to convince themselves a good, honest job awaited their poorly educated daughter. Better than the truth: confinement in a Thai brothel, forced to lie with twenty customers a day, one hundred baht a coupling, no protection. Their daughter would never have heard of AIDS. When the chronic coughing and the fatigue came, she continued to work, desperate to claw out of debt. When the sickness could not be hidden, she went home to die, only to be turned away by the *bu seh*, the Akha headman, who could not allow bad magic to pass through the village's sacred *lok kho* gate, who would set clay dolls afire, even butcher dogs and then impale their heads on stakes to ward off evil spirits.

The daughter now was doomed to wander the valleys, cadging food in the *talaat*, sleeping in the sois, begging for baht in the night bazaar. She was not alone in her estrangement. Burdened by poverty, constrained by vanishing forest, tempted by encroaching Western culture, bedeviled by AIDS, at the mercy of drug addiction, the nomadic hilltribes of Thailand were in a state of slow, inexorable collapse. Rejecting the backbreaking, subsistence labors of their parents, detribalized youths flocked to the cities for work. But their poor fluency in Central Thai and their rudimentary education marked them as *kariang*, rubes or hicks to be overworked and underpaid. Reluctant to return to the mountains—they regarded their elders as embarrassing rustics; their parents returned the scorn by treating them as lazy shirkers—they drifted through the cities. They identified neither with the Western culture they aped nor with their elders whose heritage they had discarded. Adrift and in despair, foundering without the village support system of mutual help and collective responsibility, they often sought comfort from heroin.

Increasingly, their opium-smoking parents also turned to heroin. Development programs and Western trekkers had brought baht to many poor villages, and the cash attracted drug dealers who had the medicine to chase away the stress of warp-speed modern life. Ironically, Thailand's poppy-eradication and crop-substitution programs, while decreasing the availability of raw opium, had driven hilltribe addicts to more potent, more accessible heroin that was produced just over the border in Burma. A 1992 report of the U.N. International Narcotics Control Board noted the disturbing rise in heroin use among these tragic nomads, and blamed the increase on increased availability of heroin and social and cultural upheaval.

"Any tribe, they are using more heroin," said Sompong Potpui, director of the nonprofit Grassroots Development Institute, who worked with Thai addicts in Bangkok. "The hilltribes have more and more money. Their country has had a lot of change, has become urbanized. They lost their values. They have more and more become city people."

━━━━━

A watcher of the skies with a new planet swimming into ken. A stout conquistador, silent upon a peak in Darien. Reginald Le May knew the thrill of their discoveries. In 1914, the British diplomat traversed northern Siam on the back of an elephant to arrive at the confluence of the Mekong and the Ruak River, an eastward-flowing tributary separating Siam and Burma.

"Below my feet the river bank went sheer down for fifty feet; the river itself was a mighty expanse of water flowing swift and clear," he recounted in his 1926 book, *An Asian Arcady*. "On the left, the river took a wide bend to the west, and on the right, another sweeping bend to the east, and in front the great gaunt hills rolled down to meet the river at either bend. This was the very apex of Siam. North lay British territory, the southern Shan states, and to the East, across the blue expanse, were the Lao states, which are now French soil. What a magnificent boundary to have for one's country!"

The years had blurred Le May's pastoral vision of Sam Liam Tongkham, the fabled Golden Triangle. The eternal Mekong now flowed quick and dirty between Burma, the Lao People's Democratic Republic, and Thailand, and all the krathong in the Orient could not appease the river goddess for its sullied state. The jungles of rustic Chiang Saen (the name meant "trumpeting elephant"), which held tiger and rhinoceros in Le May's day, had been cut down decades ago. Every *rai* of level ground in the Thai district had been cleared, tilled, and planted in rice or bananas. The big animals of the forest had been hunted out, their skins sold to collectors, their bones and horns rendered into Chinese tonics and aphrodisiacs. Trails worn by thousands of elephant caravans had been widened, leveled, and paved to accommodate huge motor coaches.

Every day, lumbering buses carried middle-aged farang on day-trips from Chiang Mai and Chiang Rai up to the infamous Triangle. The coach potatoes sat at *howdah* height in padded, air-conditioned comfort, dutifully videotaping the blur of rice fields, wats, and monks for the folks back home. Their anticipation grew as the road turned north from Chiang Saen, hugging the tan bluffs lining the west bank of the Mekong. English-language road signs counted down the distance: Golden Triangle 10 km, then six.

Arrival was anticlimactic; Le May's superlatives no longer applied. Along the Thai apex of the triborder area stretched Ban Sop Ruak, a village of thatch-roofed souvenir stalls and unsanitary restaurants. Less than a mile upriver, the scaffolding and concrete-reinforcing rods of the Golden Triangle Paradise Resort, a ten-million-dollar, Thai-financed facility complete with a gambling casino and an eighteen-hole golf course, erupted like thickets of bamboo along the Burmese riverfront hamlet of Ban Pak He. While human-rights concerns had deterred all but a handful of American firms, primarily oil companies, from investing in Burma, no such morality affected the decisions of the Thai, Chinese, and Singaporean governments, which had forged a business-first policy of "constructive engagement." Through ventures like the casino, SLORC appeared to be winning the test of economic and political wills.

The undeveloped Lao bank held nothing, save for trees, befitting the sleepy, socialist Albania of Southeast Asia. Little more than a quarter-century ago, these hills had thundered with gunfire and the sky had churned with wild napalm flames when a mile-long drug caravan belonging to Khun Sa had been attacked by Kuomintang troops near the Lao lumber town of Ban Khwan. An anachronism straight out of "Terry and the Pirates," the 1967 Opium War had raged until the duplicitous Lao general who had contracted for the drug shipment called in air strikes and paratroopers, then took the spoils—sixteen tons of opium—once the combatants retreated across the Mekong.

A generation ago, the area was a crossroads of criminal activity where opium was exchanged for ingots of gold. Now the Golden Triangle was a dreary roadside attraction, trading on its former notoriety, marketing its mystical cachet. The outlaws and opium kings had relocated beyond the western horizon, in the hills that tumbled down to the border crossing at Mae Sai, Thailand, and Tachilek, Burma. The former stronghold of druglords now contained a Le Meridien resort hotel. The pop of AK-47 automatic rifles had been replaced by the whirr of autofocus 35-mm. cameras. The unpardonable action had become the banal memento. Souvenir stalls sold wood-and-aluminum "opium pipes," bolts of poppy-theme printed cloth, cheap poppy-theme T-shirts, poppy-theme postcards, and one-baht Burmese cheroots. From a sandy landing, long-tail boats charged two hundred baht to carry passengers on a quick three-nation circuit. After some desultory bartering and a high-speed river cruise, visitors paid their ten-baht entrance fee and wandered through the modest exhibits of the House of Opium. Having come this far only to stare at a sanitized, commercialized, less-than-magnificent boundary they damn sure planned to see everything, including the self-styled "fabulous collection of poppy." It would be the only opium that all but the most foolhardy of tourists would see in Thailand. The museum's collection included antique opium-smoking sets of solid silver, pipes of jade and ivory, and sized weights of handcrafted bronze. In the mountains of the Triangle, merchants and traders used a *viss*-and-*tikal* system for opium, for any market good. One viss—about 1.6 kilograms, or three and one-half pounds—equalled one hundred tikals, and the weights, usually fashioned into animals, ran in size from one viss down to one-eighth of a tikal, about two grams. These measures of human misery—prides of patinated lions and flocks of oxidized ducks—could possess a terrible beauty.

A promontory overlooking the river held a crumbling temple, more souvenir stalls, and a gazebo with a panoramic view of the Mekong and the mountains of Burma and Laos. This Kodak moment was thoughtfully labeled with a poppy-theme English-language sign. Thai children scampered about, clad in hilltribe garb, badgering tourists. No farang photo was complete without the Golden Triangle sign and several faux-hilltribe girls wearing bright, yarn-dyed Lisu headdresses that resembled Victorian lampshades.

"You want photo complete? For you, 20 baht."

———

"I love border areas."

We were three or four Singhas into Chiang Mai, and Barry Flynn was feeling expansive. We sat at Fang Ping, the open-air restaurant owned by Keutsada "Noi" Panyatipaya, nursing a pleasant buzz, luxuriating in the mild upland weather, admiring the view of the wide, slow Ping River and Noi's impressive collection of American cowboy memorabilia. Framed pictures of John Wayne and Clint Eastwood hung near the cash register. The wreckage of a huge lunch—*plaa noong manao*, river fish steamed with garlic, green onion, and red chilies, khao phat kai, and *meht mamaung himapahn tote*, an appetizer of fried cashews tossed with salt, chilies, and onions—littered a low wooden table. I had handed off Flynn's suitcase and Khun Sa's rubies, and been repaid my $250. Thai Airways 192 was a distant memory. It felt good to be in a local joint, far from tourist hotels and trekker guesthouses.

A friend of Flynn, Prasert "Jackie" Wiboonjak, was pitching jewelry. He pushed back the shoulder-length hair that fell across his face, reached into the pockets of his matching white-and-navy striped shirt and pants ensemble, and produced silver rings set with glittering diamonds and sapphires.

"You like?"

The effect was ridiculous: a hippie in prison clothing coming on like a Patpong tout.

"Maybe on the way back," I demurred.

Fat chance. I had a backpack full of old Levi's to trade for pigeon's-blood rubies inside Shan State.

"I don't want to be near farang," Flynn said. "I want to be far away and live comfortable. I don't want to even see them. My office is this restaurant. I just want to be by myself. I come here and drink. People know where I'm at, because if I'm not at my house, I'm here. I think I'm living my own fantasy."

Ever since grade school, when he told his mother that one day he would live in China, the dream of Asia had burned in his imagination. In junior high, Flynn studied tae kwon do and washed dishes in the China Clipper, a restaurant owned by a

Chinese friend of his father. In Hollywood, he dated a string of Far East beauties with names—Selita, Harmeet, and Mizuko—to match their exotic features. Bo Gritz had given him the chance to taste the Orient; Khun Sa had given him a reason to stay. The money was irregular, but the adventure guaranteed. Life in the shadowlands, in the cusp of betrayal and distrust, where nothing counted but bullets and balls. Flynn didn't speak much Thai, even less Tai Yai, the language of the Shan. He preferred to brass it out, improvise. Drop a few names from his impressive black book, flash a wallet-sized photo taken with Khun Sa, and, if need be, buy his way out of trouble. Just show a Purple King and do whatever he wanted.

Khun Sa also acted with a measure of impunity. In Chiang Mai, the warlord maintained an office and staff, including bodyguards and intelligence personnel, and a warehouse to store and trade his Kachin jade. Although Khun Sa stood accused of ordering the bombing of a KMT general's compound and the murder of a local DEA agent's wife, he was even rumored to travel from his Burmese camp to Chiang Mai for medical checkups at a city hospital, where his soldiers were also treated.

At the Chiang Mai airport, a kiosk distributed complimentary guides to the city that included a full-page ad sponsored by the local Rotary Club. "Warning!!! Drugs and Chiang Mai Don't Mix!!" In no uncertain terms, the ad rumbled about the consequences of a drug arrest: "In Thailand, the penalties are heavy, and the courts not beyond death sentences or life imprisonments." A few meters away, I had seen a newsstand that stocked two self-published books—*Khun Sa: His Own Story and His Own Thoughts* and *General Khun Sa: His Life and His Speeches*—both by the man alleged to be the world's largest single heroin trafficker, a man who seemed immune to arrest and prosecution in Thailand.

Au Cheng and Mook Keaw Kam also sat at our table, picking through the fine bones of succulent, aromatic plaa noong *manao*. Slightly built and barely five feet tall, Au Cheng guarded a simple-minded nephew of the general who lived in Chiang Mai. Although he spoke slow, thoughtful English, Au Cheng remained quiet, depressed about his painful divorce proceedings. He deferred to Mook, who held a higher position within the Shan organization.

Raised in Keng Tung and educated in Taunggyi and Rangoon, Mook Keaw Kam supervised mining operations for the Shan State Restoration Council. As such, he was Flynn's invaluable link to the jade and gems that filtered from northern Burma along the trails controlled by Khun Sa's Mong Tai Army. Mook, too, was quiet during the rounds of Singha, preferring to leaf absently through the pages of his new *Peterson's Rocks and Minerals Field Guide*, our thank-you gift for his assistance in solidifying this adventure. Mook had just returned from Khun Sa's headquarters, where he had overseen preparations for our arrival. Khernsai Jaiyen had given orders to his people to postpone our trip, Mook related matter-of-factly. "Do not worry," Mook said. "There will be no problems. I left orders you are in camp as my guests."

Mook probably wished he was home making love to his new wife, whom he had spirited out of Rangoon the week before, particularly since we had previewed footage of *The Chameleon*, our gift to the General, for him. There was Tori Welles, porn star, diamond stud through her flared left nostril, heaving implanted breasts, moaning for April West and Peter North to bring her to climax. So beautiful, Mook had said as he gazed at the farang goddess of sex, so beautiful.

At four o'clock, Noi himself finally roared off Changklan Road and slid to a stop in the restaurant's gravel lot. We crammed our packs into the trunk of his golden Super Saloon

Toyota sedan and shook hands with Mook. *The Chameleon* in hand, he was going home to his wife; Khun Sa would have to wait for his blondes. We cruised through Flynn's neighborhood, passing the villa of his neighbor, Colonel Vichit Vechasart of the Border Patrol Police. Flynn rolled down the window, leaned out, waved.

"We are going to see criminals, Colonel!" he cackled. "Bye!"

Noi popped in a bootleg cassette of cowboy music, the larruping theme from "Bonanza." Head 'em up, move 'em out. We were off to see the warlord, the wonderful warlord of smack.

7

The Land Above the Clouds

Noi drove into the mountains with the panache of a Paris-to-Dakar wheelman. We slid and skimmed along Highway 108, following the southwesterly folds of the Ping River watershed, then turned westward at the town of Hot to trace the Chaem River Valley. On a road as thin and crumpled as a molted snake skin, we scattered pedestrians and untethered livestock, raced past paddies and pasture, then entered the lush forests of Mae Hong Son Province. King Chulalongkorn was our talisman in these sylvan hills. Along with an assortment of cologne bottles, the sedan dashboard held a framed picture of the beloved monarch who had brought paved roads to Thailand. Glinting in the fading light, his portrait guarded us from head-on collisions with overloaded teak trucks and packed song thaews.

At home, I had read the brief, wire-service reports of international disasters—"24 Die in Fiery Thai Pickup Plunge"—and wondered about the accuracy of the body count. One truck? And twenty-four fatalities? A few hours on mountain roads in the Thai hinterlands and the carnage made perfect sense. Every hairpin turn held an encounter with an oncoming song thaew, its brakes squealing like a terror-stricken market pig, its roof brimming with fuel drums, rice sacks, and split-bamboo baskets of tumbling, squawking chickens, its bed and rear bumper crowded with several dozen passengers. One truck? Just twenty-four fatalities?

From the front passenger seat, Barry Flynn regaled us with fun facts about Shan State, shouting over the wild, warbled theme music of *The Good, The Bad, and The Ugly* and the cool upland wind whistling through the open windows. "There are fifty different strains of malaria in Shan State!" Flynn announced. "The camp doctor recommends Fansidar!"

"But my doctor prescribed Doxycycline!" I replied. "She said there's resistance to Fansidar!"

"When the jungle people tell me to take a pill, I take it, because they fuck with this every day!"

"Any pharmacy that stays open late in Mae Hong Son?"

Flynn smiled. Who knew? It dawned on me that, Xanax aside, I was going in to Burma woefully undermedicated. My first-aid kit held only a few Motrin, a couple of Tylenol, several Immodium, a tube of Neosporin, and a jar of multi-vitamins. More than a century earlier, Holt S. Hallett had packed a portable pharmacopoeia before settling atop his elephant to explore the unforgiving terrain of northern Thailand:

> The medicines, purchased by me chiefly in England, were the usual ones carried in Indo-China. They consisted of quinine, Warburg's tincture and arsenic for fever; ipeca-cuanha, Dover's powder and laudanum for dysentery, Eno's fruit salt, Cockle's pills and chlorodyne for lesser ailments; pain-killer for dispelling the agony of bites from noxious insects such as the huge dairy-keeping red ants that milk syrup from plant-lice, centipedes and scorpions; Goa powder for ringworm, the most general and conta-

gious plague of the Far East; and vaseline and Holloway's ointment for abrasions of the skin and ordinary casualities so frequent on a journey.

The closer we got to Burma, I realized, the more miserable things there were that would crawl, swim, or fly into our lives. Absolut, which we had in abundance, would have to be our panacea. Sullivan was already pouring the first cocktail-hour measure of the evening into plastic cups that vibrated violently on the rear floormat. We felt confident, nearly cocky, on the threshold of enormous, certain success.

"Tonight's specialty is vodka and Fanta," Sullivan announced. "No twist, no ice. Shaken, not stirred. You're gonna love it, Au Cheng."

Our bodyguard, a confirmed Maekhong rice-whiskey man, regarded his sloshing cup as if handed a live grenade, then cautiously sipped.

"Is it good. No taste."

Au Cheng sipped again. Soon, this lovelorn gun for hire, so upset about being cuckolded by his adulterous wife, was recounting old war stories.

"I was born in the north, in Wa State." Au Cheng grinned, made a slitting motion. "Headhunters. I start fighting when I am twelve. My brother was assassin for hire. Killed by Chinese Wa. I fight as mercenary for Group 04, to get Thai I.D. card. We fight with Communists. Battles in Chiang Khong, Phitsanoluk. Now I am offered money to fight in Bosnia, but I don't like Communists and I don't like Muslims. I like freedom and Americans."

He sipped his cocktail.

"America has best weapons, too. M-16 is Number One. Is very strong. Look is not so beautiful."

On the tape deck, Gene Pitney wailed "(The Man Who

Shot) Liberty Valance." Au Cheng, who fancied himself a singer of American cowboy music, settled into the middle of the rear seat and closed his eyes, meditating on frontier justice. To the west, an orange-red sun floated through rose and lavender pastels, then fell like a dying flare behind the rising hills.

Somewhere over the sunset simmered a decades-old war between the Burmese and the White Karen, a minority people who lived along the border. Repeated dry-season Burmese campaigns had driven Karen soldiers to strongholds hugging Mae Hong Son and Tak Provinces and sent tens of thousands of Karen civilians into "hidden" jungle villages or refugee settlements in Thailand. It was a conflict notable for its domestic brutality and its international invisibility. As part of its "Four Cuts Strategy," designed to sever rebel sources of food, funds intelligence, and recruits, the Tatmadaw followed the traditional Burmese tack for scorched-earth ethnic subjugation: looting homes, plundering fields and animals, raping women, dragooning anyone to slave as a porter or human shield in the annual offensives against the Karen, the related, hill-dwelling Karenni (or Red Karen), and the Shan.

The army had forcibly relocated hundreds of thousands of Karen civilians from their villages to "strategic hamlets," then declared the cleared areas to be free-fire zones. Thousands of Shan and Karenni were driven from their villages to crude, unsanitary slave-labor camps and forced to construct a one-hundred-mile-long railroad line from Aung Ban south to Loi Kaw. In southern Burma, the army had just decreed that thousands of Mon, another ethnic minority people, must work as unpaid corvée labor on the Ye-to-Tavoy railway. The one-hundred-ten-mile extension was being built to solidify government control of the coastal area and to serve offshore oil and gas exploration by American firms. Working conditions on the railroad echoed those of the Allied POWs who had hacked the

Death Railway through a nearby stretch of Burmese and Thai jungle fifty years before. Short rations. Unrelenting heat. Landslides. Dirty water. Scant medicine. Frequent beatings.

In spite of the Tatmadaw's treatment of millions of its own citizens, the ethnic cleansing of the frontiers, and pitched battles involving artillery, armored vehicles, and thousands of troops, only an occasional wire-service story appeared in the international press. The spotlight fell instead upon Somalia, Yugoslavia, Iraq, and South Africa. Editors could apparently summon public indignation against only so many dirty wars and outlaw regimes. Aside from a handful of relief workers and a scattering of diplomats, few people in the West took notice.

At Mae Sariang, the largest town in southern Mae Hong Son Province, Highway 108 turned north. Swerving up the valley of the Yuam River, our bodyguard suddenly lurched forward, put his head between his knees, and unceremoniously vomited upon his cheap Chinese sneakers. Then he sat back, eyes glazed, mouth agape. Not a good idea, the vodka. All the cologne bottles in Chiang Mai could not mask the sweet-and-sour stench rising from the floormats. Noi turned up "Mule Train," gunned the engine, and we crashed through the night like a rogue elephant.

Our driver performed a remarkable feat, delivering us to Mae Hong Son by 9:30 p.m., nearly four hours faster than any death-wish song thaew jockey. By then, Au Cheng had nearly recovered from his Absolut encounter and Sullivan and I had acclimated to his acrid effusion. Flynn felt a brief tour of town was in order. Noi cruised through the darkened streets, past the new Holiday Inn, the city hall, the local prison, and into the town center. Flynn pointed out the local attractions that Fodor's neglected to mention: the small, in-town hotel that Khun Sa once owned; the teak bungalow near the airport where the warlord's younger half-sister, Khun Nittaya, still lived; and the office next to a police barracks where another Flynn friend, Somwang Oonman, ran the local headquarters of Khun Sa's political organization, the Shan State Restoration Council.

"As long as there's tea money," Flynn said with a chuckle, "there's no problem."

As Noi drove to Kai-Mook, a restaurant near our hotel that specialized in Shan food, Flynn spoke of the good old days in Mae Hong Son, before trekkers descended in droves upon the smugglers' Shangri-la, before an honest living seemed possible. "Whenever VIPs flew to Mae Hong Son, they'd just close off the gates to secure the airport for Khun Sa's meeting. It was the wild, wild West days. You'd go into a bar, there'd be a .45-caliber pistol on the table. Now it's just a regular old town."

He laughed. "But we'll be going to the other kind of town tomorrow."

Mae Hong Son had not strayed far from its colorful past. According to local legend, the town owed its existence to an elephant hunt. In 1831, the king of Chiang Mai sent out a party to capture wild elephants. The luckless hunters slogged westward over the gnarled mountains and did not trap a herd until they were more than one hundred miles away, in the thick jungles near Burma. Reluctant to drive the wild beasts back to the capital, the hunters built an elephant *kraal*, and Mae Hong Son was born. The province, the remotest in the kingdom, was established only in 1893, after a Thai-British party surveyed the border with Burma. Their demarcation was immediately ignored by the roving traders, bandits, and hilltribes to whom borders were merely states of mind. Mae Hong Son, the end of the elephant trail, became Siam's tropical equivalent of Siberia, a favored internal exile for provocateurs, criminals, and scandal-tainted government officials. Their legacy lingered still, an unsavory current beneath the town's paradisiacal façade.

At the open-air Kai-Mook, we ordered spring rolls, river crab, fried rice, and chicken with cilantro, then settled in to listen as Flynn talked of his work on *Air America*, the 1991 movie starring Mel Gibson and Robert Downey, Jr. The black comedy about two pilots flying for the CIA's secret airline, dropping supplies to mercenaries fighting a covert war in Laos, was filmed almost entirely in northern Thailand. The Vientiane bar scenes were shot in Chiang Mai; the action and aerial scenes were filmed around Mae Hong Son and Mae Sariang, where the terrain was a better match for the untamed landscape of north-central Laos.

Flynn had answered a Bangkok casting call and landed several small, nonspeaking roles in the barroom and special-operations-room scenes: he played the pilot who wore his hat backwards; the pilot who didn't wear a hat; the pilot who always hovered near Mel Gibson. Tricks of the trade, said Flynn, to stand out in a crowd or keep from being cut out of a tight shot. Why work without being in the movie? He also provided "logistical assistance" when the production filmed in Mae Hong Son.

"Khun Sa said he was going to cause trouble unless he knew where exactly all the airplanes, all the trucks, everything was during location filming, because the DEA was flying planes over Khun Sa's territory to provoke him to shoot down an airplane. Then they could say Khun Sa was attacking the set of *Air America*."

To keep an eye on the Hollywood production, said Flynn, many of Khun Sa's Mong Tai Army troops "came right from camp" to play extras. Their movie roles did not call for much of a character stretch—they played soldiers under the command of a corrupt Royal Lao Army general trafficking in heroin.

"They even kept their own weapons, which were loaded, during filming just in case a C-130 decided to head off into the sunset," Flynn said. "After the last day of filming, me and Somwang raided the wardrobe department for uniforms. You'll see some *Air America* uniforms when we get to camp tomorrow."

I could hardly wait for tomorrow, for the predawn Zero Hour to arrive. It had been two years since my first conversation with Flynn. In the interim, I had searched out obscure magazines and out-of-print books, spent thousands of dollars on overseas telephone calls and airline tickets. I had become junkie-consumed, as obsessed with Khun Sa as Sullivan was in his search for POWs. The dragon, Sullivan liked to say, had bitten me on the ass. The chase had brought us to Mae Hong Son, all the way to the edge of Indian country. The word would come at four o'clock. Khun Sa's local factotum, Somwang, would send a truck to pick us up before five. Delivered to the mule camp at Ban Mae Suya, Thailand, just a few miles south of the border, we would be saddled and on the trail before dawn. By sundown, our long chase would be over, the dragon finally flushed from his lair. Tomorrow night would be spent under a big, Burmese sky. I could visualize the story already. Date-line: Ho Mong, Burma. It would look sensational on page one, above the banner.

════

The word never came, the truck never showed. Not at four, not at five. By six o'clock, the night's spell was broken. The cries of invisible songbirds and strutting roosters, the cacophony of mongrel dogs and poorly lubricated motor scooters cut through the cool, smoke-scented mist. It was too late today to take the trail to Burma. I donned the clothes I had worn since leaving Boston three days before: blue jeans, black T-shirt, long-sleeved olive-drab shirt, hiking boots. Sullivan spoke in a muffled voice from beneath the pillow covering his face: "Rulenumberthree, buddy."

No, this morning had not gone as planned. Now we would have to wait while Flynn sorted out this latest mess. Might as well get the lay of the land, I thought, and rousted Sullivan. The morning sun was barely peeking over the eastern mountains as we walked north on Khunlumprapras Road towards the talaat, the daily market that is the axis of morning activity in every Thai village. The two-lane road was clogged with businesses—trekking agencies, gift shops, and restaurants—catering to Mae Hong Son's booming tourist industry. For farang who found Chiang Mai too Westernized, this town was the new end of the road. A sour-faced antiques dealer dusted his stock of gramophones, treadle-powered sewing machines, and Burmese temple artifacts. A brass temple bell? For you, 250 baht. Cowbell, 150 baht. Take or leave, he seemed to shrug. There would be another trekker along shortly, someone willing to pay his exorbitant prices. We hacked our way through souvenir thickets of sequin-beaded baseball caps, split-bamboo conical hats, and hand-loomed cotton vests, kept to the path marked by grocery-store cairns of biscuits and bottled water. Red silk flowers, made to dress the artificial *Air America* poppy fields, had found a second life in many window-box planters. It would not be long before Mae Hong Son, too, seemed tame and spoiled.

The talaat stood behind the newly repaired Wat Hua Wiang, a temple in the Burmese style: teakwood walls and a gabled, three-tiered roof known as a *yama* rimmed with filigreed ironwork. Surrounding the market were small shops that, in the Asian fashion, stocked identical inventories of cheap goods: bolts of cotton fabric, plastic sandals, packets of Lux soap and Tonic shampoo, stainless-steel shears and machete-like *dah* blades, aluminum cooking pots, pirated cassette tapes, and knockoff baseball caps.

In front of the stores, vendors displayed Thailand's bounty of fruits, arranged carefully on mats and newspapers. Sweet-scented, crayon-colored pyramids of oranges, papayas, mangoes, pomelos, sapodillas, limes, and lychees. Shopkeepers sang the praises of their fried bean curd, boiled quail eggs, and steamed sticky rice. They beckoned shoppers to sample their homemade honey cakes, freshly shredded bamboo shoots, and aged fish sauces. Other greengrocers hawked garlic and onions, chilies and ginger root, chickpeas and lentils, cashew nuts and sesame seeds, cinnamon sticks and turmeric powder. In a raised, central pavilion, chain-smoking butchers dismembered chicken and pig carcasses into pale joints and slippery chunks. Fishmongers arranged cords of split, smoked eels or gutted writhing catfish, their cleavers flashing crimson blood and translucent scales. Pariah dogs lurked on the perimeter, intent on snatching the offal. Solemn, saffron-robed mendicants walked through the morning tumult, cradling their alms bowls.

"Know where that chicken you ate last night came from?" asked Sullivan. He made a clucking sound. "Now you know why I only eat peanut butter and crackers over here."

The cool market air smelled of jungle orchids and overripe fruit, pungent tobacco and fresh death. Tattooed Shan men in baggy *gon* trousers sauntered through the clamor, their turbans rakishly angled, their dahs secured in leather scabbards. Their women smiled cryptically, sweet-smelling faces streaked with straw-colored *thanaka*, a cosmetic paste made from the crushed bark of the orange jasmine bush. An exquisite frisson of Burma. If Mae Hong Son was this wondrously alien, how fantastic would Ho Mong seem?

We left the market and walked south, through a short, narrow alley where Lisu girls sold cheap, faux-opium souvenirs, to

Thanon Singhanatbumrung, the main east-west road. There, thank God, we found a pharmacy that stocked Fansidar. For good measure, we bought a sample of every antimalarial measure in stock, including a can of FlyPel mosquito repellent and a box of Chinese-made mosquito coils. The dragon cast a long shadow: the store also stocked the tools of the heroin habit. A glass showcase near the entrance was filled with rubber gloves, glass syringes, brass syringe cases, Chinese- and Japanese-made hypodermic needles, and face masks, which protected jungle chemists from inhaling fumes during the final refining stage. A junkie could put together a user's kit for less than one hundred baht, about four dollars.

When we returned to the hotel a few hours later, Flynn confirmed the distressing news: Because we had arrived in Mae Hong Son so late, our trip to Burma had been delayed. Nothing to do but wait. Why did I think anything would go as planned, that Mae Hong Son would somehow be different from Bangkok or Chiang Mai? We took a tuk-tuk to an old *Air America* haunt, the riverside restaurant of the Mae Hong Son Resort, for breakfast. While I wrote optimistic postcards—*We go in tomorrow!*—Au Cheng spoke of his revered leader, whom he referred to as "K.S.," and his role in the heroin trade.

"Hong Kong traders get villagers to plant poppies," he said, loudly. Nearby, a resort worker was singing along, badly, with a karaoke machine. "But to transport opium to refineries, they need security and mules, so they hire K.S. After opium refined, they need security to protect heroin and refinery. They need permission to make a deal. Security to guard field. Security to guard mule trains. They hire K.S. They pay tax to K.S. He tax everything that go through Shan States: opium, jade, rubies, teak, cattle. Tax on one cow is two hundred baht."

Below us, long-tail boats sped down the fast-flowing Pai River, ferrying tourists toward a frontier village of several dozen Padaung families. These long-neck Karen had fled the ethnic pogrom in neighboring Karenni State, a small, mountainous region of eastern Burma nestled between Karen and Shan States. A trumpeting elephant forded the river, his Shan *mahout* goading him with a hook-like *ankus*, then lumbered into the forest carrying a howdah full of farang to gawk at hill-tribes. Everywhere I looked, farang were having exotic adventures; Sullivan and I were treating our erstwhile guides to their third free meal.

"Instead of hiring mules in Ban Mae Suya we could have driven in," Flynn said after breakfast. "The Thai charge twenty thousand baht to allow a vehicle with farang into Shan State."

"If I had an extra eight hundred dollars to burn, I might have thought about it," I replied. "But I'm print, not television."

"It's two hours by truck from Mae Hong Son to the border," Flynn added. "There are five Thai checkpoints. From the border to camp, the drive is more than four hours, with three Shan checkpoints. At least the trip is in hours in Shanland. You go to Laos and ask someone how far somewhere is, and the answer is 'Ooohh.' If the answer is 'ooooohhhhh,' you know the distance is really far."

We tuk-tuked back to the hotel and parted company. Flynn and Au Cheng headed uptown to meet with Somwang Oonman at the Shan State Restoration Council's office. Sullivan, true to form, decided to nap. I opted to walk off the khao phat kai smoldering in my stomach by hiking to the hilltop temple, Wat Phra That Doi Kung Mu. I followed a rocky path that climbed the western slope of the valley through palm and tamarind. Near the summit, where the uneven path finally became paved, I nearly stepped on a small, khaki-colored mongrel that lay on its side, drawing shallow, rapid breaths through its fox-like snout. There was nothing to be done.

Dukkha, or pain, was one of the three fundamental principles of Buddhist life.

The mountaintop temple, painted a bone-white and topped with a golden *hti* umbrella, commanded a sweeping view of the lush oasis of Mae Hong Son. Forested mountains and *naa*, the checkerboard of wet-rice paddies, crept to the edge of town. The midday sun had dissipated the morning haze and improved the view. To the south, brief-lived *bua tong* flowers, which bloomed for just two weeks every November, covered hillsides like new temple gilding. To the north, the mountains swelled, blue-gray waves in an angry autumnal sea. The largest, faintest peaks belonged in Burma, belonged to no one. Monks regarded the vista silently from a bench inside a cliffside pavilion strung with Christmas lights.

This was the intoxicating, untainted Asia touted in slick travel brochures and moldy memoirs, as picturesque as a Chinese paneled screen. The tableau barely masked the outlaw activity to be found in these mountains, where boundaries were rumors and laws little more than wishful thinking. It's not my favorite place, a dealer of Asian antiquities had told me, but if I was a heroin addict I'd probably never leave. A place where smackworks were sold openly and brazenly, where trekkers searched for guides to take them to hilltop villages for the chance to "chase the dragon," to smoke opium in a culturally correct setting. A place where the bounty of Burma—priceless antique temple carvings, immense, old-growth teak logs, and pure jins of No. 4 heroin—seeped through mountain passes on well-worn jungle trails and officially nonexistent roads.

When I descended, the rabid dog had died. It lay in a pool of foamy saliva spreading across hexagonal, blood-red tiles, its dark eyes as glazed and uncomprehending as those of an opium addict. Death in paradise arrived arbitrary and anonymous. A happy Thai couple posed nearby for a photograph against the perfect backdrop of unspoiled Mae Hong Son: a stir-fried mix of overseas adventurers and local smugglers, hilltribes and anthropologists, ethnic rebels and undercover intelligence operatives, civic boosters and HIV-positive massage girls.

8

Border Problems

When I returned to the Baiyoke Chalet, Sullivan had the shuddering air conditioner cranked to full and a paperback action novel opened on his lap.

"You cannot take too many naps or bring too much reading material to Thailand," he said. "You spend 90 percent of your time here sitting around, just jerking off. Waiting." He pointed to the day's English-language Thai newspapers, *The Nation* and the Bangkok *Post*, in a heap on the floor. "Nothing ever changes," he groused. "They had the same crap the last time I was here."

I picked up the papers: photo-ops of beloved King Bhumibol greeting some foreign dignitary, breathless coverage of snooker and badminton tournaments, a pissing contest between politicians over corruption charges. The only diversion was the Honey Watch. The papers splashed daily updates on Honey, a two-year-old female elephant that had been struck by a truck near Chiang Mai while on her way to play in an elephant soccer match. A tearjerker headline—"Agony Continues for Honey"—

with a pathetic photo to boot: a pair of concerned zookeepers hovering over reclining, panic-stricken Honey.

While I mulled the deep Thai love for elephants, Flynn and Au Cheng entered the room.

"We spoke with Somwang," said Flynn. "The real reason we couldn't go in today is because there's fighting on the trail. It won't be clear until tomorrow."

"Fighting with whom?" I sputtered. "I thought the General sent out a patrol yesterday to sweep the trail for our arrival."

Flynn shrugged. "You never know," he said. "We can still go today. We can walk in on an old road I know. It breaks off the highway before the mule camp at Ban Mae Suya. The road is mined on the Thai side, but the villagers know where all the mines are. They've been flagged."

Au Cheng did not seem enthusiastic about this hike. "Today is too late," our bodyguard said. "At night, we still walking on trail. Villagers see three farang, they maybe attack. Think you set mines, or you are DEA. No good."

"Let's just hang tight," I replied. "We could still get word tonight that the trail is open."

"The mines are no problem," Flynn persisted. "But whatever you want to do."

He and Au Cheng left the room.

"Fifty-fifty we get in," Sullivan said. "First we arrived too late, then it's fighting on the trail. We're being jerked around. I don't know how many times Phoumano told me he'd sent a guy up to the Mekong River to get a photo or a letter out of Laos and it never happened. You ask later and the answer is always, 'Border problems.' It's the all-purpose excuse. Border problems, fighting on the trail—it's the same thing.

"Something smells," he continued. "Let me tell you a story. When I was in 'Nam, I had to go from Phan Rang to Cam Ranh Bay, about 150 clicks up Route 1, to pick up the payroll for all the indigenous employees. About one million piasters. The morning I'm supposed to leave, my Vietnamese driver calls in sick, which was rare. I got another driver for the truck and hooked up with an armed convoy. On the way up, we passed a truck that had been hit by a B-40 rocket and some recently killed Viet Cong. A bridge had been blown the night before and we had to make a forty-five-minute detour, driving on paddy dikes.

"We made it to Cam Ranh Bay, picked up the money and turned back. No convoy this time, just me and my driver. About halfway in on the detour, it began to get dark, and only two things came out at dusk: mosquitoes and V.C. I flashed back to my driver not coming to work. He *knew* the V.C. were going to hit. It was a perfect setup. I had one guy with me and I'm off on this rice paddy with one million piasters. He drove like hell and somehow we made it back to the main road without getting hit. A few minutes later, I saw a V.C. patrol, heading exactly where we had come from. We just missed them. The lesson was, I knew something was wrong, that I could have been set up. It's a sixth sense. Do I make myself clear?"

Something smelled all right, far worse than any stagnant klong. But there was nothing to do but wait out of the midday heat. I leafed through the Thai newspapers, wondering what would happen to Honey. Sullivan began working on the collection of paperbacks in his rucksack. In the evening, we summoned the energy to walk downstairs to the hotel bar, where we found our guides running a tab.

"Khun Nittaya is coming at eight o'clock," informed Flynn. "Did you bring gifts for her?"

What do you bring the half-sister of the world's most powerful opium warlord? I trotted upstairs to fetch her a pair of gold-leaf-and-pearl earrings and small flacons of French perfume. I also grabbed copies of several *Herald* stories that bore my byline.

Khun Nittaya arrived promptly, seated on the pillion of a Japanese motor scooter. She met with us in a corner booth of the bar while her driver/bodyguard idled outside the hotel. Several years before, Flynn told me, Burmese agents had shot her husband to death practically across the street from our hotel. Now she took no chances. With her broad face, small, piercing eyes, and rosebud mouth, the youthful woman bore an uncanny resemblance to her notorious older half-brother. If Barry Flynn could not deliver an audience with the warlord, he would damn sure deliver the kingpin's sister, if only to prove his connections.

After the proper introductions and gift giving, Flynn described our border problems. To buttress my credentials, I laid out the *Herald* articles. Khun Nittaya was unimpressed by my dispatches from Vietnam and Laos reporting on a fact-finding trip by the Senate Select Committee on POW/MIA Affairs. The Kennedy name had worldwide recognition, yet she ignored the profile I'd written on Massachusetts congressman Joseph P. Kennedy II. The one piece she stared at approvingly reported a Boston promotional appearance by Elizabeth Taylor. Khun Nittaya, an apparent fan of Liz, regarded me across the banquette. I met her gaze, thought I saw a flash of respectful approval. I tried to remain cool and vaguely bored, as if I was a bigfoot journalist, someone not to be trifled with. Khun Nittaya smiled, and Au Cheng translated her decision.

"Not to worry," she said, standing to leave. "I will drive into camp tomorrow to prepare everything for your arrival."

Thank God for old-time Hollywood glamour. We confined Au Cheng to Maekhong rice whiskey and passed the evening in the bar mixing Sullivan's vodka with fresh-squeezed orange juice. The house band phonetically sang "Somewhere Over the Rainbow," "Imagine," and "Yesterday." Our troubles seemed very, very far away with the warlord's sister pleading our case.

Flynn recounted more fringe show-biz tales: how he dated Lee Marvin's girlfriend; how he got the part as Paul Koslo's homosexual lover in *The Stone Killer* after his agent sent the film's producers a picture of him clad only in underwear; how he and his Middle Eastern friends used to take women aloft in Adnan Khashoggi's private jet for "Thirty-five-thousand-Foot Parties."

"We'd take the plane over Salt Lake City for two hours," Flynn laughed. "Suck, fuck, or jump."

We were going to enjoy Ho Mong, he promised. His Shan friend, Sengjoe, was anxious to meet us and to sample vodka for the first time. There was a massage parlor staffed with fifty-baht-a-trick Thai girls, diesel generators, and satellite television. "We can sit in camp," said Flynn, "drink Shan whiskey and Singha beer, and watch Larry King."

Hello, Chris from Burma. Go ahead, you're on the air. . . .

Hours later, Sullivan and I lurched upstairs, relieved of one thousand baht and one liter of Absolut. Dreams came to me that night, full of besotted paranoia and malarial delirium: I was in a teak-paneled room, kneeling on a large bed beneath the white, cascading folds of mosquito netting. I was not alone. A naked woman lay before me, arching her back to meet my feverish thrusting. Not Tori Welles, not even Bin, but Khun Nittaya. We were not alone. Maniacal laughter filled the room; through the silken shroud I could make out an amused voyeur. Barry Flynn. I awoke, fully clothed, sweating. 4 a.m. The word would not come, not today.

———

An agitated Flynn burst into our room in mid-morning. The fresh air couldn't dissipate the odor of failure.

"Give me copies of all your paperwork, and correspondence with Khernsai."

I complied and, for good measure, also tossed him my Liz

Taylor feature. Like sister, I hoped, like druglord. Perhaps he could pick up "Entertainment Tonight" on his satellite dish or had seen a bootleg copy of *Cleopatra*.

"What's the word, Barry?"

"The General's in a very bad mood," replied Flynn, heading for the door. "Everyone's afraid to speak with him. Maybe Khun Nittaya will have word tonight."

When Flynn had left, Sullivan spoke from beneath his pillow. "This is what's called the Bangkok Shuffle. I've been dealing with this for seven years."

Broken plans, border problems, mercurial druglords, Absolut hangovers, sententious sidekicks. It was time for a change of scenery. I walked down to Jongkhum Lake and hired a driver and a guide to take me into the distant hills. I wanted to meet the long-necked Padaung women I'd seen staring from T-shirts, postcards, and posters all over town.

We headed north from Mae Hong Son on Highway 1095, a serpentine, alternate route that swung around to Chiang Mai. The men I'd hired for the day were English-speaking White Karen, refugees from Burma. A lowland people who earnestly converted to Christianity with the arrival of Bible-bearing British missionaries (their myths predicted the appearance of a younger "white brother" who came from across the sea to return the lost Golden Book about Y'Wa, the creator), the Karen harbored a centuries-old distrust of the Burmese. The British had only inflamed tensions by recruiting the Karen into the colonial army and police forces, especially as Indians dominated the civil service, and Chinese merchants controlled trading. Most ethnic-majority Burmans were rootless peasants. Their resentment festered until World War II, when Japanese occupied Burma. The collaborationist Burmese Independence Army then exacted ethnic revenge, massacring hundreds of Anglophile Karens and Indians. After the war, the wary Karen had revolted against the Burmese government even before independence was declared. Among the ensuing Burmese atrocities, the worst was the slaughter of more than eighty Karen attending Christmas services in Tavoy District in 1948. The enraged Karen then very nearly ripped Burma asunder, capturing Taunggyi and Mandalay and coming within ten miles of Rangoon before being driven back. Their war had dragged on ever since. If the Tatmadaw had an order of battle, the Karen topped the list. Western diplomats regarded the Karen conflict as the purest, most acceptable revolt against Rangoon. The Karen, who lived in hills far south of the poppy belt, levied taxes on passing caravans and traded in teak; drug trafficking was a capital offense. Tropical hardwoods and ancient hatred had bolstered Karen resolve for more than four decades.

"In 1948 we start fighting, until today," said my guide, U Thai, who had served eighteen years as a corpsman in the rebel army commanded by General Bo Mya, the corpulent leader of the Karen National Union. "Not finished, not defeat. The Burmese control townside. The countryside, all revolution. No one can win. A long time, forty-six years. I am not born. My father decided to fight with them. Now I fight with them."

We crossed the tea-colored Pai River, then turned west onto a red-dirt road. U Thai took slices of betel-palm nut from a bamboo box blackened with use, wrapped them in a betel-pepper leaf smeared with slaked lime and cutch, a dye extracted from the catechu tree, then popped the teabag-sized quid into his mouth.

"Just now, I'm old and I stop," he smiled, flashing pointed teeth the color of dried blood. "I rest."

After six miles of sadistic road, we passed through the gated entrance of Ban Nai Soi, a palisaded rice-farming village with tidy houses bedecked with phlox and bougainvillea. A hand-painted sign pointed the way to the nearby village of the long-neck women. Two jarring miles on, we arrived at Mu Ba Karen Koyong, a village of forty-five Padaung families who fled from Burma in 1984 to escape the wrath and the press-gang roundups of the Tatmadaw.

The custom of encasing the necks of Padaung women has endured for centuries. Legend had it that the spiraling brass rings protected the women from tiger bites, but the practice of this hill-dwelling Karen subgroup actually began as a form of elective mutilation. The Padaung men hoped the radical disfig-urement would dissuade raiding parties of lowland Burmese from carrying off their women. For the same reason, the Chin living in the hills along the Indian frontier often tattooed the faces of their women.

When a Padaung girl turned five, the *bedin-saya*, or village shaman, consulted the entrails of a chicken to determine the date for the full-moon *waso* feast, when five brass coils were permanently applied to the girl's neck. Successive rings were added annually until a woman reached her late teens. Because of the enormous weight of the *jeiw*, or neck rings, which could tip the scales at more than thirty pounds, other brass loops, called *hakaw*, girded the calves to act as counterweights. "Long-neck" was a misnomer. While it was believed that the rings stretched the neck, X rays of a Padaung woman revealed that the heavy collar—sometimes as many as twenty-five loops—actually increased downward pressure, drastically displacing the ribs and collar bone. The resulting appearance, an elongated neck and sloping shoulders, suggested a champagne bottle, according to one nineteenth-century British observer. The deforming rings became indispensable. Underlying neck muscles atrophied and could not support the weight of the head. (Ring removal, a guaranteed death by suffocation, was a traditional Padaung punishment for adultery.)

To the Padaung, the constricting rings connoted beauty, status, and, more recently, prosperity. The swan-necked women from the hinterlands of Karenni State had become a Thai tourist attraction. Before entering Mu Ba Karen Koyong, tourists had to register at a Thai Border Patrol Police post, then pay a 250-baht entrance fee at a booth staffed by a normal-neck Karen girl. Part of the fee, fifty baht, would go to the Thai police, my guide said; an equal amount would go to the Karenni Army, yet another ethnic insurgent force locked in endless warfare with the Burmese. The balance went to the village chief, who then distributed money to the families. The steady cash had altered life drastically in the village. The Padaung traditionally grew rice, tea, and tobacco, but none of the indolent men in Mu Ba Karen Koyong appeared to retain an interest in subsistence farming. What was the point of breaking your back for a few baht when your long-neck wife and daughters earned far more money posing for photographs and selling trinkets?

Nearly every household had a raised platform, made from split bamboo, where the women—clad in black skirts, white smocks, and blue jackets, their Clara Bow–like bobbed hair covered in magenta *kakao* scarves, their legs sheathed in blue-cotton puttees against leeches—sat patiently for pictures with tourists. In faint, strangled voices, each woman also hawked souvenirs: thin brass bracelets, handwoven shoulder bags, cheap *dah*, even long-neck figurines to hang on Christmas trees. There was no sense in bartering on the cost. Every family charged the same price. You like ornament? For you, for everybody: 50 baht.

Just a few years ago, the brass wrap was considered a vanishing cultural idiosyncracy among the Padaung. Yet the baht to be made from Thai and foreign tourists had sparked a long-neck resurgence in this remote hamlet. A majority of the young girls in the two-room schoolhouse now bore the brilliant brass shackles of custom and greed. The raison d'etre of disfigurement had been inverted; now, the intent of the rings was to attract outsiders.

The first vanload of coach potatoes marched into the village that was at once a quasi-zoo, an airport gift shop, and a carnival sideshow lacking only a two-headed calf. I felt ashamed my curiosity had brought me to this unsettling spectacle. We left hurriedly, retracing our route to the Pai River, then turned north and followed a tributary, the Sa Nga River, climbing past the spectacular seven cataracts of Namtok Pha Sua Forest Park. In the mountain valleys beyond Pang Tong, the royal summer palace, and the Hmong village of Meo Naphapak, women with ancient sickles cut wide swaths through swaying fields of wet rice.

The road fizzled into uneven, muddy tracks in Mae Aw, a windswept, fly-blown hamlet where the old, tattered remnants of the Kuomintang, the once-mighty soldiers of opium, were fading away. It was difficult to walk the dusty, narrow lanes, scattering flocks of geese and greeting amiable KMT sexagenarians, and hold these rustic retirees culpable for the global scourge of Golden Triangle heroin. But forty-five years before, these men and their commanders were not nearly so benign. Loyal to Nationalist Chinese leader Chiang Kai-shek, they had been members of the KMT's 93rd Division, the "lost army" driven from Yunnan Province into eastern Shan State by the People's Liberation Army of Mao Zedong.

Adrift and unwelcome in Burma, in need of revenue to sustain their military operations, the KMT decreed that hilltribe farmers pay an opium tax. They also began charging ferry fees at river crossings and dunning passing caravans—acting, in short, like modern-day warlords. Although isolated between the Burmese and the Chinese Communists, the KMT soldiers under the command of General Li Mi were by no means desperate. Their salvation took the form of heroin and the CIA. In the aftermath of World War II, the Agency was climbing into bed with all manner of rough trade, in the name of building a bulwark against Communism. In the KMT, the pragmatic CIA found a trained, motivated asset to gather intelligence, conduct covert operations, even mount disastrous invasions of southern China in 1951 and 1952. Dependent upon the KMT for control of this obscure, yet crucial region, the CIA, at the very least, turned a jaundiced eye as the KMT, with the assistance of the Thai military, transformed opium from a locally consumed crop into an international commodity.

The symbiotic bond between smugglers and senior Thai military commanders dated from Thailand's annexation and military occupation of southern Shan State during World War II. The KMT's opium soon moved along wartime supply routes under the protection of Thai police commander General Phao Siyanan, a corrupt, but valued, CIA asset. The Burmese Army finally dislodged the KMT from Shan State in 1961, with little effect. The exiled KMT soldiers, now disavowed by Taiwan, regrouped just over the Thai border in Tam Ngop and Mae Salong, two mountain redoubts north of Chiang Mai. With quick, military precision, the KMT soon cornered the local opium trade, outlawed in Thailand two years before. But the Thai weren't about to hobble this illegal KMT enterprise. The opium army provided steady "tea money" and acted as a buffer against Communist forces in the northern frontier. Drug trafficking was a small price to pay for such peace of mind.

In a 1967 interview, KMT General Tuan Shi-wen explained

the drugs-for-weapons rationale: "Necessity knows no law. That is why we deal with opium. We have to continue to fight the evil of Communism, and to fight you must have an army, and an army must have guns, and to buy guns you must have money. In these mountains the only money is opium."

Gradually, however, the grand KMT dream of reclaiming mainland China gave way to the exclusive pursuit of narco-dollars. The KMT settled Mae Aw in the early 1970s and soon cleared the surrounding hills for poppy production. But the killing fields had since vanished. The Thai frowned on a contraband crop grown uncomfortably close to the palace of a beloved monarch trying to wean his people from the drug trade. The KMT veterans now trafficked in tea, coffee, and potatoes. Mae Aw was clean, with the exception of a small plot of poppies dutifully grown for the benefit of the few tourists who made the two-hour, thirty-mile drive from Mae Hong Son. Visitors found no raffish intrigue, only an unremarkable village in terminal decline. Less than one hundred KMT veterans lingered in Mae Aw, their grand vision of a free, Nationalist China a lost dream.

"A long time ago we got care and help from America," said Lu Chang Tong, sixty-three and a former KMT signalman. "Now we have not enough men to go back."

I left Lu Chang Tong with his sunny CIA memories and drove west, through a scrubby pasture dotted with cow dung. After a half mile, we halted at the crest of a small hill. U Thai led me across the defenses of an abandoned KMT outpost, now overgrown with creeper and bramble. A tattered, sun-bleached Thai flag fluttered from a cracked bamboo pole. At the summit, my guide made a sweeping gesture toward the valley below, where cattle grazed near a Red Karen village.

"Burma," announced U Thai.

To the south, a distant hilltop commanded by the rebel

Karenni Army. To the north, about three miles across the valley, a mountain ridge bearing the manmade striations of the Mong Tai Army's resolute trenchwork. The king of that unassailable hill, of the jungle and the seven-thousand-foot mountains beyond, was Khun Sa. The Tatmadaw, Burma's armed forces, were nowhere to be seen. This land was all revolution, cooled by breezes scented with wildflowers and cattle feces.

I was getting close.

When I returned in the gloaming to Mae Hong Son, Flynn and Au Cheng were waiting in my room with Sullivan. There were more border problems. Our *laissez-passer* to Khun Sa's territory had only been good for yesterday, our original entry date, Flynn explained. Now we would have to go through the ordeal of obtaining a new pass, and only Khun Nittaya had the courage to approach her moody sibling.

"I think the answer is yes, though," said Flynn. "Au Cheng threatened Somwang that if we don't hear today, we return to Chiang Mai. Somwang said, 'No, stay, stay.' We're waiting for Khun Nittaya to return from camp."

Somwang Oonman knocked, then entered. He was a small, thin man who possessed an admirable Clark Gable–style mustache and the harried air of a low-level manager. The stuffy room was redolent with the sweat of expectation. Who had the laissez-passer? When could we go in? What trail would we use?

Somwang sat down heavily on the edge of the bed, his head bowed.

"No," he said.

Flynn dropped his head, put his hand on Somwang's shoulder.

"It's not your fault," Flynn said softly.

I wanted to put my hands around Somwang's neck, but felt

too weak. A deadly undertow pulled me through a crashing surf, toward a deep, uncertain sea. I fought to breathe, my throat burning with gastric juices, my ears throbbing with warm temple-bell waves. I could faintly hear Au Cheng translate Somwang's excuses.

"Somwang knew last night," Au Cheng related, "but he was afraid to tell us. The letter came last night. He try again today. The problem is the border. The Thai army comes to the border, so it is difficult to cross the border. The Thai army waits on the border. So if you cross, very, very danger. If something happen, they are very concerned about you."

"Last week, Mook said it was all clear," Flynn responded. "The General sent down troops to clear the trail."

"The Burmese army always change," Somwang said. "The border always change. It change yesterday. Maybe it will change again tomorrow. You understand? I'm very sorry it happen like this. You come from far away. You are very close and cannot cross. We try and try again, but the Thai government has very strong control of the border. They wait in the jungle."

I struggled to pull my way to the surface. "Is it possible the border situation will change soon?" I asked.

"It could change tonight, it could change in two days," said Flynn. "We just don't know. The trail was clear on Saturday. Right now, they say we can't go in. It's best to return to Chiang Mai. You can stay at my house. We can monitor the situation from there. You can interview Prince Mahasang. He can tell you all about the Wa.

"Could Khun Sa invite Mister Jay and Mister Chris back?" he asked Somwang. "Khun Sa to pay expenses? They were invited in. They came here at their own expense. If they come back, the General should be paying their expenses."

I shook my head at Au Cheng and Somwang. Impossible. No junkets.

The contrite Somwang shuffled out of room, still muttering apologies. A *Loi Krathong swan*, a delicate sky lantern sent aloft to carry away misfortune and unhappiness, had just crashed and burned on the Baiyoke Chalet. Thousands of dollars had netted us only one sad truth: our sure thing was a petulant phantom.

"Barry, you said this trip was 100 percent!" I raved. "You personally guaranteed it!"

"We were *late!*" Flynn shot back. "There's fighting on the trail! We can still walk in if you want to. I *know* the trail. We'll find out what the problem is. Something's going on in the camp. I called the office in Chiang Mai. I couldn't get hold of Mook. They told me he was going to Bangkok."

"Barry, watch your ass," said Sullivan. His sixth sense had flashed. "There is something here that is more than it appears. 'Problems at the border'—I've heard that a hundred times."

Flynn and Au Cheng left for Khun Nittaya's house to get a better explanation. The General's sister had avoided meeting with us again at the hotel. She had lost face, having promised to get us into camp, then failing to do so. Sullivan and I drifted downstairs to the bar, numb, incredulous. Eighteen months of cajoling, planning, and reconfirming, nearly four thousand dollars out of pocket, and I had been rebuffed just a few maddening miles from my goal. I had no story. There was only the reality of a depleted bank account, a long, brooding trip home, an uncomfortable meeting with my editors.

We got your postcard, Cox. What happened?

In the bar, the house band played last night's same, uninspired set. Mae Hong Son was conclusive proof that hell came complete with a bad lounge act and tepid beer.

"I spoke with Cal Bowden in Tampa while you were out

smelling flowers," said Sullivan. "He said Phoumano is very optimistic about the POW video. Phoumano told him he is dealing with people in very high places. The guy—Phoumano calls him Martinez—*speaks* on the video.

"You gotta know when to hold 'em, know when to fold 'em," he continued. "Hell, let's get outta here. We'll go back to Bangkok and give Phoumano's deal our best shot. If Barry clears up these 'border problems,' we're only an hour away by plane. I don't want to go back to Chiang Mai and drink with these guys and have Barry's friends try to pawn shit off on us. This place, this place is a cluster fuck."

9

The Official Stories

The only Shan leader I saw during our stay was a bronze likeness of Phraya Singhalat Racha, the first ruler of Mae Hong Son. Clutching a dah, the turban-topped saopha struck a Resolute Founder pose in an afterthought of a park outside the town jail. Bored guards watched as Sullivan photographed my audience with the statue. Then we trudged to the airport under the weight of our enormous, now irrelevant backpacks and the burden of dashed dreams. We felt violated by this predatory town. To our chagrin, Mae Hong Son was not yet through with us. Since our return date had changed, we would have to fly standby back to Chiang Mai. Our names went atop the list for Thai Airways 191, the first flight of the day. When departure was announced, the small waiting room became a frenzy of trekkers, package tourists, and hotel touts. Then a Thai businessman pushed his way to the Thai Airways counter, spoke to the agent, flourished a wad of baht, and fled with the lot of boarding passes. Apoplectic, I jabbed the agent's standby list. He looked at me blankly.

"No passes," he lied. "I no lie."

We could stay at the airport and allow other Thai travelers to bribe their way ahead of us onto further flights and thus miss our connection to Bangkok. The only alternative was to get aboard the next thing smoking to Chiang Mai. At a nearby trekking agency I threw down four Purple Kings to charter a minivan and a driver to carry the four of us to Chiang Mai. I was in a foul mood, but it would not do to leave Flynn and Au Cheng to arrange their own passage home. I had spent half the night concocting a salvage operation, and Flynn was still my only connection to the General.

We pushed our luck on rollercoaster Highway 1095, a northerly route that paralleled the Burmese border, wending for hours through a nerve-wracking landscape of karst pinnacles, before dropping south to Chiang Mai. Noi had avoided this road on the outbound trip, although it was at least sixty miles shorter than the southern drive along Highway 108. There was no way to cut any time off the six-hour passage on Highway 1095, where rarely one hundred meters passed without a switchback or a grinding gear shift. The van labored over pine-topped mountain ridges, crept around blind, unrailed curves, then dove headlong into vine-choked valleys.

"We would have taken this road to get to the mule camp," said Flynn. We traveled in the morning shadows along the southern rim of a long, narrow valley holding Ban Huai Pha, a carpet of lush, golden paddy and stilted rice sheds that extended to the base of a soaring limestone massif. It was achingly gorgeous, and I didn't care. Ban Huai Pha was not part of my original itinerary. I stared glumly through the tinted glass, catching only snatches of Flynn's running commentary. Tham Plaa . . . fish cave . . . sacred blue carp . . . deadly curse. Beautiful, useless local color.

I came around a few miles later, when Flynn pointed out a dirt road breaking north into the mountains.

"Built by Thai logging companies," he said. "It goes all the way into camp. Of course, it doesn't officially exist. Khun Nittaya drove this road yesterday. She went in to Ho Mong and even she couldn't speak with K.S. She's the General's sister and she was stopped."

Au Cheng shook his head.

"Au Cheng and I visited Khun Nittaya's house last night," Flynn added. "She was inside with the Thai border police. She met me out on the porch and told me, 'Barry, don't even try to go to the border.' "

The danger did not belong with the Thai, Khun Nittaya had intimated. The danger came in Burma. It would be foolhardy to push our way along a smuggling trail, knowing neither the rules of engagement nor the reception we might receive should we make it to camp unharmed. Once inside Ho Mong, a confrontation seemed inevitable.

Khernsai Jaiyen had crafted an elegant scheme to place Flynn in this undignified position. As the foreign-relations officer who handled all press inquiries about Shan State, Khernsai must have been insulted by Flynn's successful, back-channel appeal through Mook Keaw Kam to obtain our invitation. Only now did I realize what a loss of face our invitation must have been for Khernsai. We thought we had the deal wired, and now we were paying for that hubris. Khernsai had left himself room to spring this surprise tactic. My letter of invitation to visit Ho Mong, which Khernsai had been ordered to type, had included his own clever caveat: *subject to conditions prevailing at the time of your entry.* My request had been accepted. We had traveled to Mae Hong Son, then been forced to wait while Khernsai's minions fed us excuses. We were late. Our pass was only valid for one day. There was fighting. There were border problems.

Payback. It was a painful lesson.

Now, Khun Nittaya could not speak with her brother.

Mook, our only other hope to plead our case directly to the general, could not be reached in Chiang Mai. He couldn't overrule what had happened in camp and, to avoid a confrontation, had probably decided not to take Flynn's calls. And Khernsai had left Ho Mong. His distance allowed him deniability; he could explain away our rebuff as some sort of miscommunication. Flynn had been isolated, neutered. Even worse than defeat, he had also lost face. Each roadside kilometer stone only reinforced the humiliation.

"The mule camp's on the right," Flynn said brightly. "Ban Mae Suya."

I should have ridden a snorting beast through the village gate, across Highway 1095, then into the valley leading to Burma. Instead, I was in full retreat; worse, I now had to endure a passage through the landscape of my defeat. Not a soul stirred in Ban Mae Suya. Beyond the highway, the Thai Border Patrol Police outpost appeared equally langorous. I found it impossible to believe that border problems bedeviled this corner of the kingdom.

The highway began to climb out of the peaceful valley. A few miles further, a dirt road branched northward from the highway into dense forest. Several Thai soldiers lounged in the shade of a simple shelter at the junction, guarding a turnpike.

"The special road to camp," said Flynn. "Only for Khun Sa and VIPs."

VIPs bought teak and gems, sold weapons and political favors. I trafficked only in information. I would not be taking the special road. We ordered the driver to turn off at the next overlook. Hundreds of feet below, Khun Sa's exclusive highway snaked through the forest canopy, then vanished in the folds of the crumpled hills that crested into fantastic knob-, fin-, and coxcomb-shaped summits. Flynn noted the peaks and valleys we should have traversed on our way to Ho Mong. The slopes of the nearest mountains were pockmarked by the fires of hilltribe swidden farmers. In a few years, the soil exhausted, they would move on, perhaps toward the distant, tourmaline-colored Shan highlands that remained unscarred, their virgin state almost a taunt. I had gotten close, but that was no solace. I might as well have been twelve thousand miles away, back in Boston, for all the good it did to stand on that hill and look across the jungle to where I should have been that galling morning.

I told Mook as much that afternoon in Chiang Mai. Having survived Highway 1095 with nothing worse than a few near-misses with overloaded, oncoming song thaew, we were toasting our small fortune at Noi's Fang Ping Restaurant. "We traveled halfway around the world at personal expense and personal time and we get to Mae Hong Son and we don't get in," I complained.

Mook nodded gravely. In the aftermath of our border-crossing fiasco, he had come to the restaurant to hear our complaints.

"We were lied to, outright," said Flynn. "They say there's fighting along the border. I called Colonel Vichit. He says no fighting, no Thai police along the border. No commandoes. They lied to us."

I had played the Good Scribe. Now I became the Bad Scribe. I had nothing to lose. I called upon the power of the press. Surely the General understood bad publicity.

"I've researched Shan State for more than a year. I want to do an objective story. Now, whatever story I write, the only comments I'll have will be from DEA, the United Nations, the State Department."

I handed Mook a confirmation letter from the regional

director for Southeast Asia of the United Nations International Drugs Control Program. The U.N. would have plenty to say about the heroin situation in Shan State.

"I have interviews in Bangkok set up with the U.N. and DEA. I will write a story. I will go to Bangkok and I will talk to those people. I'm not blaming you, Mook. I just want you to communicate this."

"The whole country will be aware," said Flynn. It was hyperbole, sure, but I wasn't going to correct him. "Now all they're going to get are Khernsai's lies."

"I will talk to Khun Nittaya," said Mook.

Now Flynn laid down his ace: Lord Charles Brocket, Member of Parliament. The youthful, polo-playing peer, an old Etonian who counted Prince Charles as a friend, boasted an antique-car collection valued at twenty million pounds, and led the lush life with Lady Brocket, former *Vogue* covergirl Isabell Lorenzo, had become an obsession of Khun Sa. Flynn had met the nobleman through his second cousin, Rick Furtado, a classic-car expert who worked at Brocket Hall, the M.P.'s five-thousand-acre Hertfordshire estate. The Brockets had traveled to Chiang Mai, where they bought sapphires, and Flynn introduced them to Khernsai and Mook. The jetsetters gave the warlord's associates a brochure about Brocket Hall. Khun Sa was mightily impressed with the Brockets and their forty-eight-bedroom, thirty-bathroom manse. Think of the public-relations victory if a British M.P. was to visit Ho Mong. But first, Lord Brocket would need to feel comfortable, at home in Shan State. What better welcome than a replica of Brocket Hall? If the warlord built it, the Brockets would come. And so a home inspired by the Brocket's eighteenth-century mansion, once the residence of Victorian prime ministers Palmerston and Melbourne, was rising in the Burmese jungle.

"The General wants Lord Brocket to come," said Flynn.

"Lord Brocket's not going to come until there are reports that something's being done in Shan State. If we show the United States is listening or communicating with Khun Sa, I can give the story to Lord Brocket. Then Lord Brocket shows the House of Lords. That could be an excuse for Lord Brocket to come. See? Now Lord Brocket won't come."

"You can come again," said Mook, his eyes solicitous, hopeful.

"This trip I paid for myself," I replied. "If I come over again, I would also have to pay for myself. If I come to Mae Hong Son again and nothing happens, that's more money. Last night, Mister Barry made an offer to pay for my expenses. It was generous, but I cannot take money. How could I write an objective story?"

Mook nodded, no doubt wishing he was with his bride rather than three irate farang. Khernsai had dealt him a bad hand, given him big problems. Who would tell the General that Brocket Hall East was going to be a white elephant?

"I think we can solve the problem if the General gave us the 43,000-carat ruby," Sullivan cracked. "Then we have no problem."

The laughter eased our foul moods. We had vented our displeasure upon Mook for being shat upon from a great height. There was nothing more to do but drink Singha, nibble Noi's fried cashews, catch the last flight of the day to Bangkok, then begin salvage operations tomorrow. What would it take to succeed in getting into Shan State? How much tea money? How many gifts? How many XXX-rated videos? Even Tori Welles had failed to open trails.

========

As was his habit, Phoumano Nosavan had promised far more than he could deliver. We met at Villa Champa, the walled, plumeria-shaded compound his late father had built in the northern suburbs of Bangkok, to view his touted POW tape. It was a depressing fraud. In the video, a Filipino-looking man supposedly under the control of Khmer Rouge soldiers in Battambang Province of west-central Cambodia sat on the floor of a hootch. The scene was surreal, pathetic: pictures on the wood-plank walls of Hun Sen officers, Michael Jackson's Top 40 hit "Remember the Time" blaring from a boombox. "Martinez" spoke in halting, British-inflected English: "Please sir, I want to go home. I come from California. I don't want to live in Kampuchea. I want to see my mama. I want to see my papa. Hubba, hubba, sir."

I was now zero-for-two in cloak-and-dagger deals. It was time to try my luck with the good guys, to gain a little leverage, then to apply pressure on Khernsai, the clever factotum who had cheated me out of my story in Burma. It was time for a second round of payback.

William F. Beachner, regional director of the U.N. International Drugs Control Program, met me in his organization's high-rise offices adjacent to the Royal Military Academy. The tinted windows framed a view of Dusit Zoo and Chitralada Palace, the moat-girdled royal residence. The pale walls of Beachner's sparely furnished office held maps charting his agency's efforts to wean the hilltribes of Thailand and Laos off the poppy. There was no such map for Burma—or Myanmar, the appellation used only by diplomats and the ruling State Law and Order Restoration Council.

"There's no question that opium production has significantly increased since 1988," said Beachner, a short, trim, buttondowned American who, at fifty-nine, still had an enviable shock of silver-gray hair. "We've just begun to work in Myanmar. We've got a long way to go before we start to make any inroads into the opium cultivation."

He delicately allowed that opium eradication in Burma would be much more difficult than in the relatively remote areas of northern Thailand and the Plain of Jars in north-central Laos where the U.N. had implemented small agricultural development projects.

"The Myanmar government does not really have control of much of the Shan State, particularly the areas where much of the opium is grown and where the opium is being processed into heroin. . . . The writ of the government does not really fully apply in these areas."

The Shan rebels, however, were not the only group involved in the opium business. The Burmese government had reached political accommodation with ethnic Wa and Kokang Chinese narco-insurgents along the remote Sino-Burmese border and claimed these accords would end the region's reliance on opium production. In truth, the exact opposite had occurred. Lacking the logistical capability to battle Khun Sa's Mong Tai Army along the Thai border, SLORC had followed a classic, cynical form of Asian statecraft: empower one foe, then turn him loose against another enemy. Rangoon had employed the United Wa State Army as a proxy force against Khun Sa since 1989, with the antithetical goals of improving its sorry international image and of wresting control of the booming heroin trade from the renegade Shan warlord. In return for their fealty, SLORC legitimized the Wa, granting them carte blanche to increase poppy acreage, construct new heroin refineries, and develop China's Yunnan Province as an alternate drug-trafficking route. Only SLORC's enemies needed to worry about counter-narcotics efforts. Beachner chose his words carefully.

"They obviously should have a political interest in stopping opium production and heroin trafficking because it has, in the past, provided the wherewithal for some of their opponents."

He smiled wryly. "It is a difficult subject to discuss very openly."

The following day, Donald F. Ferrarone, director of the U.S. Drug Enforcement Administration in Thailand, ushered me into his office in a high-security wing of the American Embassy. The white noise of afternoon rush hour on Wireless Road pulsed through the second-floor window. Ferrarone, forty-six, balding and athletic looking, had decorated the room with an assortment of foreign police caps and, with a wink at zero tolerance, a large pipe taken during a raid on a Chinese opium den. In quiet, measured tones, the Springfield, Massachusetts, native, a twenty-two-year DEA veteran, spoke about the kingpin who topped his agency's most-wanted list in Southeast Asia. He quickly dismissed the freedom-fighter persona that Khun Sa cultivated so assiduously.

"He's a guy who's got the propaganda game figured out," Ferrarone said. "But beyond a shadow of a doubt, he gains 50 percent of his income by manufacturing heroin and selling it worldwide. He's a ruthless guy. His discipline is final, quite often. . . . Our intelligence in this area is absolute. We know what he's doing. We know his moves."

Knowledge of Khun Sa's operations was one thing. Action against that criminal activity was an altogether different matter. Ferrarone described a drug empire that cut a swath through several hundred miles of Shan State, from the Wa States adjoining China all the way south to Mae Hong Son. By his own admission, the DEA was "not in this game" until the heroin crossed into Thailand. Even then, the agency seemed hindered by Thai law-enforcement and military authorities. It was a frustrating subject that Ferrarone declined to discuss on the record.

Although Thailand had outlawed opium production in 1959 and officially condemned the drug trade, the kingdom remained the primary conduit to the west for Golden Triangle heroin. According to annual reports of the BINM, "widespread police and military corruption, expanding narcotics trade with Burma, and the involvement of influential Thai and Sino-Thai private citizens and government officials" had undermined counter-narcotics efforts in Thailand.

"Elements of the Thai military and police" maintained contacts with Khun Sa's Mong Tai Army, the report continued. "They also tolerate arms and precursor chemical sales to the [MTA] and some other trafficking groups, as well as the licit trade which sustains their illicit activities."

Politicians, policemen, and military officers were thought to funnel billions of dollars a year in "black money" profits from drug trafficking, prostitution, and arms smuggling into stock and real-estate transactions. The investments weren't difficult to arrange; Thailand had no money-laundering laws. Progress in major drug cases still depended largely on U.S. government initiative and direction, according to the State Department.

Politics and profit shaped Thailand's ambivalent enforcement approach. The kingdom had feuded with Burma since 1569, when Ayutthaya fell. When the Burmese again captured the city in 1767, the Siamese established a new capital further down the Chao Phraya River. Over the centuries, as Ban Makok, the Village of the Wild Plum, grew from a tiny fishing settlement into the sprawling metropolis of Bangkok, the Thai never forgot nor forgave the Burmese for destroying glorious Ayutthaya.

By trading with Shan, Karen, and Mon insurgents, the Thai created a buffer zone with Burma (General Bo Mya, the White Karen rebel leader, once likened his soldiers to "a foreign legion" of Thailand), preoccupied the military strategists in Rangoon, and fostered a state of controlled anarchy—ideal for illicit trade—along the turbulent frontier. Just as there was a steady business between elements of the Thai military and the

Khmer Rouge, who traded timber and gems for weapons and supplies in Cambodia, there was a fortune to be had along the porous Burmese border. The rebels of Burma required the same revolutionary staples and would pay in any coin of the realm: baht, teak, jade, rubies, or, as was alleged in Khun Sa's case, heroin. Despite receiving millions of dollars in American funding, the Thai waged a halfhearted war on drugs. With a fortune to be made in trade and tea money, it made little business sense to Thai authorities to completely support American counter-narcotics efforts. The Thai masterfully walked the middle path, cooperating just enough to ensure that DEA made some high-profile busts, but not so vigorously that the lucrative black-market trade was irreparably damaged. No one, in the Asian phrase, wanted to see his rice bowl broken. "Arrangements" were made. In the early 1980s, Khun Sa had actually run his empire undisturbed from Ban Hin Taek, a Thai border village north of Chiang Rai. I had already seen the office that Khun Sa's political organization kept in Mae Hong Son and the roads to his jungle headquarters built and guarded by the Thai. None of this could have existed without the complicity of the very people who officially wanted Khun Sa captured.

"Do we have this thing under control?" Ferrarone asked rhetorically. "No, this thing isn't under control."

———

The DEA agent's frustration was understandable. The taint of drugs has touched the highest levels of Thai government. In the spring of 1992, there had been an uproar when Narong Wongwan's nomination for prime minister was scuttled when the United States charged that the influential politician and timber magnate had close links to drug traffickers and denied Narong an American visa.

Mai pen rai. It was all right, the Thai saying went. It didn't matter. Despite being part of the Golden Triangle and party to the shipment of most of Southeast Asia's heroin, many Thai authorities considered the drug and the addiction it fostered to be a Western problem, just as AIDS was seen as a disease of the unclean farang. Sompong Potpui, the director of the Grassroots Development Institute, knew better. His country has an estimated 340,000 heroin users and an additional 35,000 hilltribe opium addicts. While public officials might be in denial about drug abuse, Sompong has firsthand knowledge of the damage done by heroin in Klong Toey, the ramshackle Bangkok slum built on marshy land adjacent to the Port Authority of Thailand.

Just two miles east of the sexual playpens of Patpong, Klong Toey is the Thailand that few tourists encounter. Outside Sompong's simple storefront office, cattle forage in rotting piles of garbage and children play in fetid muck left by the warm afternoon rain. Adults, primarily unskilled peasants from rural Isan, lounge in rickety, raised houses built of scrap wood. This luckless place is the center of Bangkok's netherworld. The slum's narrow alleys and unregistered houses, its desperate inhabitants and proximity to contraband shipments, make Klong Toey ideal for criminal activity.

In 1986, according to Sompong, the slum of thirty-five thousand had more than one hundred fifty heroin dealers and nearly one thousand addicts. An equal number of transient addicts came to score in Klong Toey. His aggressive, community-based prevention program had chased pushers and slashed the number of addicts by 75 percent. But as Sompong acknowledged, there are few antidrug success stores in the rest of Thailand. In the far north, heroin abuse is rampant among hilltribes; in the far south, great numbers of Muslim fishermen also inject the drug. The HIV-infection rate among heroin addicts, who often share dirty needles, is at 35 percent and swelling. Mai pen rai. The epitaph of a kingdom.

The Thai drug trade, like nearly every major business enterprise in Southeast Asia, is dominated by ethnic Chinese. Yunnanese muleteers handle the grunt work of cross-border smuggling in the north, leading caravans on ancient trails through slick-sloped mountains. South of Chiang Mai and Chiang Rai, the thrifty Chiu Chao, whose seafaring ancestors immigrated in the mid nineteenth century from the coastal Swatow region of China, see to finance and distribution. If it is difficult for DEA to work with Thai law enforcement—in effect, the DEA has to bid against drug dealers for their services—it is impossible to penetrate the secretive, family-run crime groups that launder money through a web of legitimate businesses or informal banking systems, that conduct business solely with relatives or trusted intimates, that communicate in arcane Chinese dialects, and that enjoy cozy relationships with powerful Thai officials.

After consolidating loads in northern Thailand, the untouchable Chiu Chao syndicates bring the heroin to Bangkok. With its modern communications, banking, and transportation systems and its pliable officials, freewheeling Bangkok is an ideal entrepôt. Routed to ethnic Chinese brokers linked to the Triads, the heroin leaves the capital on trains heading for Malaysia, planes bound for Taiwan or Hong Kong, and aboard ships that might drop anchor anywhere from Singapore to New York City. Having smuggled contraband for generations, the Chiu Chao possess a genius for elaborate deception. In August 1993, just a few months before my trip, U.S. Customs agents in New Orleans had seized 361 pounds of heroin, with a street value of $200 million, in tins of "Hand Brand" lychee nuts. Ferrarone termed the smuggling methods of the Triads "far more elaborate and probably more effective" than those of the Medellin and Cali cocaine cartels.

"They've been doing it for centuries," he said. "It really doesn't matter what it is. This century it happens to be narcotics. It could be anything in the future."

Illegal drugs, illegal aliens, illegal weapons. Business is business. And business is very, very good.

If their job isn't difficult enough, U.S. law enforcement now has a new player to contend with: Nigeria. Through control of air-courier networks departing Bangkok, then transiting through Lagos to Europe and the United States, Nigerian traffickers have become the DHL of the drug-delivery service, responsible for an estimated 35 to 40 percent of the heroin bound for the West. Official corruption is so bad in Nigeria, money laundering so extensive, counter-narcotics efforts so paltry, that the nation is one of just a handful decertified for its failure to comply with the goals of the 1988 U.N. Convention Against Illicit Traffic in Narcotic Drugs and Psychotropic Substances.

The Nigerians favor an "ant army" approach to smuggling and are willing to suffer enormous casualties. Black Africans are conspicuous in Thailand and body-packers, after picking up the drugs in Bangkok, often find themselves sitting upon the "Nigerian pot" at the airport until they pass the condom-wrapped evidence. But the Nigerian cartels reason that the majority of their human wave, recruited among the desperately poor, will still slip through Thai customs with a fortune in heroin. The chance at quick money is enough to lure countless West African mules to Bangkok. The Africans linger in the lobbies of low-end hotels and guest houses throughout the city, but nowhere more than Khao San Road, a downtown block catering to the hip, hirsute farang doing Thailand on the cheap. It is all for sale on Khao San Road: bootleg cassettes and clothes, tattoos on demand, silk suits in just a few hours, fake identity cards—student or journalist, take your pick—while you wait, even heroin, which some tuk-tuk drivers offer for 30 baht a shot. The West Africans keep to themselves, frequenting a hotel near a billiards hall on a narrow soi perpendicular to Khao San Road, biding paranoid time for hours, for days, in a ground-floor vegetarian restaurant.

The Nigerian Connection illustrates the problems facing DEA's overwhelmed Thai operation. With no in-country linguists who could decipher a wiretap in such West African languages as Hausa and Yoruba, Ferrarone was forced to find translators in Lagos, then dig deep into his budget to bring them to Bangkok.

"Think about it: we're struggling here, although it's a good choke point," he told me. "No one was willing to give us the extra money back home . . . we put this pick-up softball team together and get on the line, start listening, and Holy Christ. You know what we found out?"

The DEA found that the Nigerian "ant army" had overrun Bangkok. A quick airport survey revealed that West Africans had voluntarily declared one hundred million dollars upon arriving in Thailand. How much drug cash was actually carried into the country was anybody's guess. The towering one-hundred-million-dollar figure, like the tip of an arctic iceberg, was both a breathtaking revelation and an ominous indication of a giant, unknown problem.

"They're very familial, tribal groups," Ferrarone added. "You grab them, they won't say a thing to anybody else. They go to jail and do their time. You could fill the jails with these people. They're running all over the place."

Was this thing under control? Hell, no.

When I returned to Boston in mid November, Khernsai was in full cover-your-ass mode. A faint fax awaited me, written on the letterhead of the Shan State People's Representative Committee, née the Shan State Restoration Council. The dozens of squabbling factions in Burma agree on only one course of action: they change the grandiloquent names of their rebel groups as often as possible. The Karen National Union begat the Karen People's Liberation Army, which begat the Karen National Liberation Army. And at one time, both a United Nationalities Front and a Nationalities United Front issued communiques. On his destined-to-be-obsolete stationery, Khernsai's superior, Khun Lurn, chairman of the Subcommittee for Foreign Affairs, blamed the Thai for my problems, then extended an invitation to return after the new year "when the border guard is less strict." Khun Lurn was full of hale reassurance: "Even if you are arrested they will not give you any trouble but only have to release you."

I wrote tough, two-page letters to Khun Sa and to Khernsai, lengthier versions of the rant I had dumped on Mook in Chiang Mai. I had been invited to Ho Mong. I had traveled to the border. And I had been betrayed. Although denied an audience with the General, I had not been denied a story. I had the U.N. and DEA officials to thank for that. I still hoped for Khun Sa's comments and was willing to try again, but only with his personal, written guarantee of quick, safe passage to Ho Mong. I did not want his money for any expenses I would incur; I only wanted his words.

I was ready for the *Herald*'s managing editor, Andrew F. Costello, Jr., to rip into me for my failure to get into Burma, but he let me off the hook. After all, I'd agreed to do the story on spec, so the red ink flowed from my checking account, not his news budget. I laid out for Costello what I thought I had. Local color along the Thai border and in Bangkok, comments from DEA and U.N. officials, interviews with academic experts and Boston junkies.

"I can write a story, Andy, if we want to go now. I've done 90 percent of the reporting. I can pull some old Khun Sa quotes, fax some questions to his office in Thailand, then go with his responses. But whatever I write will lack that last 10 percent, the holy-shit stuff. I can't get that unless I get into Burma. If I write it now, I think it'll read like boilerplate. I really need to get to ground zero. There's a chance. I'm leaning on Khun Sa and his people. If I get the green light, I'm willing to go back and try again."

"What are your expenses so far?"

"I'm at the break-even point."

Costello thought for a minute.

"There's no rush on this thing," he said. "I think you're right. Let's wait and see if you can get in. If you can get another invitation, we'll up the freelance payment to cover your airfare and expenses for another trip. Sound fair?"

It was the first good news I'd had in many weeks. And any year now, Khun Sa might reply. Perhaps Flynn would, too. I had tried reaching him in Chiang Mai but he seemed to be forever out the door, an expat on the fringe, trying to make a quasi-legal living—traveling to Malaysia to help sneak the mother of his friend, the Wa prince Mahasang, into Thailand; flying to London to meet with Lord Brocket about gemstones.

My official reply finally arrived in mid January, in a three-week-old letter written on the stationery of the Shan State Restoration Council. Even by Burmese standards, the Shan State People's Representative Committee was short-lived. The typed message was pure, crawfishing Khernsai:

You have to understand first of all that it was neither I nor any of my subordinates who had barred you from visiting us. On the contrary, it was the misguided policy of our neighbors and your own administration who had stopped you right across the border. I told you that our neighbors were usually lenient during the New Year's celebrations and accordingly invited you to come that time but you will recall that you had insisted on coming before the celebrations and you yourself found out how tough the situation was. . . . I hope the New Year spirit shall stay for some time. Please advise me in advance of your arrival so that my aides can arrange for your safe transit.

> Happy New Year.
> Sincerely,
> Khun Sa

So there it was, the letter I'd wanted. An invitation, with no restrictive clauses that could suddenly mutate into "border problems." The missive had been written in exculpatory fashion by Khernsai, but it carried the General's personal signature, which would be my precious key to his kingdom. I called Sullivan and gave him the good news.

"Pick a date," Sullivan replied. "Hell, I'm ready to go now. I never unloaded my backpack."

We were back in the saddle again, praying for hope to triumph over experience.

10

Getting In

Six weeks later, on March 1, 1994, Sullivan and I returned to the Thai frontier. Checking again into the Baiyoke Chalet felt like donning a dead man's musky clothes. Our room was a familiar, lonely place: cool parquet floors, empty white walls, bone-colored lampshades. I lay on a short, hard bed, mocked by the bitter, gnawing ghosts of Mae Hong Son. A pall of oily candle smoke clung to the ceiling, a benediction. Too late for sleep. Boston. Detroit. Tokyo. Bangkok. Chiang Mai. Mae Hong Son. In a few hours, perhaps Burma. No border problems; the word would come soon. It had to.

Nothing had changed in our absence. Not the traffic, not the heat, not the politics. Nothing but Honey, the baby elephant, who had died despite an outpouring of public support, even the patronage of Queen Sirikhit of Thailand. Honey's death was a foregone conclusion—the truck that had struck her had crushed her hind legs and damaged her spinal cord—but Thai reverence for elephants, the Buddhist concept of dukkha, and precepts against the taking of any life had inhibited veterinarians from euthanizing the tormented animal. Death came to

Honey only after a long winter season of enforced, yet atten-
tive, agony. That was Thailand, mindfully courteous to a fault.
In a legendary case, a favorite wife of King Chulalongkorn had
fallen into the Chao Phraya River and, because her subjects
were forbidden to touch royalty, no one had lifted a hand
while she drowned.

The word came at four. Flynn strode into the room, smiling.

"The truck comes in an hour," he said, then left to pack.

Time for a cold, bracing shower to chase fatigue and fear,
then to don the raiment of my previous Far Eastern failure: blue
jeans, black T-shirt, long-sleeved olive-drab shirt, hiking boots.
Snapped thick rubber bands around the ends of my pant cuffs,
protection against water-borne leeches we might encounter
crossing streams. Still wired, I confirmed the contents of my
boogie bag for the third time that night, retightened the straps
of my camouflaged backpack, then poured Absolut into
unbreakable plastic bottles. No margin for error.

You're going into a war zone.

I hefted my fifty pounds of equipment and liquor and
stepped outside onto the Baiyoke Chalet's second-floor gallery.
Sullivan followed, grunting beneath an even more enormous
load. Woe unto our luckless pack mule. Through the mountain
mists, the red warning lights of the radio and television anten-
nas atop Doi Kung Mu winked like rubies. Bracts of yellow-,
pink-, and fuschia-colored bougainvillea pushed through the
dew-streaked teak balustrade. Sand-colored geckos scrambled
like antic shorthand along the pale walls.

Au Cheng had not made this trip. If he went to Ho Mong,
he feared the General would prevail upon him to go fight the
Burmese on the front lines. It was best that he remain in
Chiang Mai. So this time around, there would be no one to
ride shotgun. There would be two Shan mule skinners, neither
of whom spoke English, to lead three unarmed farang—who

spoke no Tai Yai—to the heart of the Golden Triangle. Some strategy: stumble through the bushes, waving Khun Sa's laissez-passer at any creature drawing a breath.

Not to worry, Flynn had insisted. Everything had been prepared for our arrival. And so far, he was correct. Our return trip had gone off like clockwork, even the domestic Thai Airways flights. Somwang Oonman, the bearer of such bad border tidings in November, had been the consummate host in Mae Hong Son, meeting us at the airport with a truck belonging to the Shan State Restoration Council, arranging for our pickup ride to Ban Mae Suya, confirming our mule-train departure to Burma.

"*Sawasdee,*" said Flynn. "Good morning."

He was dressed smartly in pressed jeans and a black-satin Nexus Productions jacket. Befitting his extemporaneous nature, our man from Chiang Mai carried just two small gym bags. He traveled light, just as he lived. Flynn led us down the gallery, the sound of his steel-toed boots causing the lizards to dart even more frenetically along the walls. He turned at the top of the hotel staircase, then disappeared in a chorus of thuds and obscenities. We rushed to find him sprawled below on the staircase landing, clutching his back and sucking air between clenched teeth. His boots had slipped on the dew-slick tread of the wooden steps.

Bile burned my esophagus. Not again. Not another star-crossed trip to Mae Hong Son. I could see my editors, incredulous. *First border problems and now . . . stair problems?* For the rest of my newspaper career I'd be entrusted to write nothing more demanding than obituaries and lost-pet stories. Before I let that happen I would piggy-back Barry Flynn all the way to Ho Mong. He grimaced, then—all praise to Lord Buddha—gingerly stood.

"Lucky I landed on my bag," Flynn said.

He didn't know how lucky. Bad back or not, he was going to take us into Burma. Downstairs, a deserted lobby, an empty street. We stood on darkened Khunlumprapras Road, as blasé as three foreigners loaded with gear and about to embark on an illegal border crossing could appear. Lisu men wearing dark, woolen balaclavas against the predawn chill drifted by on scooters, implacable hilltribe ninjas on their way to lowland labor. Our transport, a white, battered Toyota pickup, rumbled to a stop at five o'clock. Flynn took a seat in the cab while Sullivan and I tossed the gear into the shell bolted atop the truck bed, climbed inside, and grabbed secure handholds. The driver, undoubtedly a blood relation of Noi, then took us on a mad, twenty-six-mile dash to Ban Mae Suya. The roadside banana groves and second-growth teak trees, the empty *sala* pavilions and shuttered snack stands of Highway 1095 soon dissolved in a howling blur. I closed my eyes and imagined the Bangkok *Post* headline: "Three Farang Die in Fiery Thai Pickup Plunge."

We crossed the Pai River six miles north of Mae Hong Son and the police waved us through a highway checkpoint. The driver barely slowed; the Thai authorities rarely searched jitneys like this song thaew. VIPs and farang intent on illegal activity rode in comfortable Toyota minivans or Land Cruisers, not in overloaded deathtraps patronized by rustic locals. Sullivan and I huddled against the rear of the cab, seeking the lee against the wind. In the hills, the temperature hovered around 55 degrees Fahrenheit; the mercury dipped a good ten degrees when we fell into the fog-bound valleys.

In the light of a three-quarter moon, tree-covered ridgelines bristled like hairs on a watchdog's back. Slumbering Ban Huai Pha, the looming mountain of Tham Plaa Forest Park, the sliver of surreptitious side road. We were getting close. The song thaew crested a rise, then everything went gray and silent.

We ghosted downhill with the engine and lights off, crossed a small bridge over rushing water, left the hum of the highway for the crunch of a dirt road, then crept beneath the wooden gateway cut into the bamboo palisades of Ban Mae Suya. I checked my watch: 5:45 a.m. Right on schedule.

In the darkness, the Shan muleteers set about squaring away our gear. After a lifetime of loading and unloading clandestine caravans, they quickly had our baggage lashed to an A-shaped wooden freight saddle, covered with a mildewed, olive-drab canvas tarpaulin to guard against rain—and, more importantly, prying eyes—then tied down again. On the trail, conspicuous trekking gear could be a dead farang giveaway.

The Shan hamlet, with stilted wooden houses and Toyota trucks, seemed prosperous and well kept. In the moonlight, I could make out a flagpole, a basketball backboard and hoop. A pariah dog ambled up, sniffed the farang, and urinated in the dirt. Mules snuffled, shifted nervously as thin blankets and hard saddles were mounted and cinched to their swaybacks. I counted the huffing apparitions.

"We've only got four mules, Barry. We'll need another one just for Jay's vodka."

An unseen rooster crowed. The village chieftain watched silently, his Krong Thip cigarette glowing like a beacon. He gave a curt order and the trail boys led the tethered mules out the gate. We moved to follow, but the chief held up the palm of his hand. He pointed at his glowing watch dial: 6:10 a.m. Timing was critical. We could not be linked so obviously to the caravan. Two Shan men driving mules, that was an everyday occurrence. Add three farang, people started asking questions.

Five minutes later, the chief nodded. Go now. Flynn thanked him, in Thai, and we walked out of Ban Mae Suya. We paused at the highway to reconnoiter the Border Patrol Police camp.

No smoke. No lights. No cars. On a sloping hill beyond a quarter-mile of naa wet-rice fields, the police settlement slumbered. Hats off. Nothing to call attention to our silhouettes. Move out. Quick. We scuttled across the empty macadam, then crabwalked to a row of cassia trees between the rice paddies and a newly paved access road. Hidden from the BPP camp by the treeline, we walked toward the narrow entrance to a valley flanked by two sheer-faced karstic massifs.

I felt my heart pounding, my bowels churning, the warm, heavy surge of adrenaline. Keep a normal pace. Keep quiet. Across the creek, the stirrings of a rural morning inside a peasant's thatched-roof hut. The growing smell of smoke, then two Thai laborers squatting at roadside by a small, bamboo fire, casting long looks in our direction.

"Sawasdee," Flynn said in greeting.

"Sawasdee," muttered one of the workers. They watched until we had rounded a bend in the road.

"We'll have to move a little quicker," Flynn whispered as we passed. "When the border police come out on patrol, they'll ask those road workers if they saw anybody on the trail. 'Oh, nothing,' " he mimicked. " 'Only four mules and three farangs last seen heading toward Khun Sa.' "

We strode for twenty minutes, then turned west from the main road, which continued north through paddy and pasture to a monastery and the shrine of Tham Wua, or Cow Cave. Wide enough for an ox cart, our rutted path led through dry, tangled, second-growth forest. The upland sky, the color of scullery water, in the last minutes before sunrise, was filled with birdsong. A glossy black hill myna perched on the nearby branch of a dead tree, flashing yellow lappets, piping its cautionary call. *Ti-ong. Ti-ong.*

We had just walked away from any plausible excuse that we were simply tourists out for a ramble in northern Thailand.

This trail led only to Burma. Despite the maddening urge to walk briskly, the need to put as much distance as possible between our party and the Border Patrol Police camp, Flynn slowed our pace. I had an appreciation of the "pucker factor," the soldier's measure of sphincter-tightening fear.

"We have to keep the mules several hundred yards ahead of us," Flynn explained. "The border police put out sitting patrols for ambushes. This way we'll spring their trap. If they stop the mules we'll know, and we can escape."

Meaning a mad, assholes-and-elbows sprint through the woods and, if caught, playing dumb.

"If we're stopped, let me do the talking," Flynn said. "You just say you don't speak Thai. You don't know anything. I took you into the jungle. If they arrest us, first they have to call in to Mae Hong Son, and those are all my people."

Some plan. If we were stopped in the forest, I could only hope it would be by the Thai BPP. These borderlands swarmed with all manner of armed, foul-tempered men—the Burmese Army, the Mong Tai Army, the Kuomintang, the United Wa State Army, as well as brigands and dacoits—none known for their hospitality to strangers, particularly well-outfitted farang. They might smile and conduct us further, or they might smile and chamber a round. I had seen the video that Flynn shot of a 1990 battle between Khun Sa's troops and the fearsome United Wa State Army in this very region. After the Wa had been routed, Flynn explained, MTA troops made bad, mocking magic with the enemy dead. They decapitated the corpses, then mounted the heads on stakes in the jungle, so their spirits would never rest. Now, I hoped we would not wind up in the skull grove of a wet-head Wa who bore a grudge. I placed my Varig Airlines baseball cap back on my head. The hat seemed vaguely martial and official, a deep Navy blue cotton with gold braid on the bill. The "egg salad" might earn me a VIP salute, or mistakenly label me as CIA or DEA.

Sullivan eyed the terrain warily.

"I think we just reached Indian country."

We crossed clearings marked by the ashes of recent BPP campfires and strewn with the cigarette butts of bored sentries. Flynn pointed to a towering, bullet-shaped karst formation in the east. Shan lookouts occupied the summit, he explained, and alerted caravans bound for Ban Mae Suya of Thai sitting patrols. A banner flew if the trail was clear, but the sentries could not help convoys bound for Burma. My heart continued to pound.

An hour after leaving Ban Mae Suya we finally passed the last empty BPP laagers. A few hundred yards later, we caught up with the trail boys, resting with our mules. We mounted, then proceeded Indian file along the path covered with dead leaves. The pack mule took the point, goaded along with bamboo switches by our two Shan guides. Flynn followed, then Sullivan. I took drag position in the rear, glancing nervously over my shoulder for the first sign of hot-pursuit Thai soldiers, urging my stubborn steed forward by shaking the reins and slapping his flanks. My equestrian form—I had not ridden in more than twenty years, ever since cantering a nearly blind horse into thorns in Panama—was worse than that of a dude-ranch rookie.

Our path hugged a mountain stream, fording its quick, clear waters a half-dozen times within a mile, then left the valley, punched through a thicket of bamboo to a gradual gradient where all the undergrowth had been put to the torch. Only tropical hardwoods, including teak trees, remained. Their massive, fluted boles, clear of branches for nearly one hundred feet, rose as tall and strong as the stone columns of a Gothic cathedral. Despite the Thai ban on logging, the trunks of these regal trees were numbered, marked for death by lumberjacks who had littered the ground with crumpled Fritos bags and empty Fanta cans. The air already held the distinct, old-leather odor of fresh-cut teak.

There is hardly a wood as perfect as the heavy timber from *Tectona grandis*: strong, unshrinkable, nearly impervious to insects and fungi. Teak's allure, like a narcotic, drowns all reason. Men search malarial jungles, risk jail, take up weapons, all to cut teak. In the nineteenth century, with the Malabar forests of India dwindling, the British had seized Lower Burma partly for the teak stands near Moulmein and Pegu. And they had used a petty dispute over a teak shipment as a pretext to conquer Upper Burma in 1885. Better than oak in marine environments, teak-constructed ships lasted for ages. The wood was so durable that the *Success*, a one-time prison ship built of Burmese teak in 1790, was seaworthy enough to sail across the Atlantic in 1912. Today, the insatiable tropical-hardwood market has hastened the harvest, pushing loggers into remote pockets of Thailand and areas of Burma held by Mon, Karen, and Shan rebels.

We left the doomed trees and crossed a small, naked valley. A Hume's pheasant, a blur of dark blue and chestnut panic in the first rays of sunlight, took wing near an empty rice shed, skimming above gray fields of fire-scorched stubble toward the curtain of green forest. Our mounts picked their way through dead ashes, dry, harrowed earth, and crumbling paddy dike, the last hint of human habitation before we entered the folds of primeval jungle that draped the hills. Sullivan began humming "The Ballad of Paladin," the theme song from an old television show of his youth, "Have Gun Will Travel." A knight without armor in a savage land. . . .

In upland fashion, the trail soon rejoined the stream. We

ducked through lush tunnels of *wabomyetsangye* and *wapyu* bamboo that shot from the humus to explode overhead in pyrotechnic cascades of delicate green and yellow leaves. Above the floral shower, a few faint chords of light fell through the tracery woven by the leaves of teak, *pyinkado*, and shingly *kanyin* to dance on the blue, iridescent wings of butterflies. Dark mountain walls gradually constricted the wild gorge. As the ravine narrowed, we began tacking upstream through the rock-strewn creek bed. The very air teemed with life: the mist of sparkling water, the scent of unseen orchids, the cries of hidden birds.

Progress through this majestic old-growth forest was slow, painful work. I tore my way with glove-clad hands at the gauntlet of flaying branches and sharp-toothed fan palm leaves, bounced upon a hard saddle only slightly more comfortable than a prostate examination, forced my aching feet to remain wedged into the short, tight stirrup irons that banged against my fat, flea-ridden mule. The obdurate beast seemed intent on personally denuding the forest, nipping at vines, leaves, and fruits along the trail. I looked ridiculous, like Sancho Panza, needled Sullivan. I dug my knees into my mule's ribs. He brayed, then fitfully deposited another load of steaming dung in his wake. Let the BPP step in *that*.

The jungle continued. False violets, red-veined begonias, wild banana trees sprang from the wet, black earth; delicate, lavender-colored flowers burst from elephant creepers strangling the sinewy, silver trunks of bombax trees. Sunset-colored flowers of the *mai-kao*, the Shan flame tree, ignited other suffocating stretches of flora like Chinatown fireworks. We dismounted, clawed our way over a steep, moss-slick rise. My mule's girth strap came free during the slippery descent and the empty saddle tumbled through the undergrowth like an animal in flight. I had been fortunate. Even a minor injury could turn serious in the jungle. The last thing we needed was a first-aid emergency at the very edge of Thailand. During the hasty remount, the amused muleteers let out the stirrup leathers from Asian- to farang-length and advised me, the city slicker, about Shan horsemanship: I should ride with my heels resting in the stirrups, Friar Tuck style.

Two and one-half hours on, we finally left the stream bed and began climbing out of the lush ravine to rolling, open forest. Oriental turtledoves cooed from creamy-flowered catechu and *thitsi*, the black-varnish tree used for lacquer. We moved quickly now, the trail following a natural colonnade of teak, pyinkado, and yellow-flowered *padauk*. The guides, although shod only in cheap thong shoes, kept a brisk walking pace while smoking our gift-pack Marlboros. The Shan had a deserved reputation for stamina; Khun Sa's "iron-legged soldiers" were famous for their long, rapid marches. It was a point of pride for our guides to walk, not ride.

"If these trails could talk," Flynn said. "They've been used for decades, if not centuries, to smuggle everything from gems to drugs to weapons to rice. There are at least fifty trails from Shan State to Mae Hong Son Province. That's why it's impossible to stop the flow of anything."

I don't know what I had expected. Perhaps a grand gorge, a wild ridge, a raging river. Something to delineate clearly chaos from order, kingpins from kings, summary judgment from the rule of law. We topped a slight hill and the guide pointed to a low, bed-sized platform fashioned from tree branches and split bamboo to the right of the trail.

9:15 a.m. Burma.

Around us, the same clear, trackless, sun-dappled forest, but less one splitting headache. If the Thai Border Patrol Police had been tailing us, that chase was officially over. But to guard against unofficial law-enforcement initiative, we kept pushing into Shan State. Within a mile, we skirted the remains of a border customs post. As if to make a point during the 1990 war with the Wa, said Flynn, Khun Sa allowed the Burmese, who had a notion to tax the Shan caravans, to build the remote compound. When construction had finished, Khun Sa's troops then raided and burned it. Now, only a few building stakes remained, already choked with feral creeper. Out here on the perimeter, the writ of Rangoon did not apply.

=====

"That was the easy part," Flynn announced.

We were resting in banana-frond shade by a cool Shan stream, gulping water from canteens and devouring wheat crackers slathered with peanut butter. The mule skinners had declined our strange farang luncheon and our bottled water, preferring to smoke Marlboros and drink from the creek. They kept a wary distance; my microcassette recorder had already stolen their laughter.

In these borderlands, travel came in just two categories: under fire or undercover. We had lucked into the latter, although we still had more than halfway to go—and all of it seemed vertical. The guides had turned the mules loose to climb the mountain; we followed on foot, laboring for the next half-hour up an overgrown path that clung for life to the forty-five-degree slopes.

We finally caught up with our Shan State Land Rovers, bored and nibbling bamboo shoots in a saddleback along the ridgeline. Remounting, we continued the arduous ascent into the Doi Larng Range. To the east, about fifty yards off the trail, I spotted wooden slats running up the trunk of a teak tree toward the crow's nest of an MTA lookout. These hills had Khun Sa's eyes. The trail, a series of hundreds of switchbacks to conquer the devious cant, was sutured into the spine of the mountain. The mules stepped in bucket-sized holes worn between the rocks by countless caravans. A half-dozen steps, a steep, acute turn, then a half-dozen more steps, then another sharp about-face. A mountain, said a Burmese proverb, was climbed by degrees. I gripped my saddlehorn, heels light in the stirrups, fighting vertigo, prepared to jump. My struggling mule snorted, his flared nostrils nearly buried in the haunches of Sullivan's mount. For the first time in my life, I was literally up someone else's ass.

At more than three thousand feet in the equatorial highlands of Southeast Asia, the mixed deciduous forest of teak and bamboo soon gave way to temperate evergreen flora: Burmese pine, oak, chestnut, and cycads. Python-thick lianas choked tall, elegant *mai-song* trees, squeezing the fragrance from their white, camellia-like flowers. Other trees were drenched with a profuse, crowning climber the Shan called *Hko-mak-nim*. Bracken fern, Chinese rhododendron, impatiens, and *milla*, a medium-sized shrub with violet flowers and aromatic leaves, blanketed the mountainside. The steep grade grew more rational, and occasionally the track even dipped briefly, but we were steadily gaining altitude.

"Just when you think you've reached the top, you start climbing again," said Flynn. "I've ridden through here some mornings when you're above the clouds. You look out and all you see are the tops of mountains."

The great range poured southward, its sharpened ridges as impregnable as the skeletal armor of some primordial, Lost World creature. A century earlier, while surveying the countryside for a possible rail route linking coastal Burma with southern China, Hallett had concluded that the Shan mountains were so imposing "it is in the uttermost degree unlikely it will ever be traversed from west to east by a railway." Nothing had since happened to alter that opinion. Cloaked in virgin forest, the hills sheltered wildlife—Asian elephant, Malayan bear, Bengal tiger, ethnic rebels—eradicated from much of the remaining subcontinent.

Somewhere over the jungled ramparts of the western horizon, the Salween River tumbled toward the sea. The mightiest rivers of Asia—the Mekong, Yangtze, Yellow, Irrawaddy, Brahmaputra, and Salween—all formed in the Central Asian plateau of western China, stormed out of the mountains through narrow gorges, then spread paper-fan deltas from the Bay of Bengal to the Yellow Sea—all except the Salween, which retained its original, untamed character nearly to the Andaman Sea, more than seventeen hundred miles from its headwaters. The daunting succession of steep mountains and deep defiles, the unhealthy jungle, and the raging Salween had been emphatic enforcers of isolation, dictating pockets of habitation, speech, religion, and politics. The very terrain of Shan State bred suspicion, conspired against peace.

The ridgeline mercifully leveled after a two-hour climb that brought us nearly seven thousand feet above sea level. The highland pine forest segued into a second-growth savannah of sharp, head-high elephant grass, the useless, untillable aftermath of swidden agriculture. A faint path branched off to the right, then was swallowed by the swaying field. Ahead, and hundreds of feet above us, a Mong Tai Army redoubt crowned the mountain, complete with earthworks, huts, and bunkers. There was only the sound of wind in the grass. The sentries had gotten word of our passage, Flynn explained, or we would have been under mortar and machine-gun fire.

Our trail broke to the west, then began a steep plunge along the slope. What went so painfully up necessarily came uncomfortably down. For the next two hours I clamped the saddlehorn in my left hand while I leaned back at a forty-five-degree angle and clutched the cantle in a death grip with my right hand. Accosted by branches and slapped by sedge, I could do nothing but endure the ride. Knapsack straps gouged into my shoulders. My buttocks grew numb. My thighs ached and chafed against the steady pounding. The muleteers smiled, lit fresh Marlboros, and, just to twist the knife good-naturedly, began singing. Tough? This wasn't tough. Farang, this was a walk in the sun.

The vegetation gradually grew denser, more verdant; the mule-trail footholds became shallow and slippery. The path, barely a ledge amid a sheer wall of humid, emerald jungle, wound along the mountain's serpentine contour. Far below and across the valley, the road to Ho Mong appeared briefly through the canopy. How I wished my editor, Andy Costello, had sprung for enough money to cover a bribe that would have put me in a truck on that road. Malkoha birds, green-feathered rumors, rustled in the thickets. We forded a spring where tigers came to drink; the mud, thankfully, held no pawprints. In the midst of these wild woods the MTA had posted a sign. In blood-red paint, the Thai, Tai Yai, and English letters carried the same simple announcement: BORDER. I looked to Flynn.

"Believe it or not, we've been walking through Thailand for the last couple of miles," he said.

Another ten minutes along the trail, another sign, a more ominous message. A red skull and crossbones and, in English, the warning: DANGER AREA. A bit redundant, given the political climate in these hills. Noise in the undergrowth, and then a young Shan man stepped ahead of us onto the trail. The militancy of his olive-drab uniform was undercut by his Kawasaki baseball cap and his ancient, flintlock rifle. An off-duty MTA soldier out hunting for small game, he was the first human we had encountered since the road workers near Ban Mae Suya. Dumbstruck by the sight of three *na poek*, or "pale faces," on a jungle trail in remotest Burma, he stood aside and allowed us to file past. We rode another half mile, passing several stilted, birdhouse–sized shelters constructed as resting and feeding places for the *nat* spirits of the forest. The guides then motioned us to dismount.

"For safety," Flynn said. "Punji sticks. Stay on the trail."

We carefully followed the mules through scrub forest, then a tangle of thorns surrounding an empty MTA blockhouse built of timber and earth. All vegetation then ceased. We stumbled down a hellish, clear–cut valley of thick stumps and gray, barren earth to a whitewashed wooden gateway flanked by empty guard shacks. We had endured a twenty–mile death march through triple–canopy jungle and over saw–toothed mountains because we could not drive through this border gate without handing out enormous bribes.

1:30 p.m. Welcome to Shan State, Burma. Despite my doubts, Flynn had delivered.

"If the Boston Marathon is a ten, that trail was about an eight," reckoned Sullivan as he mopped his brow.

"On foot, that trail would have been an eleven," I countered. "Heartbreak Hill had nothing on that mountain."

A graded dirt road led to Ban Nam Ong, a lowland Shan hamlet flanked by fallow rice fields and trafficked by wandering buffalo. The sun glowered in a cloudless dry–season sky. The landscape felt alien but vaguely familiar, like the backdrop of California canyons in a "Star Trek" episode. Ban Nam Ong appeared abandoned. The villagers were either working in distant fields or sleeping late in observance of Peasants' Day, the March 2 holiday.

"We've just entered the outskirts of Never Never Land," Sullivan said.

The Shan rebels had their own bureaucracy, so we had to seek out the border commander. We found him in a small, roadside shelter, lounging out of the midday heat and waving away the dust kicked up by a Ho Mong–bound Thai truck loaded with rice sacks and caged pigs. Flynn flourished Somwang's letter of passage. The officer, a thorough man with an industrious wife who earned pin money selling drinking water, soda, and beer from a stand inside the open-air building, considered our permit carefully. I bought two bottles of warm water, cutting the rebel red tape immeasurably.

Through pantomime and pidgin Thai, Flynn deduced that there were no more vehicles headed for Ho Mong. We could take an additional twelve-mile walk or. . . . We chose "or." We would wait in the commander's home while he radioed headquarters for a truck. His house was a simple, one-room affair brightened by an incongruous poster for McEwan's Scotch Ale. For the next two hours we lay on his cool, earthen floor, sipping weak, tepid Shan tea.

It wasn't until after four o'clock that a blue Toyota pickup finally roared up to the house. We paid our patient trail guides one hundred baht each—the best four-dollar value in Southeast Asia—added a big-spender tip of one hundred baht and a fresh box of Marlboros apiece, and the five-hundred-baht per mule rental fee. No drop-off penalty. The indefatigable mule skinners smiled, grabbed bamboo switches, and began trotting toward Thailand.

We weren't quite through doling out baht. Rule number one: Nothing was free. The two Shan men with the truck had sized up the three fatigued farang and the pile of baggage. They wanted six hundred baht, about $24, for the ride to camp.

"Five hundred baht," I countered.

"No, six hundred baht."

"Five-fifty," I offered.

"For you, six hundred baht." The driver smiled. We had no leverage. We had requested the truck and would pay whatever price he set. The alternatives—walk or wait to hire another vehicle, perhaps not until tomorrow—would be huge insults.

"Deal," I said wearily. "For me, six hundred baht."

"Yessssss."

I pulled another Purple King and some smaller notes from my thinning wallet, and we crammed into the jump seats in the rear of the cab. For the next hour, we shook, rattled, and barely rolled along the thin lifeline of Khun Sa's revolution, kicking up rooster tails of fine, powdery dirt, scattering jungle birds with house music that throbbed from the truck's tape deck at distortion level. The MTA guards manning checkpoints along the road waved us through without a second glance. Before noon, I had astounded two Shan muleteers by the simple act of recording their speech and laughter with my microcassette recorder. Now, other, more worldly Shan used the same technology to fill my life with headaches.

The forest surrendered to hills that had been put to the torch in preparation for the planting season. The seared fields soon gave way to dilapidated peasant huts, which fell to orderly, numbered homes, complete with garden plots, belonging to MTA officers. We had reached Ho Mong, the thriving heart of the global heroin trade. The town rippled across the long, thin mountain valley, laid out with a military precision anomalous in rural Asian villages: parade grounds, orderly barracks, a grid system of residential streets. The gated entrance held a sign written in earnest, albeit fractured, English: WARMLY WELCOME. The General did not miss a public-relations trick. At our destination, the External Affairs Department, a complex on the eastern slope of the valley, the walls were decorated with framed deep-thought slogans written in English and Tai Yai: "Be nice to the little people. You're still one of them."

Khernsai met us in the office's sala pavilion, offering

unctuous greetings. Flynn could barely hide his contempt. I said diplomatic things to Khernsai about Somwang, the trail boys, the drivers from Ban Nam Ong, but I politely declined the drab rooms he had planned for our stay. They seemed far removed from whatever hubbub and tumult Ho Mong had to offer.

Flynn directed us to town center, as far from Khernsai and as close to the limited nightlife as possible. We landed at a no-star guest house. The new building already possessed the faded, desperate look of shoddy construction and unrealistic schemes, but it did have a cement foundation and a location near the morning bazaar. Our spartan room contained unpadded, wine-colored carpeting, one small window, a queen-size mattress, a flimsy table, an even flimsier rack for hanging clothes. An uncovered electrical outlet dangled from the wall; we were promised generator power from six to ten o'clock in the evening. The lavatory teetered behind the building, a wooden shed with a "Shan shower"—a plastic bowl and a fifty-five-gallon oil drum brimming with cold mountain water—and an American Standard squat toilet, a porcelain fixture set into the cement floor that demanded a defecation position that was any-thing but standard in America. A bowel movement in rural Asia, unless one had experience as a baseball catcher, was an equilibrium-defying adventure.

No concierge, no continental breakfast. No room service, no wake-up calls. Boiled water in the morning, bed lice all day long. Cash only, U.S. dollars preferred. Had I seen this guest house in Mae Hong Son, I would have immediately turned my back. In my mule-muddled state, however, the place seemed nearly as welcoming as the Hyatt Hotel's Regency Club. And the prospect of nocturnal shitting in a land with the world's highest snakebite mortality rate presented an irre-sistible challenge.

"Deal," I sighed. "Two hundred baht. For everyone."

Our innkeeper shook her head, held up two fingers. Two hundred baht for me. Held up four more fingers. Two hundred baht for Mister Jay. Two hundred baht for Mister Barry.

"Okay. For me, six hundred baht."

"Ooookaaay."

More Purple Kings fluttered from my fingers. Having jump-started the local Shan economy, I went to my room and promptly collapsed on the thin, louse-infested mattress. I had paid for location, not atmosphere. Through the window's dust-caked glass louvers, the sun spread golden fingers across shards of fading, pastel-blue sky. I felt filthy, exhausted, famished. I had made it to Burma, to Shan State, to the edge of the earth. No anxiety tonight, no Xanax. No need for dreams, only sleep. And Immodium.

II

Hidden Fortress

In the morning I reset my watch. Although Shan State was in revolt against Rangoon, the region still observed official Burmese time that, due to some unfathomable quirk, was one-half hour earlier than Thai time. But I could have spun my watch's hands counterclockwise nearly forever; Ho Mong appeared out of a world several centuries earlier than Bangkok. We had awakened to a Dalí dreamscape, a feudal city-state nonetheless equipped with Toyota trucks and automatic weapons. Pickups droned by carrying armed, uniformed Mong Tai Army soldiers. In their dusty wake, Lisu hilltribe women walked toward the market bearing stacks of broad, ovate *thanat* leaves and bouquets of maroon-tinged eugenia gathered in the jungle and sold as cheroot wrappers and temple offerings. Shan girls strolled along in ruby-red sarongs, hummingbird-blue jackets, and indigo turbans, swinging tassled shoulder bags in which to carry the day's shopping. We followed, our trail-sore muscles gradually loosening during the early morning walk. On our first full day in Burma, we would get a thorough tour of

Ho Mong from Flynn and one of his closest Shan friends, Sengjoe.

Sengjoe's dirt-floored house stood on the south side of the market, a profitable location for the noodle restaurant and small dry-goods store his wife ran out of the large, open front room. Still sleepy, presumably from carousing the previous night away with Flynn, Sengjoe extended a long, tattooed arm to shake hands, then bade us to sit. His wife brought clouded drinking glasses and a Chinese thermos brimming with weak, scalding-hot Shan tea to our table.

"How was your sleep, gentlemen?" he asked. His English was courtly and British accented, the product of a childhood spent in a Keng Tung missionary school run by Italian priests.

"Never better," I replied. The jet lag, the pent-up anxiety, and the mule ride had knocked me into flat-line sleep for ten hours.

"It is the Shan mountain air."

Sengjoe popped a fifth-generation bootleg cassette by country singer George Strait into a tape deck powered by dying batteries. The sound was pure Nashville on Quaaludes. Fifty years old, his India-ink hair combed straight back, and standing a rangy six feet tall, Sengjoe carried himself with a patrician grace and a wistful touch of the poet. He settled onto a bench and fumbled absently with a pack of Krong Thips. I made his morning with a fresh box of Marlboros.

"Some breakfast, sirs," he said, lighting the first of what would be many cigarettes that day. "Then we begin."

While his wife fed us sticky rice, Sengjoe regaled us with tales of his CIA mercenary past. As a young man he had enlisted as a rifleman in the force of Khun Myint, a rebel commander with the Keng Tung–based Shan National Army. To get arms and ammunition, he explained, Khun Myint contracted the company to a CIA subsidiary. His mission: fight Communist-backed guerrillas in northwestern Laos.

"We were hired as machineries," he recalled, although he meant "mercenaries."

"We fought on behalf of the CIA. The company was called Scope. The pay was very poor but we have a lot of things. Air drops full of ice cream, full of meat canned. We have lot of arms and ammunition from the Scope people."

Deployed to Muang Meung, a Laotian town near an ancient caravan crossing of the Mekong River, Sengjoe's unit had engaged in a classic bout of Asian shadowboxing. Again, rule number two: Nothing was what it seemed.

"We rarely fought each other," Sengjoe confessed. "Actually, the Pathet Lao and our corps had a mutual understanding. In the night we'd both do shelling to get more ammunition for ourselves. The Pathet Lao, knowing we were not a Laotian force, did not attack. It was like a cheating game."

"We were hired guns," he added. "We didn't get killed. Most of the soldiers suffered from syphilis. There were a lot of tribal girls, Lahu girls, all around." He smiled at the memory. "We should say we were lucky."

Despite the nocturnal artillery "duels," Sengjoe continued, the Scope advisers had an inkling their Shan hirelings were not fighting and had a gentlemen's agreement with the Pathet Lao. If there was heavy fighting, why weren't there any body counts?

"They tried to detect this with a lie-detector machine," he said. "But our officers were very smart. Whenever they were summoned, they took some balls of opium. The machine didn't have any effect on them. They just passed the examination smoothly. There was no trace. No fluctuation in blood pressure, no sweating."

He sucked in a lungful of Virginia tobacco, then exhaled fit-fully. Hilltribe women stood near the talaat, gaping at us.

"The Scope contract was a year, but after eight months we had enough. We returned to Shan State, full of arms."

His dislike for the Burmese became stone-cold hatred in the late 1970s, he said, when his wife and a daughter were killed in an air raid in eastern Shan State. The loss still cut through his military reserve. Now remarried with two young children—a handsome boy hobbled by a minor brain injury and a cute daughter with a thanaka-streaked face—he worked as a transla-tor for Khun Sa and served as the mayor of Ho Mong.

"I want to retire," he said with a sigh. "It's a bloody hot job." Five hundred baht a month couldn't lessen the headache of arbitrating constituent complaints about garbage, noise, and wandering buffalo. Sengjoe stubbed his cigarette butt, adjusted his Australian bush hat to a rakish angle, then set out to show us the armed town that Khun Sa had carved out of the deep forest.

＝＝＝

To arrive in this distant corner of Burma, Khun Sa had charted a life course resembling a harsh Akira Kurosawa epic. He was born Chang Chi-fu on February 17, 1934, the son of Khun Ai, an ethnic Chinese living in Hpa-perng, a village under the dominion of the saopha of Mong Yai in northern Shan State. After Chang's father died in 1937, his Shan mother, Nang Saeng Zoom, remarried the hereditary chief, or *myosa* (a Bur-mese term literally meaning "town eater"), of nearby Mong Tawm. Young Chang was soon entrusted to the care of his paternal Chinese grandfather, who tutored him in tea cultiva-tion and horse breeding. It was a lonely childhood.

Although he received little formal education beyond the instruction at a temple required of every Buddhist boy, Chang possessed a flair for leadership, a talent for reading the political winds, and enormous business acumen. By his mid twenties, he was authorized to form his own local, government-sanctioned militia, or Ka Kwe Ye (KKY) unit. Overwhelmed by a host of ethnic insurgents, KMT troops, and Burmese Communist Party rebels in Shan State, the Burmese military concocted a plan that allowed almost any armed group that pledged fealty to Rangoon to become a KKY outfit. Without funds to pay, clothe, or supply these soldiers, the government permitted KKY commanders a powerful perquisite: use of government-controlled towns and roads to transport contraband, including opium.

Chang set himself up in north-central Shan State, a major locus for poppy cultivation, and soon built his KKY unit into a heavily armed force of eight hundred men. Chang also adopted a new name: Khun Sa, The Prince of Prosperity. By 1964, the ambitious young Sino-Shan commander cut his ties with Rangoon and relocated to Vingngun in the far eastern reaches of Wa territory, just a few miles from Yunnan Province, to establish his own poppy-growing fiefdom. Within a few years, his force had grown to two thousand soldiers. The KMT generals settled along the Thai borderlands north of Chiang Mai, who then controlled 90 percent of the opium trade, began to take notice of the young Turk in the distant hills.

The inevitable showdown occurred in 1967. During the February opium harvest, Khun Sa issued a brash ultimatum: KMT caravans passing through the Wa states would have to pay the same tax that he had to pay whenever his mules transited KMT territory on their way to Thailand and Laos. The following June, Khun Sa's opium convoy headed south from Vingngun for Ban Khwan, a Laotian village in the Golden Triangle where the buyer, General Ouane Rattikone of the Royal Lao Army, operated a heroin refinery. In the trackless mountains east of the Salween River, the armed column linked up with a secondary shipment from central Shan State to create an enormous opium caravan of three hundred mules that stretched single-file for more than a mile. For the KMT, the implications of this sixteen-ton drug shipment were enormous. If the opium got through, Khun Sa would have the revenue to place another one thousand men under arms. That would put his private force almost on equal footing with the KMT and threaten its stranglehold on the caravan routes. An expedition of one thousand KMT troops was assembled quickly and ordered into Shan State to intercept the pack-mule train.

In mid July, the KMT sprang an ineffective ambush south of Keng Tung, then pursued the opium caravan to Ban Khwan. As a showdown loomed, General Ouane ordered both parties out of Laos. Neither side budged. The KMT attacked the entrenched Shan on July 29 and an intense firefight raged into the next day before General Ouane, in full face-saving fettle, called in his air force for two days of bombing and strafing runs. The Shan retreated by boat across the Mekong to Burma; the KMT fled north and were soon captured by Lao soldiers. The wily General Ouane retained his honor and the spoils of war: sixteen tons of unpaid-for opium, courtesy of Khun Sa, and a seventy-five hundred–dollar repatriation fee for his KMT prisoners.

While a humiliating episode for the KMT, the 1967 Opium War was an even heavier blow to Khun Sa. He had lost dozens of men, weapons, and mules, and half a million dollars' worth of opium. Troops began to drift away from his command. To recoup power and prestige, he met secretly in September 1969 with Shan rebels to discuss the formation of an anti-Communist resistance. Tipped off by the KMT, the Burmese Military Intelligence Service arrested Khun Sa the following month and imprisoned him for high treason.

As Khun Sa languished inside Mandalay Palace, a moated, century-old fort on the broiling Irrawaddy riverplain, the power vacuum in northern Shan State created by his incarceration was filled by Lo Hsing-han, another KKY commander who had used his government-approved smuggler status to swell his fortune and his firepower. By 1972, American narcotics officials labeled Lo the "kingpin of the heroin traffic in Southeast Asia." But it all fell apart for the Lashio-based druglord the following year. In the face of international outrage over the heroin boom in Burma, Rangoon abolished the disreputable KKY program. Lo then defected to the Shan rebels and was arrested in Mae Hong Son Province.

As Lo's luck ran out, Khun Sa's fortune improved. In April 1973, his loyalists entered Taunggyi, kidnapped two Russian doctors who had come to the Shan capital to inspect a Soviet-built hospital, and then demanded Khun Sa's freedom. After an unlikely go-between, Thai General Kriangsak Chomanan, negotiated the release of the Russians, Khun Sa was discharged from prison. In short order, he resurfaced in northern Thailand in command of a new force, the Shan United Army. His headquarters in the village of Ban Hin Taek was just a short stroll away from a Thai Border Patrol Police camp, but his close relationship to General Kriangsak, who became prime minister in 1977 following a military coup, allowed him to operate undisturbed.

Khun Sa's five-year incarceration in Mandalay had provided him time for reflection and strategic planning. Laying claim to his maternal lineage, he began positioning himself in the media as a Shan nationalist, a leader who reluctantly trafficked in opium to earn his people's freedom. In a savvy move to garner credibility, he convinced a prominent Shan poet and intellectual, Long Khun Maha, to relocate to Ban Hin Taek, going so far as to buy him a printing press. The self-styled "King of the

Golden Triangle," began floating a bold drug-eradication plan in return for international help in negotiating Shan State's independence from Burma. All the while his army consolidated control of the Golden Triangle and its illicit riches.

Khun Sa's illegal operations and indiscreet pronouncements so infuriated Kriangsak's straight-arrow successor, Prem Tinsulanan, that the prime minister ordered an assault on his headquarters by Thai Rangers in January 1982. After a furious battle, Khun Sa relocated several hundred miles to the west, to the mountainous Shan forests just north of Mae Hong Son Province. He displaced a rival rebel force, the Shan State Army, from the old caravansary and tax station of Mong Mai and began rebuilding his opium empire in the nearby hamlet of Ho Mong. The upland-valley settlement was an ideal site for an insurgent's citadel. Its strategic border location allowed Khun Sa to control the major Shan caravan routes to northwestern Thailand. The Salween River, just twelve miles away, formed a daunting natural barrier to any attacks on his northern and western flanks. To the east, the jagged, rebel-infested Doi Larng Range posed a similar physical obstacle. And a web of jungle trails led south to Thailand, his major trading partner and, if things got too dicey in Ho Mong, his rear supply base in the Shan village of Ban Mae Suya.

To hasten his comeback, Khun Sa may even have cut a pragmatic deal with the Burmese military, with whom he had maintained a relationship—somewhat strained by his five-year prison term—since his KKY days. Several sources indicate that in March 1984 the Tatmadaw offered Khun Sa and his Shan United Army free rein in the opium trade in return for attacking other narco-insurgents and ethnic rebels. Shortly after the alleged accord, a SUA truck bomb blew up the Chiang Mai mansion of a KMT general. The power play continued. The headquarters of several other factions were overrun by SUA troops. Other rival leaders died violently. Khun Sa also pursued a longstanding vendetta. In March 1985, he allied with Khorn Jern, leader of the Shan United Revolutionary Army and a staunch nationalist, opium trafficker, and former KMT ally. To emphasize its ethnic connection with neighboring Thailand, the new Shan force was renamed the Tai-land Revolutionary Army. Following rebel custom, the name was short-lived and soon changed to the Mong Tai—or Shan State—Army. Khun Sa had severed the KMT's opium and jade routes, had appropriated its proxy army in Burma, and had finally exacted his revenge for the 1967 Opium War. Just three short years after being chased from Thailand, the King of the Golden Triangle had returned, stronger than ever.

=====

Ho Mong, the General's redoubt, had a population of more than ten thousand people, according to Sengjoe, made up of nearly six thousand civilians and almost five thousand MTA recruits training at two camps. Despite its size and its amenities, which dwarfed those of nearly every town in southern Shan State, Ho Mong did not appear on any national maps of Burma. The outlaw city-state we cruised through in a rented Toyota pickup did not officially exist.

Sengjoe directed our Shan driver toward the northwestern base of the valley. About one mile from the talaat, we stopped at a complex of cinderblock buildings. This was Ho Mong Hospital, complete with operating rooms and wards. The General had built the facility to treat MTA casualties who could not be evacuated to hospitals in northern Thailand and to minister to the local civilian population, who received free medical care. New wards were being erected, boosting capacity from ninety to two hundred fifty beds. It looked like the

General was bracing for either an epidemic of disease or a major military engagement.

Inside the main hospital building, a young MTA soldier lay on a canvas stretcher on the floor. His delirious moans echoed off the cool gray walls. Flynn gave him wide berth.

"Has he been shot?" I asked.

"Blackwater fever," said Flynn. "Don't let him spit on you."

"Ho Mong is a place highly infested with malaria," said Sengjoe. "And in the past eight months we have a lot of trouble with dysentery. Eighteen people died. It comes from the black-water fever. In this season we have more influenza and cholera and dysentery, because the water system is contaminated. We have to educate our people to boil water before drinking. It helps, but still we have a lot of disease around."

I had been warned about the biological environment I would face. Somehow, mountains always seemed salubrious. H. N. C. Stevenson, a colonial-era administrator of Shan State, had tried to disabuse lowland farang of the same notion in his 1944 pamphlet, *The Hill Peoples of Burma*:

> It was fashionable for people living in the hot plains of Burma to describe the hills as a healthy paradise in which diseases of the plains had no place. The great evacuation of 1942 has changed all that and the hill areas are known for what they really are—the home of malarial mosquitoes more deadly than most, the haunt of leeches so fantastically innumerable as to have become legend, the stamping ground of typhus ticks and the place of sneaking winds which strike down the unwary with pneumonia.

I hoped I didn't end up face down on the floor of this jungle clinic, pissing blood, heaving bile, and wondering, should I survive, how Blue Cross would handle my claim. To guard against malaria, I was taking daily Doxycycline pills, and, on Flynn's advice, Fansidar. In the morning, I had doused myself with FlyPel; the previous night I had fumigated the room with noxious mosquito coils. And all day long, I intended to pray.

The hospital had seven surgical wards, two operating theaters, and a pair of X-ray machines, although one was broken. In the jungle, said Sengjoe, it was hard to get parts and medicine. There were five doctors on staff: two Shan and three Chinese.

"One of the Chinese doctors is wanted in Hong Kong on charges," Flynn related. "He didn't tell me the charges, but they must be serious. He told me, 'Best I stay here for a long time.' "

We pushed through swinging doors and walked down a hallway lined with glass windows looking onto the operating theaters. A medical team prepared for major surgery in one of the rooms.

"One of the Shan doctors comes from the front lines last year," said Sengjoe. "We have a lot of patients, a lot of casualties from Doi Larng, when we have a pitched battle with the Wa. We save a lot of money treating patients here. Usually it costs between fifty to one hundred thousand baht for each patient being treated in Thailand. We prefer to do our own operations. It saves a lot of lives."

An electric fan blew dusty air through the surgical theater. The frosted-glass louvers were open to admit light; no screens covered the windows. A young boy lay face down, ether-oblivious, on the operating table. Two nurses struggled to place a soiled cotton sheet beneath his unconscious frame. The boy's diagnosis: a meningococcal infection. My prognosis: not good, in an unsterile environment with few antibiotic medications, no matter how skilled the physicians.

Just north of the hospital stood Pang Seua—Tiger Camp—Khun Sa's original Ho Mong headquarters. Here the General trained and educated the Noom Suk Harn, the Young Brave Warriors. The name was a clever choice: the Shan resistance movement formally began in 1958 when a group of university students founded an identically named cadre. Hundreds of boys, some as young as eight, most not yet in their teens, had come from all corners of Shan State to Tiger Camp. When they reached sixteen, they became combat soldiers. Inculcated from an early age with MTA dogma, they were the true believers in the cause, and in Khun Sa. It was from the Noom Suk Harn that the warlord plucked his retinue of loyal bodyguards.

During their years at Pang Seua, the Noom Suk Harn lived, fifty to a dormitory, in one dozen long, low barracks of split, woven bamboo arranged around a large, dirt parade ground. Inside each dormitory, a raised wooden platform kept the boys' thin reed mats and rough woolen blankets off the ground; a single wooden shelf held their meager personal belongings. It was a hard life, but a peasant's life had always been spartan in Shan State. The recruits ate rice and vegetables, studied mathematics, English, and Shan history, and dreamed of the moment they would be issued a rifle. It was a momentous rite of passage for any boy of the hills, the day of the gun.

Twenty percent of the boys had been sent by parents too poor to feed them, said Sengjoe, while an equal number had been "recruited" by the MTA. "If you have three children in a family," he explained, "we take one and leave the two." However, Sengjoe added, the majority of the child soldiers were orphans whose parents had been killed by the Burmese Army, which had achieved international condemnation for its brutal treatment of ethnic civilians.

"Their parents are used to serve as porters, used to serve as minesweepers," said Sengjoe. "They are made to walk into the minefields. They are just killed at random. They are not given adequate rations like the Burmese people. At times, even ladies are being recruited as porters. In the day they have a big burden, they have to carry a lot of weight. At night, they suffer mass raping. After that they are just killed. Many have died in the process."

Behind the barracks complex, the hillside was dotted with what appeared, but for the timbered lintels, to be the mouths of dozens of small caves. Air-raid shelters, Sengjoe explained. He pointed to the top of the ridgeline, several hundred feet above the valley floor, where an antiaircraft battery equipped with .50-caliber machine guns guarded the western flank of Tiger Camp. Similar posts occupied high ground around the valley of Ho Mong and provided the withering, interlocking firepower that dissuaded Burmese air attacks. Sullivan eyed the shelters with the same disdainful look he gave to cheap vodka.

"I'm hoping we won't have a chance to experience this."

Rows of open-air classrooms were situated east of the barracks. Inside, the Noom Suk Harn sat ramrod straight upon wooden benches at long, rough tables, their arms crossed and their eyes fixed on the blackboard and the day's English lesson:

He is jumping. She is clapping. Is she opening the window? Is he closing the door?

The students used Burmese textbooks for their English classes, although I doubted the language credits from Tiger Camp would ever transfer to a Burmese school system. I surveyed the room. Two dozen boys, ten to thirteen years of age, some with hair shaved to prevent lice, all carrying the hard, untrusting stares of childhoods stolen by war. It was difficult to imagine these future soldiers ever having occasion to say, in English, "She is clapping."

Sai Ching was a typical Tiger Camp student. He was thirteen and had not been home to his village in Loi Kaw township, a five-day walk to the west, since his parents sent him to Khun Sa more than two years ago.

"I came here to fight the Burmese," he said. Sai Ching spoke Tai Yai and Sengjoe translated; the boy's fierce ambition could not be articulated from the English-language phrases of his Burmese textbooks.

"They came to my village," said Sai Ching. "They beat the villagers and looted the chickens and pigs. I want to become an MTA officer." The Shan conflict with the Burmese had endured for decades. Sai Ching, I felt, would probably get his wish.

The contradictions surrounding Khun Sa were seeping to the surface. A global pariah, the warlord lived a high-profile life by the standards of international fugitives. Narcotics were the lifeblood of the MTA, yet Khun Sa had tendered a plan to abandon the heroin business in return for Shan independence. Cast in the Western press as a cruel, petty tyrant, he provided free medical care, however primitive, and free education, albeit with a rebel bent. He controlled the lion's share of the world opium market and yet drug use was forbidden among members of his organization.

Doubling back toward the center of town, we paused to view the special-forces parade ground. The camp was under the command of Khun Sa's eldest son, Cham Herng, whom everyone called "Number One" or "The Principal." According to Flynn and Mook, Number One had received military training in Taiwan and, under an assumed name, had also attended Arizona State University. Now the son had been brought into the family firm and groomed for a leadership position. Number One lived adjacent to the parade ground in his father's old house, a tidy red-brick bungalow set behind a picket fence bordered with a low, clipped hedge, a trellised gateway, and grounds planted with banana trees, aloe, and bougainvillea.

Number One oversaw a training regimen that lasted one full year. Officers and soldiers received leadership training, studied infantry and guerrilla tactics, and learned to handle the General's entire arsenal, from M-16 and AK-47 rifles to M-79 and RPG-7 grenade launchers. Several company-sized groupings of uniformed soldiers stood at attention on the sun-burned field as a bullhorn-wielding officer addressed them from a reviewing stand. The Tiger Camp flag—a blue banner emblazoned with a red M-16 rifle, a fountain pen, and an open book—flapped weakly in the slight breeze.

"The flag means that wisdom and the pen are sharper than the sword," Sengjoe said.

"No," corrected Flynn. "It means read, write, and shoot."

There would be soldiers, many more soldiers, to see. We left the special-forces troops and rode north for a mile, beyond the outskirts of Ho Mong, and turned onto a secondary road blocked by a turnpike topped with a red stop sign. Sengjoe spoke with the armed guard at the checkpoint, the pole was raised, and we drove through the gate of the limited-access Shan State Drug Rehabilitation Center.

"This was created by the General himself three years ago," Sengjoe said. "A lot of people get cured in this encampment. We try to get rid of the opium addicts. Most of the guys under treatment are opium addicts. They cannot afford money to buy heroin. Heroin is so costly. But it's easy to get addicted to opium. At first, they want to take about three balls. But soon, if they want the same feeling, they have to multiply the balls. They have to smoke six, ten balls. In a day you can take about fifty to sixty balls. Then you are really in the groove of addiction."

Thirty men, soldiers as well as civilians, were currently being treated. The center could accommodate one hundred patients.

"Some are volunteers for treatment," Sengjoe said. "Some

have been caught by the authorities. The village headmen have to send all the addicts to the center to be treated. Also the commanders in the front lines have to send the soldiers here. Most of the military people in the front line have no medicines. They smoke opium for relaxation or for illness. At first, it's a miracle cure. But then they repeat very often and they get hooked. So many of the officers and soldiers from the front lines come here for treatment."

Elderly addicts, however, were exempted from the drug-treatment program.

"People over sixty are allowed to have the addiction," Sengjoe said. "As long as he doesn't extend his opium pipe to the youngsters, it's all right. He can keep. He's happy. If you cut off the old man, it's like killing him."

We parked at the foot of a small knoll. A young man, his head shaved clean, greeted Flynn. He was an errand boy at the Shan State Restoration Council's office in Mae Hong Son. But for more than a month, he had been confined to rehab, locked in the throes of opium withdrawal.

"He's a good boy," Flynn said quietly. "I didn't know he had a problem."

We climbed to the hillock's summit, which was ringed with trenches. On the southern slope, just below a small MTA garrison guarding the inmates, stood four simple lean-tos. Beneath their sheet-metal roofs, wooden crosshatches lay inexplicably on the ground. Sengjoe walked to the nearest shelter, stooped, then lifted the heavy, hinged hatch. Beneath the lid was the dark, gaping maw of an oubliette, the centerpiece of the General's simple, brutally efficient detoxification program.

"It's about sixteen feet deep," Sengjoe said. "Underneath the gate it's like a ball. The mouth is small, but inside it's a big space. It's a black pit. The opium addicts are put in the pit for treatment. We leave them there for seven days and nights. We give them only water and rice. These poor guys wriggle, they shit a lot, they sweat a lot, they cough a lot. When they are hauled from the mouth of the pit, really, it's a gruesome sight. They have a bath and after that, they have to stay in a cell for a month."

He pointed downhill to a cluster of windowless wooden buildings. Nearby, a half-dozen men, with heads shaved like monk novitiates, struggled to drag away a giant log.

"Then they are allowed to move freely in the compound. They have to work all day to harden their muscles. We encourage them to have a lot of baths every day. Some have to go under treatment for six months to a year. It depends on how long they are addicted to opium."

While at hard labor, patients were permitted weekly visits by relatives. The MTA guards searched all visitors and packages for illicit drug fixes.

"In the past two years we caught some persons trying to smuggle in opium," Sengjoe explained.

"Do they get the pit, too?" I asked.

"They get killed," he replied. "Death penalty. Serious."

The center claimed a success rate of 80 percent. To deter recidivism, the General had enacted a draconian three-strikes policy. For a second offense, patients received fifty lashes, then got the black pit, isolation, and hard labor. For a third transgression, they were put to death. Decapitation, with the stroke of a dah sword.

"The drug treatment works wonders," Flynn chuckled. "We always say, 'Don't lose your head over it.' "

We had been invited to a memorial feast hosted by the field commander of the MTA, Sao Kan Zet, to honor his recently deceased brother, and so we left the involuntary ascetics and drove south, passing the Ho Mong talaat, now quiet in the midday heat. A brown patch of a soccer field spread to the west, alongside a concrete basketball court. Flynn had introduced the game in the late 1980s to Tiger Camp. The General, who was intrigued by Western culture, had wanted recreation for his soldiers. Basketball, which required only rudimentary equipment, seemed a good way to build troop morale.

"There can't be too much dunking," I said. "The only Shan taller than me is Sengjoe."

"Sure, they can dunk," Flynn cracked. "They load the ball in an RPG-7 and shoot from half-court."

Beyond the playing fields lay brown, fallow paddy. The General was thinking of leveling the rice fields, remarked Flynn, building an airstrip, then purchasing a C-130 cargo plane. But he would never consider felling the gargantuan tree that caused the two-lane dirt road we now traveled to split around its thick trunk. Khun Sa might have absolute power over Shan life and limb, but the sacred Bo tree was not within his bailiwick. It was under a *Ficus religiosa* that Prince Siddhartha had renounced all earthly passions and become the Buddha. To fell the Bo was a sacrilegious act that also invited the wrath of the tree's nat spirits, and so we lurched along an undulating detour around the tree.

The memorial banquet was laid out inside a breezy pavilion, just beneath a Buddhist temple at the foot of the valley's eastern slope. The commander had gotten leave from the field to host the event and at least seven hundred people, some from as far away as Chiang Mai and Mae Hong Son, had traveled to Ho Mong out of respect. The career soldier, a short, barrel-chested man with Brezhnev-thick eyebrows, bade us to sit at his table as honored guests.

"We always have a great expectation that the Western world will take a stand and give us some moral support or help," said Sao Kan Zet, as Sengjoe translated. I offered an innocuous, optimistic reply while his aides descended upon the table with brimming porcelain bowls of curried chicken and potatoes, pad thai and pumpkin, bean-curd soup, boiled rice, fried river fish, and two-liter bottles of Sprite. Flynn and Sengjoe helped themselves to the food like starving men; Sullivan and I doled a few spoonfuls of rice and morsels of chicken onto our plates.

"Mister Jay and I do not have jungle stomachs," I explained.

Sao Kan Zet nodded. I hoped we had not committed a grievous offense that would land us in a rat pit or on the front lines. Then Khernsai materialized, hoping our new accommodations were adequate, still apologetic for any past misunderstandings, quickly taking his leave. For the duration of our stay, he was to remain invisible.

Sullivan and I ate farang-style, with spoons. Some banquetgoers ate with chopsticks, in the Yunnanese manner, while most dined in traditional Shan fashion, with their fingers. As the feast concluded, MTA soldiers and civilians formed a human "bucket brigade" nearly one hundred yards long to pass dirty dishes and cutlery back to the kitchen for cleaning. Sengjoe remarked offhandedly that General Khun Sa was just uphill, visiting the monks inside the temple. The dragon had surfaced, surreptitious, unannounced.

We scrambled up the bouganvillea-shaded slope. A matched pair of late-model white Toyota four-wheel-drive trucks were parked outside the temple, outfitted with complete war-wagon packages: tinted windows, knobby tires, fog lamps, and raised chassis. Song thaews with attitude. Dozens of local Shan milled around outside while a trio of armed soldiers stood near a side doorway, smoking Krong Thips, regarding all observers with lidded, shoot-first eyes. The red strips of cloth dangling from their rifle slings like fishing lures identified them as Khun Sa's personal bodyguards.

Through an open temple window I could see a golden Buddha image seated upon a raised altar, the glow of candles, the familiar hue of Purple Kings stuffed in glass offering jars. An MTA soldier armed with a Panasonic videocamera was recording the General's audience with the monks. The sweet, lazy smell of joss sticks drifted from the room.

"Don't make any sudden movements," Flynn whispered. "The guards are very nervous."

A near-electric ripple of anticipation swept the crowd hoping for a glimpse of their leader. MTA soldiers trotted from the temple and swung into the Toyota truck beds. They bristled with hair-trigger firepower: .45-caliber pistols, M-16 rifles, M-79 grenade launchers.

And then General Khun Sa ambled from the temple. The warlord's loose, cream-colored dress shirt nearly hid the slight paunch pushing over his brown slacks. I don't know why, but I thought of Marlon Brando in *The Godfather*, the old Mafia don playing in the garden with his grandchildren. From a distance, Khun Sa seemed benign, nearly bemused by the commotion. Maybe the comfort of ready automatic weapons did that to a man. The General spotted Sullivan videotaping his exit and stopped. That's it, I thought, black-pit time. But the warlord raised his right arm, waved in our direction, and smiled.

"Bye-bye," said the Prince of Death, in English. Then he stepped into the Toyota's cab and was gone.

12

The Kings of the Sunset

We walked downhill, coughing the dust kicked up by Khun Sa's departed convoy.

"The General is a very busy man," Sengjoe explained. "He is preparing to fight with the Burmese. And everyone comes to him with their problems. Tomorrow, we will speak with him."

Twelve thousand miles, I thought, an eighteen-month chase, and a ten-second sighting. And now K.S. had left the building. The time, location, and duration of our upcoming meeting would be revealed in the fullness of time and would be subject, of course, to "border problems" and the superstitions of the Burmese Army, rumored to be massing for an assault on the national holiday of March 27, Tatmadaw Day, which celebrated the army's about-face against their Japanese allies in 1945. We walked through the empty banquet pavilion to a wooden, two-story building that held the Shan Human Rights Center and Museum. Our guide warmly greeted the manager of the three-year-old facility, his younger brother, Sarm Tip, who was also a leader in the House of Representatives formed three months earlier by the Shan resistance.

In the Asian manner, we removed our shoes and followed Sarm Tip into the ground floor of the building occupied by a propaganda print shop. Trays of cold type filled rough-hewn wood tables. Piles of the same English-language biographies of Khun Sa that I had seen for sale in Chiang Mai stood in neat stacks on the floor, alongside booklets of Shan State history and pamphlets charging the Burmese with the aerial spraying of toxic herbicides. The center also produced Chinese-, Burmese-, and Shan-language material, said Sarm Tip, including magazines and a newspaper.

"Good," said Flynn. "I can send my letters complaining about Khernsai to the press."

The entire second floor was devoted to Shan history, especially the prewar Golden Age when the hereditary saopha princes ruled their feudal empires with little interference from the British. Sarm Tip had organized display cases with a priceless collection of silver betel-nut jars, ivory-handled dah swords, and ancient bronze opium weights shaped like lions, birds, and elephants. Black-and-white photographs of the maharajah-like chieftains decorated the walls. The word saopha literally means "prince of the sky" and the finery worn by the ancient sovereigns buttressed their celestial origins: storms of swirling turban; velvet-trimmed costumes drizzling sequins and stitching; bejeweled, Persian slippers with upturned toes cresting into heads of the Garuda, the legendary bird-mount of Vishnu.

It was a proud, ancient heritage, one that SLORC had literally sought to erase. Just last year, Sarm Tip related, the Burmese had razed the grand teak palace of the former saopha of Keng Tung. The stated reason was to erect a hotel catering to travelers who took the dreary, overpriced package tours from Mae Sai whenever rebel activity ceased along Highway 4. The unspoken need was to repress the Shan, who regarded the saophas as potent symbols of nationalism, and to convince foreign visitors that the Shan were bumpkins, nearly an uncivilized hilltribe, whose lot in life had been mightily improved under Burmese leadership.

"These people, they dismantle the Shan palace because it's of historical significance," Sengjoe said, agitated. He had grown up in Keng Tung, had known firsthand the splendor of the saopha residence. "They are scared the Shan have their own administration, their own country. So they try to eliminate everything of cultural and historical significance. They want to eliminate us, assimilate us, have a Burmanization of the whole country. That is their real intention.

"Bad people," he added. "They try to convince the world they are the rightful leaders of all the ethnic groups, but it's not true."

Sengjoe did not stand alone in his enmity toward the Burmese. The Shan and the Burmese are both Buddhist and, to the Western eye, seem physically similar, but they are markedly different people who just happen to live adjacent to one another. Antipathy between the two has existed for centuries. (The Tai-speaking Shan, who are related to the Lao and the Thai—the word *Shan* is a Burmese corruption of *Siam*—even trace different ethnolinguistic roots than do the Burmese.) The feuding began during the twelfth century, when the Shan, who were being pressed from their kingdom of Nanchao by Chinese settlers, began migrating from the Yunnan region southward to an area ruled by Burmese kings of the Pagan dynasty. When Pagan fell in 1287 to Kublai Khan's Mongol hordes, the Shan settled much of the depopulated countryside. East of the Irrawaddy River, they occupied the *myelat*, the plateau-like "middle land" extending to the Salween River; beyond the great river they kept to narrow upland valleys nestled between mountain ridges.

By the early fourteenth century, the Tai-speaking realm

stretched from Assam in northeast India to upper Tonkin in present-day Vietnam, and south as far as the Andaman Sea. Far from being unified, this ethnic empire that dominated the region for nearly three centuries was a patchwork of disjointed petty kingdoms and feudatories. The Tai era ended in the mid-sixteenth century when the Burmese king Bayinnaung conquered much of Southeast Asia. Bayinnaung and his successors treated the Shan as vassals, demanding tribute of ponies, gold, velvet, and silk, but allowing the hill people to retain their language and their saopha princes. Within their fiefdoms, the saophas wielded absolute power over their subjects. They granted land to chieftains, who then paid tribute, and reaped further revenues from bazaar licenses and monopolies on betel leaf and liquor. The money helped to underwrite the *ahmudan*, the palace retinue of umbrella carriers, timekeepers, and betel-box bearers.

The Burmese referred to these Shan rulers as Ne Win Bayin—Sunset Lords—and considered them second-tier royalty to their own Ne Twet Bayin, or Sunrise Lords. The saophas sent their brothers and sons to the Burmese royal capital to be inculcated in the fineries of court life—and to serve as hostages. To further control the Shan princes, the Burmese adopted a divide-and-rule policy, demanding each saopha's obeisance, yet forbidding them from consulting one another. The isolation only furthered suspicion and antagonism between the saophas. The Burmese also encouraged subordinate chieftains to revolt, a practice that quadrupled the ranks of principalities—from nine original city-states to forty-one feudatories—by the 1870s.

There was no unity in the hills, no sense of community with the plains. There was only chronic instability and mounting resentment against the distant Burmese rulers. Relations with the Sunrise Kings reached their nadir during the brief, cruel reign of Thibaw, the last monarch of Burma, who ascended the throne in 1878 and killed seventy of his closest relatives—and potential rivals—in accordance with a disquieting Burmese royal tradition, the Massacre of the Kinsmen. The first Shan princes broke with Mandalay in 1879; by 1882, a majority of the saophas were in open revolt.

The British, who had conquered Lower Burma in 1852 and feared Thibaw was coming under the sway of the French, used a picayune logging dispute to send gunboats up the Irrawaddy in 1885 to capture Mandalay. After Thibaw was exiled to Bombay, the riches of Upper Burma belonged to the Raj. The breakaway Shan States, meanwhile, had lapsed into civil war, brigandage, and slave raiding. It required several battles, many displays of firepower, and not a little diplomacy, but the British finally subjugated the region in 1890—with the notable exception of the Wa hills. After several unsuccessful attempts to control the headhunters, the region was euphemistically classified as "unadministered." The saophas were presented with *sanads*— a Hindi term for agreements—allowing them to retain their traditional rights and broad powers. In return, the Shan princes promised to pay annual tribute and to grant timber and mineral rights and railroad concessions. Unlike the lowlands, which were operated by the British as Ministerial Burma, the Shan principalities—which varied in size from twelve-thousand-square-mile Keng Tung to Kyong, a domain of just twenty-four square miles—were recognized as separate protectorates under the direct control of the Governor of India. The region became a cohesive entity in 1922, when the feudatories were organized as the Federated Shan States. Their administration and finances remained independent from Ministerial Burma.

"The British knew the Burmese have a different character apart from the Shan," said Sengjoe, who bore an ancient Shan wariness. "The British trusted the Shan and allowed them to carry swords and weapons. As for the Burmese, the British knew they have a hot temperament because they live in the lowland. Most of them are untrustworthy."

The British had their reasons for such hands-off administration. In the mid nineteenth century, the region had been eyed as "The Golden Road to Cathay," a back door to the enormous, untapped Chinese interior then coveted by European powers. Caravan trade had existed between Upper Burma, the Shan hills, and Yunnan for centuries. The British hoped to connect these lands by railroad, but surveys quickly revealed the daunting nature of the terrain and the staggering investment any railway would require. The British also deduced that direct rule of this mountainous, undeveloped expanse would require enormous manpower. Still, Shan State had to be kept out of the hands of the French, who held Laos and were wooing the saophas who lived between the Salween and Mekong rivers. The British chose indirect hegemony, permitting the saophas to stay on their gilded throne-platforms while the crown concentrated on exploiting the accessible, abundant riches of the western Shan States: the rubies and sapphires of the Mogok Valley; the silver, tin, and lead of Namtu; the teak from every slope.

Life in Shan State, the fringe of the empire, proceeded as it had for centuries, little affected by British rule. The Shan lived in permanent valley settlements, where they cultivated wet rice, oranges, plums, tea, and tobacco. Dozens of animist hill-tribes moved about the mountains, slashing and burning forest to grow plots of dry rice, maize, gourds, and opium. Lording over them all were the saophas, shod in their bird's-head slippers. Occasionally, a petty Shan tyrant gave the British headaches. In *Burma and Beyond*, Sir James Gordon Scott described a cruel saopha in Keng Tung who enjoyed sitting on his palace gallery with a rifle and using his subjects for target practice. The saopha's son, who encouraged Scott to pot a few peasants, was "very much of a lout," Scott wrote, "with aspirations to become as successful a shot as his father." But for the most part, the saophas ruled as benevolent despots in a timeless backwater. Elderly Shan were openly nostalgic for this colonial era of powerful, divine chiefs and their disengaged champion, a far-off English superpower that had rid them of Burmese authority.

Sengjoe saw me staring at the faded, fanciful Shan photographs.

"The Shan people enjoyed peace and prosperity during British rule, in colonization days," he said. "Still the old people mention it with tears. We remember the old days while the British were ruling. It was the best. We have peace. We have tranquility. After independence, we have only all the miseries placed by the Burmese."

Shan grievances did not mount until 1948, when the sun set forever on Britain's Asian empire. After World War II, England wanted time to rebuild war-ravaged Burma, which had suffered widespread damage to its railroads, bridges, and port facilities, before granting it self-governing dominion status. But Aung San, the strong-minded Burmese leader, rejected this course—called the Simla Plan—and lobbied London for immediate self-government. Such sentiment was not as strong among the Anglophile Shan, who had fought with the Allies while Burmese nationalists, including Aung San, had allied with the Japanese. No matter. Preoccupied with India, Downing Street allowed Aung San to dictate immediate terms: amalgamation of Ministerial Burma with the Frontier Areas, followed by independence.

"The British are big blunderers in drawing a map," Sengjoe added. "It was unreasonable. And they wanted to forget about the war. Burma was a war-torn country, in ashes. India . . . Pakistan . . . Burma. . . ." Sengjoe made a sweeping motion, as if clearing a table. "The British dropped us like a hot potato," he said. "I think the British are responsible to take some proper course, to find a solution. The Shan are entitled to freedom and to have a country of their own. But the British have poor memories. They forget us very soon."

In January 1947, Aung San traveled to England to meet with Prime Minister Clement R. Attlee, the Labour Party leader. The Burmese nationalist emerged with an agreement for a rapid transfer of power; among the document's stipulations, article eight provided for "early unification" of the hill areas with their "free consent." The following month in the Shan market town of Panglong, Aung San met with minority leaders to mollify their doubts about joining an independent Burma. On February 12, 1947, a date still celebrated as Burma's Union Day, Aung San and the ethnic leaders signed the Panglong Agreement. The crucial accord of postwar Burma, the document promised to safeguard minority rights. Aung San was willing to be accommodating; resource-rich Shan State, which comprised one-quarter of the Union's total land area, was too great a prize to lose.

A large oil painting of the Panglong conference hung on a wall of the Shan Human Rights Center. In the picture, uniform-clad Aung San signs the agreement, flanked by rows of saophas resembling a solemn, turban-wrapped choir. Seated to the Burmese leader's immediate left are two influential saophas, Sao Sam Htun of Mong Pawn and Sao Shwe Thaik of Yaunghwe, who observe the historic moment with looks that can only be described as stunned, portents of the trouble that has plagued the Shan hills ever since.

"This is the day we enslaved ourselves to Burmese rule," Sengjoe said quietly.

Just five months later, on the morning of July 19, 1947, a quartet of machine gun–toting assassins burst into a cabinet meeting and killed Aung San and six other men, including the saopha of Mong Pawn. An embittered political rival, U Saw, the last prime minister of prewar Burma, was soon convicted and hanged for the crime. The damage to the fledgling country, however, would prove irreparable. Aung San, the man who had linked the radical Burmese patriots of the plains with the conservative ethnic-minority chieftains of the hills, was gone.

Two months after Aung San's death, a constitution was adopted. For the Shan, the critical portion of this legal instrument was chapter ten, which granted Shan State the right of secession from the Union of Burma after a ten-year trial period. On January 4, 1948, at the auspicious hour of 4:20 a.m., the Union Jack was lowered forever in Burma. Sir Hubert Rance, the last British Governor, departed Government House to the strains of "Auld Lang Syne," replaced by the new president, Sao Shwe Thaik. At a more rational hour later that morning, the new prime minister, U Nu, a longtime friend of Aung San, broadcast a hopeful, conciliatory speech:

> In the centuries that passed, the groups of Burma fought among themselves, and administrative division under the British regime kept us apart. All this is over now, and, while the Mon, Arakanese, Burmese, the Karens, the Shans, the Kachins, and the Chins will maintain their several cultures, we are now one nation, under one flag and under one elected head of the Burma Union.

The optimism of U Nu, a devout Buddhist who had translated the works of Dale Carnegie into Burmese, was short-lived. According to Josef Silverstein, the retired Rutgers University professor and leading American scholar of Burma, the duality of Britain's administration of the lowlands and of the frontier areas hobbled the formation of a national outlook or identity for the Union of Burma. And without the charismatic leadership of Aung San, there was no center to hold against the powerful centrifugal forces of ethnicity and self-interest. Along with other minority peoples, the Shan soon grew disillusioned with a government dominated by ethnic Burmese, who accounted for more than two-thirds of the union's population. (The Shan, according to the country's last impartial census—conducted in 1931—comprised 7 percent of the population.) Aggrieved ethnic groups such as the Karen, Karenni, and Mon soon took up arms. In 1949, the Communist forces of Mao Zedong drove Chiang Kai-shek's Kuomintang battalions into eastern Shan State; to counter the presence of the KMT soldiers as well as homegrown Communist insurgents in the region, Rangoon declared martial law. To Shan such as Sengjoe, this decision seemed a pretext to hasten the Burmanization of their land. The Tatmadaw soldiers did nothing to endear themselves to the local populace, instead behaving like an arrogant army of occupation, dragooning peasants for work projects, raping women, and looting and burning villages.

Alienated by Burmese military abuses, their lack of influence in government, and the plundering of their natural wealth to underwrite development projects in the plains, a broad-based Shan nationalist movement soon emerged. The rumblings for independence grew louder as the end of the ten-year grace period on secession loomed. Overwhelmed by the ethnic pressures, Prime Minister U Nu relinquished power in 1958 to a military caretaker government headed by General Ne Win, who would deal ruthlessly with the Communist rebels and ethnic insurgents and make no apologies for his iron-handed approach. "The most pressing fundamental need of the Union," Ne Win said in a 1959 speech, "is law and order."

U Nu was reelected in 1960, but he soon angered the

isolationist Burmese generals with his plans for foreign investment and his efforts to accommodate the ethnic minorities.
The army could not abide his talks about autonomy with the
frontier groups, particularly the disaffected Shan. For the Tatmadaw, the prospect of secession was unacceptable. Dissolution
of the union would eliminate the fortune the government
earned from gems, minerals, and timber extracted from the
frontier areas. Furthermore, Shan independence would plunge
the lowlands into a militarily indefensible position against
China and Thailand. Such notions threatened the very existence of Burma.

Against this backdrop, U Nu convened a Nationalities'
Seminar in late February 1962. His timing couldn't have been
worse: astrologers predicted the most inauspicious alignment of
the planets in nearly five thousand years. At the seminar, the
leading voice of dissent belonged to Sao Shwe Thaik, who
now headed the Federal Movement, an attempt by the ethnic
minorities to redress political imbalances, correct constitutional
defects, and negotiate continued terms of incorporation in the
union. For two weeks, the people of the frontier aired their
grievances; U Nu had reserved the last day to give his opinions.

But on March 2, 1962, the day before U Nu was to speak,
Ne Win seized control of Burma in a military coup d'etat. The
Tatmadaw immediately suspended the 1947 Constitution,
abolished Parliament, and muzzled unions and political parties.
U Nu and his ministers were imprisoned, as were dozens of
minority representatives. Hundreds, if not thousands, of prominent Shan—community leaders, businessmen, civil servants—
were detained for years. U Nu was not released until 1966; Sao
Shwe Thaik, the nation's first president, died in November
1962 while still in military custody. And Sao Kya Seng, the
progressive, American-educated saopha of Hsipaw, was never
seen again after his arrest outside of Taunggyi. With brutal effi-

ciency, the Tatmadaw had silenced all official discussion of Shan autonomy and independence.

"Nobody is going to listen to that kind of claim," says Silverstein, "unless [the Shan] rise up, seize territory, and hope they'll be given recognition from the outside. And nobody is rushing to give them that kind of support. There has never been a unified, single command or a single leader."

Unity has never been a hallmark of Shan State, not during the centuries of rule by the independent-minded saophas, and not during the ensuing decades of disorder resulting from the dozens of armed, squabbling groups entrenched in the hills: The Shan State Independence Army. The Shan National United Front. The Shan National Army. The Shan State Army. The Shan State Revolutionary Army. The Shan National Independence Army. The Shan United Army. The Shan United Revolutionary Army. The Shan People's Liberation Army. The Tai National Army. The Tai Independence Army. The Tai-Land Revolutionary Army.

So many chiefs, so many grudges, so many communiqués, and so little progress for the Shan people—until now, the time of the Mong Tai Army. The other rebel groups had been disarmed, disbanded, or absorbed by the MTA. There was now only one Shan leader, however problematic, who could stand up to the Burmese: Khun Sa. His opium bought guns. The guns brought power. And that power might deliver independence. It was an unlikely gamble, but it was enough to sustain men like Sengjoe, even boys like Sai Ching. Become an officer. Fight the Burmese. Honor your parents. Avenge your village. In Ho Mong, thousands of men chanted this mantra.

=====

When we returned in the evening to our guest house, Sullivan made a beeline for the privy. He reappeared a few minutes later, looking slightly clammy. "I just made myself to puke," he announced. "I tried to avoid everything at lunch except rice and vegetables, but the commander kept putting chicken on my plate. I couldn't be rude and not eat it. But I'm not taking any chances now. I'm not going to wind up over at Ho Mong General Hospital, rolling around on the floor next to that poor bastard with blackwater fever." Sullivan rummaged inside his first-aid kit, then produced a pill bottle. "I believe this is a Cipro moment," he said. "Care to join me? If we escape Burma without getting sick it'll be a fucking miracle."

We gulped the large, expensive five-hundred-mg. tablets; miraculous ciprofloxacin took no bacterial prisoners. Then we set about preparing the farang feast Sullivan had carried in his backpack all the way from Dover, Massachusetts; my sidekick had eaten enough local food to test his patience and his constitution. The guest-house cook had left us a Chinese thermos filled with boiled water. We now dosed the consommé-colored liquid with three iodine pills, then pumped it through Sullivan's Pur Scout filter and into a pouch of freeze-dried beef stew. Sullivan flourished a Vidalia onion and a bottle of Ken's Italian salad dressing, which he added to the steaming muck that would be our dinner.

"I'm so good to you," he chortled.

The meal resembled raw, bubbling sewage, not the wishful, *Bon Appetit* illustration on the side of the package. I would soon be in the toilet, I thought, performing the Sullivan maneuver. We ate the effluent over wheat crackers, washed down with Tang-and-Absolut screwdrivers. I regarded my mess kit, wished I had taken more food at the commander's banquet. Rice, klong chicken, and a Cipro chaser trumped this meal any day of the week.

As he slurped down stew and cocktails, Sullivan mused

about the day's events: "We pretty much got the lay of the land. I didn't see any starving people. Either that, or it's *The Stepford Wives* around here. It's the greatest dichotomy I've ever seen. He's the world's biggest druglord, but he's built hospitals and schools. His people don't starve. Without him, they'd be nothing. They'd be living in mud huts."

I didn't disagree. Khun Sa had provided services in Ho Mong that seemed to go far beyond the purposes of press propaganda or military preparedness. He had taken particular care to win the hearts and minds of local Shan civilians as well.

After our regrettable dinner, we walked up the dusty street toward the talaat to meet Sengjoe and Barry Flynn. The sun had slid behind the wall of dark mountains; the first streetlights glowered in the brief, lambent light. Twenty diesel generators supplied nightly power to Ho Mong from six to ten o'clock, although our hosts warned that this coverage was wildly unreliable. The electrical supply was supposed to improve soon. An embankment dam had been constructed several miles south of town with rented Thai earth-moving equipment, and a manmade lake of three million cubic meters had formed after two monsoon seasons. The reservoir already functioned as Ho Mong's water supply. Khun Sa planned to outfit the dam with turbines to provide his jungle fortress with inexhaustible hydroelectric power.

We found Sengjoe and Flynn across the street from the market, in a small restaurant owned by Panthays, descended from Yunnanese Muslim traders—a legacy of Kublai Khan's Mongols—who had fled China in the nineteenth century. Flynn and Sengjoe were quaffing warm Singha over ice and eating fried *mat-pe* beans. We took seats and nibbled at the appetizer. The seeds of the *Phaseolus mungo* bush had a salty, soybean-like flavor that complemented beer. After a few pleasantries, Sengjoe stood and left.

"He went to go get whiskey," Flynn explained. "His wife won't let him keep liquor at home, so he hides it at a friend's house nearby."

Sengjoe soon returned, an old, stoppered Carlsberg beer bottle in hand.

"Jungle whiskey," he said mischievously. "The local people call it moonshine." He poured stiff shots into four chipped glasses. "Cheers," he said, then downed his drink.

There was no alternative but to follow suit. The home-brewed, 180-proof rice whiskey roared down my throat like spreading napalm. Our Shan barkeep poured anew. Ever mindful of protocol, Sullivan went to fetch the Absolut and Tang from our room. This was going to be a long night; I hoped the Ho Mong statutes for public drunkenness were lenient. As the evening devolved into endless rounds of screwdrivers and rotgut shots, Sengjoe spoke of his friend, Flynn, the farang at home in the wilds of Asia, and of his liege, Khun Sa, the strong-minded jungle warrior who had built Ho Mong into a city-state to rival that of a saopha.

"I've never seen the General as close to a European as Barry. He even has Barry's picture in his house," Sengjoe said. We toasted Flynn and Hollywood. "The General is a very sophisticated man," said Sengjoe, dispensing more whiskey.

"People call the General a druglord," I said, "a terrorist who uses heroin as a weapon. He has even said his heroin is stronger than a nuclear bomb."

"Arafat, he planted bombs all over the Mediterranean," Sengjoe replied. "The United States called him a terrorist. Now Arafat goes to the White House. He is not called a terrorist anymore. The General doesn't plant bombs, but the United States calls him a criminal. We don't use force—we use reason. For a few million dollars, we can create a drug-free region. Shan State is a very rich region, with plenty of gems and teak.

We could be a very rich people. The Shan could be the Swiss of Southeast Asia."

Terrorist or statesman. Druglord or freedom fighter. Pariah or patriot. Smuggler or narco-saint. Opinions about the half-Shan, half-Chinese strongman varied wildly.

"He is obviously more of a trafficker than he is an ethnic leader," a Bangkok-based diplomat had told me. I remembered the wry grin that followed. "In that country, the line between one or the other is hard to define."

One travel book from a widely circulated series, *Fodor's 1993 Exploring Thailand*, twice insisted that Khun Sa was dead. According to *Fodor's*, the "colorful and shady" opium king "used to be active in this area, commanding four thousand armed guerrillas at the time of his death in 1991." Khun Sa was also a perfect choice for novelists in search of a loathsome, exotic villain. A 1985 novel by John Balaban, *Coming Down Again*, about farang junkies rotting away in a Golden Triangle jail, contained an unflattering portrait of the Shan-Chinese warlord "Khan Su": "a tubby little man in green fatigues with a green peaked cap pulled down rakishly to his left ear, but much too far, so that the effect was silly." And he made a cameo in Peter Hoeg's 1993 novel, *Smilla's Sense of Snow*, as "Khum Na," a feudal prince with a standing army of six thousand men, offices through Asia and Europe, and a stranglehold on the global heroin trade.

I had read of Khun Sa's alleged cruelty less than a year before in a brief wire-service story. According to the Burmese military—hardly the most objective source—MTA troops had killed more than one hundred civilians near Mong Hsat in southern Shan State for selling opium to syndicates other than Khun Sa's organization. The MTA had hotly denied the accusation.

To U.S. Assistant District Attorney Catherine E. Palmer,

Khun Sa is nothing more than a stone-cold drug dealer, however clever, who wraps himself in the flag of Shan nationalism. "I'm sure the Shan people have a lot of legitimate complaints," she told me. "I'm certainly no expert on the politics of Burma, but I do believe he uses the problems that the Shan State people legitimately have as a very convenient cover for what I believe his primary goal to be, which is heroin trafficking. He's made hundreds of millions of dollars . . . most of which is not used to help the poor people of the Shan State.

"The money ends up in all sorts of trading companies," continued Palmer, "jade companies, jewelry companies, investments throughout Hong Kong, and probably a lot of other places and acquisitions we know nothing about. He taxes everything that goes on; he has complete control over movement in villages, even what's planted.

"Where does all his money go?" Palmer said. "Part of it goes to buy weapons. The rest of it goes to his empire. And some of the worst addiction in the world exists in the middle of the hilltribes that are being used by him to grow the opium.

"He's been indicted by a grand jury in the Eastern District of New York," she concluded, "so I think by definition and by law his activities make him accountable to the U.S. government for a large amount [of heroin] that's coming in. I think his explanations leave a lot to be desired."

Silverstein took this a step farther, arguing that Khun Sa conducts his real enterprise, narcotics trafficking, behind the convenient façade of Shan nationalism. His movement has attracted Shan support almost by default. "Who does Khun Sa speak for?" Silverstein asked rhetorically. "He is the only Shan voice left. Other Shan resistance groups have either disappeared, or been incorporated into his own, or are not doing anything. In that sense he's important."

But Shan scholar Chao Tzang Yaunghwe, who helped

found the Shan State Army resistance group in the early 1960s, considers Khun Sa more favorably. "He is a warlord, no doubt about it," the exiled Shan scholar said. "So is Ne Win. So is Bo Mya. So what? Burma is the land of warlords. There is no other form of government except through warlords and armies. . . . That is the form of politics in Burma since 1962." According to Chao Tzang Yaunghwe, Khun Sa was no latecomer to Shan independence. For decades, the General had maintained he was a Shan nationalist, even when he led a Burmese KKY militia in the early 1960s and was ordered to fight Shan rebels.

"He cooperated with me and with the SSA when he was still with the home guard," remarked Chao Tzang Yaunghwe, who once commanded a Shan State Army brigade but now lives in Canada. "He always resisted attempts to make the home guard fight rebels. When he was forced to join the Burmese in operations against us, he always gave us intelligence and munitions and logistical support. In that way his involvement with the Shan patriotic cause has been consistent. As for his patriotism, he is tied to Shan State. There is no way he can escape. He can't settle down in Vancouver or New York or Bangkok or California. He has to be there. He's a prisoner of Shan nationalism. In a way, he's the most sincere patriot—because there is no escape for him. He is tied to the politics and to the fate of Shan State."

Opium authority Alfred W. McCoy considered Khun Sa a cunning, domineering leader, a personality who is both a warlord and a freedom fighter. Khun Sa's dual, Sino-Shan ethnicity is reflected in the structure of his empire, explained McCoy. "In structure, his organization is two groups," McCoy said. "There is a self-contained Chinese network that manages finances and arms. There is also a Shan side, which is politics. The bridge between those two halves of the movement is Khun Sa. That's what's so elusive about him. He's both: the

Shan nationalist and the ruthless warlord. Although he has now dedicated himself to the Shan cause, he remains as ruthless a warlord as he ever was. He has added, not dropped. He's the man with two names—Chang Chi-fu and Khun Sa."

For all his drug-tainted notoriety, Khun Sa is indispensable to the Shan cause. "He's got the firepower, and there's not another political druglord out there," concluded McCoy. "All the Shan idealists—the purely political people who never handled opium in their lives—are now at his side, gritting their teeth. Khun Sa was the absolute antithesis of their movement for all his career. He is the ultimate warlord. By force of will and ruthlessness he's done something I never thought possible. I never thought the Shan, in any form, would be able to unify. For good or ill, he's the only one to bring them together. He can correct their weakness. He's a curious phenomenon."

Lance E. Trimmer, a former Green Beret who once accompanied Flynn and Bo Gritz to Ho Mong and now works as private investigator in Montana, offered qualified admiration: "Shit, I really kind of liked Khun Sa. He took me around, showed me all of his camp security. He was really nice and sounded sincere about all the things he wanted to do for his people. Tell you what, his people sure loved him. But you have to understand who Khun Sa is, too," Trimmer stressed. "I'm sure he'd have cut my head off if I thought anyway else."

I would get my own chance to form an opinion soon enough. I braced myself on the restaurant table, sticky with spilt Shan whiskey and Absolut vodka, and stood. We were all in our cups. Time to return to the guest house, make a list of interview questions.

"Michael Jackson went to Russia, and the country collapses!" Sengjoe told Sullivan. "Wherever Michael Jackson goes, everything is in a shambles! Bring him to Burma!"

Glasses rattled. We drank to the Gloved One and to foreign

policy. Somehow the moonshine frog-marched me through the blacked-out town to the guest house, then shoved me into a pit of mountain air, cool and black and deep as any oubliette. I closed my eyes and landed inside a Buddhist temple at an audience with Khun Sa. Three pretty, young farang women sat beside me on *zafu* cushions. Why were they here? They came here some time ago, they said, to get better. And had they gotten better? The question hung in the air. The youngest, thinnest girl bowed her head, then rolled up a sleeve of her woolen, soiled sweater. Her arm, bruised and withered as spoiled fruit from repeated hypodermic injections, was wrapped in blood-crusted bandages. No, they were not getting better. But they would not leave either.

No more questions. The words would have to come tomorrow.

13

Tribute and Tablecloths

The dawn came up like thunder, sudden and immense, rumbling ominously through the valley of Ho Mong. I fumbled for my watch: 6:30 a.m. Sullivan snored next to me, hugging a sound-muffling pillow to his face. Outside, Mong Tai Army officers counted cadence while a thousand-strong chorus of MTA recruits trotted through the misted streets, shouting down the waking jungle. As long as their cries hung on the fog, Khun Sa could defiantly flout global opinion. An enormous, well-drilled private army had brought the Lord of the Golden Triangle peace of mind. With force, guile, and perseverance, Khun Sa had survived his enemies. Now, at age sixty, the bane of Interpol occupied the outlaw equivalent of a CEO's corner office, this strategically located fortress overseeing heroin refineries and smuggling trails along the borderlands.

The martial chanting floated through the window. The Noom Suk Harn had been up since four o'clock, running, marching, performing calisthenics. They would muster on the parade grounds at seven o'clock, eat breakfast at eight, break into work teams by nine. Somewhere in the drifting mist, other soldiers stood guard upon mountaintops with machine guns, mortars, and shoulder-fired surface-to-air missiles.

Qui para pacem, para bellum. If you want peace, prepare for war.

My head throbbed as if filled with shrapnel. Our guesthouse room was a disaster. Cooled pools of candle wax on the table. Greasy mess kits, rancid onion rings, oozing packets of ketchup on the carpet. Worst of all, a pair of empty vodka containers in the corner. Two dead soldiers. If we maintained this pace, we'd soon be on half-rations, with the nearest replenishment at least a day away in Chiang Mai. A woozy walk to the privy, a tentative stance over the porcelain basin. Don't slip. Don't cramp. Don't miss.

Desultory Tai Yai and birdsong floated on the morning air. From the ceiling, a spider rappeled a dewy web, bound for night-snared prey. My bowels shuddered and loosened, confirming my worst fears. I had just put myself on an involuntary weight-loss program. The stay in Ho Mong was going to be a battle between Cipro and klong chicken, Immodium and freeze-dried beef stew.

After Sullivan and Flynn had conducted their post-Absolut ablutions with frigid, scoop-and-bucket Shan showers, we mustered at Sengjoe's house. Our hungover guide's glaring wife served us cups of Shan tea and fried rice. I begged off, saying I wanted to buy a souvenir from Burma and waded into the whirling activity of the talaat. In rural Burma, the markets often followed a five-day circuit of towns, but the daily bazaar in Ho Mong completely dominated this region. The talaat in Mae Hong Son may have boasted a greater inventory, but the sights, sounds, and smells of this market were nonpareil. There were enough different hilltribes present—Pa-O, Karenni, Lahu, Lisu, Palaung, Wa, Akha—to occupy an ethnographer for a lifetime. Spice stalls overflowed with mounds of dark, dried tamarind and sulphur-yellow turmeric, piles of pearl-grey garlic cloves and crimson chili pods. Clumps of cured tobacco, neat stacks of thanat leaves, bundles of cheroots competed with gnarled jungle roots and mysterious hilltribe legumes. The smell of dried, salted river fish and *taungtha ngapi*, the notoriously putrid paste made from pulverized, fermented fish and shrimp, hung in the air. Sweet bricks of cane sugar and towers of wafer-thin *mon-le-bway*, the whirlwind cakes of rice flour and fish powder. Steaming bamboo boxes bursting with *khao laam*, a sticky breakfast rice cooked with coconut milk and black beans, and broad banana leaves heaped with *laphet*, a Shan delicacy of pickled tea leaves, garlic, dried prawns, fried beans, and sesame. The babble of astute commerce, the nasal chant of food songs, the cries of doomed livestock reverberated beneath the market's tin roof.

I found a stall with a stock of cheap dahs, and through pantomime and pidgen Thai, cut a deal with a young shopkeeper: one sword for one American T-shirt. As I fished in my backpack for the shirt, the boy's father appeared and berated his son for his lack of business acumen. The father took the dah, then the T-shirt with the Batman insignia. He shook his head, held up three fingers.

"*Sam.*"

"*Song,*" I countered. He paused.

"Ooookaaay."

I pulled a Pink Floyd T-shirt from my boogie bag. Not bad bargaining, I thought, a deadly dah for a pair of too-small T-shirts. For a duffel of dirty laundry I probably could have walked away with an AK-47 assault rifle. When I sauntered from the stalls, a pickup was idling at Sengjoe's, ready to carry us to our audience with the General. We rumbled toward the rising sun, between rows of split-bamboo houses with backyard groves of lush banana and slender papaya trees. The road turned north at the eastern edge of the valley, where the slopes were honeycombed with air-raid shelters. After several kidney-bruising minutes, the truck pulled up to an armed checkpoint. These soldiers, judging from their beribboned M-16s, were part of Khun Sa's personal security force. We unloaded slowly, deliberately, from the Toyota. I took care to leave the dah in the truck bed. No need for these wary, loyal troops to have to fill out after-action reports because of a dumb move on my part.

Beyond the checkpoint stood several long buildings with chain-link cages built upon concrete foundations. Inside the large enclosures, ruddy Malayan sun bears and marble-skinned clouded leopards paced floors strewn with feces and chicken feathers. Derisive peacocks strutted the grounds. "Ho Mong Zoo," said Sengjoe. "The General does not allow the animals to be killed in Shan State. Orphaned animals found in the forest are brought here."

We pressed uphill, beyond an ornamental pond, "Out of Bounds" warning signs, a grass parking lot holding a dealership's worth of Toyota pickups, and purebred German shepherd dogs dozing on the front lawn. The warlord's gleaming, two-story residence overlooking the park seemed vaguely Latin: red, pantile roof, whitewashed stucco walls, cobalt-blue concrete balustrade, and ten-foot-wide satellite dish. The new house—the General had several homes in Ho Mong and hopped between them arbitrarily for safety's sake—was tastefully landscaped with crepe myrtle, bougainvillea, and banana trees. "This place should be on Nantucket," Sullivan marveled. The effect was muddied by an entranceway flanked by tacky bric-a-brac: framed portraits of the King and Queen of Thailand, absurd plastic deer heads, and what looked to be a life-sized statue of a cigar-store Indian.

"Lady Brocket," said Flynn. "It's carved from solid teak."

The expanse of lawn in front of the home was marred by an oblong-shaped crater about thirty yards long. "The General wanted a swimming pool, but he stopped building when the cost reached two million baht," Sengjoe said. "He thought the money could be better spent on his troops. It costs six hundred thousand dollars a month just to feed the army."

So Khun Sa had discovered, like so many suburban American homeowners, that a pool was nothing more than a money pit. Still, looking at the concrete walls, already cracked and blackened with tropical fungi, I pitied the contractor. The compound was also equipped with an all-weather tennis court and a covered badminton court. Despite reports of his failing health, Khun Sa seemed an avid, active sportsman.

"The General plays badminton every evening," Sengjoe announced. "Sometimes tennis as well. He was once a golf club member in Lashio, a runner-up in their tournament."

That must have been years ago, during Khun Sa's days commanding a government-sanctioned militia. Now, the General had no time to work on his tee shots, let alone his short game. There was war to conduct, a breakaway city-state to direct, an opium empire to oversee. Sengjoe gestured toward the badminton pavilion. The General awaited. We walked through trellises smothered in magenta-colored bougainvillea and entered the feudal Shan world described a century before by Sir James Gordon Scott. Inside the pavilion stood several hundred Lahu men and women, all wearing their finest ceremonial clothes. These animist hilltribers, bearing gifts of flowers and vegetables, had walked from their mountaintop hamlets in the borderlands of the Doi Larng Range to pledge their allegiance to this powerful warlord.

"The trekkers in Thailand are asking for their money back," Flynn said wryly. "No tribes are in the villages. They're all here." The audience was predominantly Lahu Nyi, the Red

Lahu, with a few dozen representatives from a Lahu Na, or Black Lahu, settlement. The two related sects were distinguished by their spectacular costumes and the different village, house, and nature spirits they worshiped. Lahu Nyi women wore short, lined black jackets trimmed in red on the lapels, bottom, and cuffs and heavily ornamented with bead patterns and embroidery. The front seams were hidden beneath large silver medallions, a proud display of the family's wealth, as were the silver torques and bracelets favored by many women. Their long, black sarongs were also bordered in red and heavily embroidered. The men wore loose-fitting indigo trousers and jackets trimmed with turquoise-colored fabric. Lahu Na women favored black, ankle-length tunics trimmed in red and a diagonal sash covered with silver buttons; their men wore baggy black suits.

"There are thousands of these ethnic people coming to pay homage and tribute," Sengjoe whispered. "Sometimes the people have to wait months to meet the General. Since February 14, the New Year, it has been like this every day. They are not being called. They come voluntarily to pay tribute to the General. This is a tradition."

The General entered, surveyed the gathering, then bade the Lahu to sit. The men squatted solemnly in the front, followed by rows of restless boys, then the women. The warlord, accompanied by the *li-goi*, the powerful Lahu village chieftain, stood in the front of the hushed pavilion beside a table heaped with a bounteous offering of melons, pumpkins, and gourds.

"So that's Khun Sa," I said, nodding toward the middle-aged man dressed in light blue pants, a white-and-blue checked shirt, and a navy-blue windbreaker.

"No, it's an actor," Flynn replied. "He has to go back now to Central Casting. Tomorrow he plays Ho Chi Minh."

"Most of these Lahu people are living along the border of

Thailand and Shan State," Sengjoe said. "They have been very intimate with Shan society for many decades." Much admired by Scott, who thought them "the best race in Indo-China" and unequaled as beaters for English shooting parties, the Lahu were a nomadic Tibeto-Burman people who lived on mountain ridges above four thousand feet, an altitude ideal for the opium they cultivated as a cash crop. Their migration had reached northern Thailand by the 1890s; approximately forty thousand now lived in the kingdom. More lived in Shan State and China's Yunnan Province.

"The ordinary people are much richer than these Lahu people," said Sengjoe. "They plant a lot of poppies, but actually they consume a lot themselves. They are addicts. Other tribes like Lisu are very smart. They plant poppies and they sell. They make money."

Khun Sa nodded approvingly at the Lahu produce. To journey to Ho Mong, particularly during the February-March opium-gathering season, was a heavy commitment by the hilltribe. Sengjoe translated the General's remarks, spoken to the Lahu in the Tai Yai language.

" 'This food will feed my army,' " Sengjoe related. " 'I encourage the Lahu people to plant more orchards. You Lahu people are living along the Thai border. You have the King of Thailand to protect you. You have peace and tranquility. Thailand and Shan State are neighbors. They are the same people. We are looking forward to the time when we will be a neighboring country. I extend my invitation that you can plant your crops in both countries. You can do trade, communications. Here you are treated as you are in Thailand. I wish you prosperity.' "

The General waved and an aide appeared with a large cardbox box. It was *hongbao* time. For the next quarter hour, the warlord, in accordance with ancient Chinese custom, passed out red envelopes. The color symbolized good luck and power, while each packet's contents—a one-hundred-baht note—represented a financial windfall to the poor nomads.

"They take it as a good omen," said Sengjoe. "On New Year's Eve the General gave every person present a red envelope with five hundred baht. A month's pay."

On this morning the General was playing one of his favorite roles, that of the gracious statesman, to a tribe whose fearsome reputation approached that of the head-hunting Wa. The Lahu had battled Shan guerrillas in the 1960s, then formed a Burmese militia and trafficked in opium, not unlike Khun Sa or Lo Hsing-han. After a falling out with the Burmese in the early 1970s, the Lahu State Army built a stronghold in the Doi Larng Range, where the smuggling trails of Burma fed into the highways of Thailand. The settlement became a haven for drugs, drink, and dice, according to news reports, with a gambling casino and a quintet of heroin refineries. After Khun Sa's forced 1982 eviction from Ban Hin Taek in northern Thailand, the warlord had clashed with the Lahu soldiers for control of the strategic mountains. Now, with an army of at least twenty thousand men and control of the frontier, Khun Sa could afford to be magnanimous.

A cool breeze blew through the pavilion, rustling the trellised vegetation. The Lahu gave the General respectful wai bows, then stood and gathered, three deep in a circle, holding hands.

"It's like a square dance," said Flynn. "Grab a partner."

A tribal elder rocked in the center of the crowd, playing a *kaen*. He was soon joined by several other Lahu men, all playing the same simple wind instrument, which was fashioned from a dried, hollowed gourd punctured with air holes, a long, curved bamboo mouthpiece, and five bamboo joints from one to more than two feet in length attached to the gourd. Tuned to the pentatonic scale, a kaen produced low, minor notes not unlike those of a mournful bagpipe. Sengjoe nodded at the hilltribe pipers.

"They can be the Scottish, you know."

Even the General's hawk-eyed bodyguard was enjoying himself. The sentinel and Khun Sa had joined hands with several comely Lahu girls and were doing their utmost to copy the ceremonial dance, a rudimentary choreography of shuffling and stamping. Sullivan and I found ourselves at the center of the dance, surrounded by blaring kaen pipers, a smiling druglord, and fantastically costumed hilltribers all swaying to the eerie Lahu tune. The ever-present MTA soldier with the Panasonic video camera recorded the scene. My sidekick and I tried to follow the footwork of a Lahu teenager wearing black Converse All-Star sneakers.

"This is the most incredible thing I think I've ever seen," Sullivan said. "Khun Sa is a father figure to these people, someone they really and truly look up to. I'm just amazed."

When the dance concluded, the General beamed. "Come early next year," he told the Lahu. "This year was too late. If you had been here we could have had a festival with you. I could dance with you for a longer time. Please come next year."

As the Lahu tribesmen drifted away from the pavilion, Khun Sa moved to a simple bench behind a large table of honey-colored teak. The surface was clean but for an ashtray, a silver drinking cup, and a bud vase holding a single frangipani blossom. We sat to the warlord's right on a long teak bench. As the first order of business, Flynn presented Khun Sa with a Christie's catalogue that featured several exquisite Burmese rubies. The stones once belonged to Khun Sa and had been sold to Lord Brocket, who then fetched a small fortune for them at auction, Flynn reported. The General nodded approvingly at the photographs. Although he possessed limited formal education and virtually no exposure to foreign culture, Khun Sa understood the Western infatuation with gemstones and hard drugs. He then turned to Sullivan and me and spoke in Tai Yai, pausing at intervals to allow Sengjoe to translate:

"Before the interview you have the key of Ho Mong and you can go anywhere," Khun Sa announced. The hospital, the rehabilitation center, the training camps, the poppy fields, the Salween River. They were all ours to see. "You have taken a lot of effort to travel over from your country to our country," he added. "So during your stay I hope you will regard this place as your homeland."

Up close, the Sino-Shan leader appeared to be at least a decade younger than his sixty years, his hair as dark and thick as lacquer, his light-brown skin smooth and unlined as a clay riverbank. His voice was a reedy tenor, the result of chain-smoking his beloved British cigarettes. His slumping shoulders and bowed posture accentuated the slight thickening around his waistline, but he hardly qualified as the pudgy, ridiculous-looking warlord of fiction. The modestly dressed kingpin, a man alleged to control at least one-third of the global heroin market, then touched upon a surprising subject: drug eradication.

"I have great expectations that you will tell the world to help the miserable people who are planting poppies and find ways to eradicate poppies," Khun Sa said. "There are a lot of problems, a lot of people who are addicted to opium and drugs. I wish you people will tell the world bodies to undertake rightful solutions to resolve the drug problem. I can say that reducing the problem is very easy. The United States should consider changing their policy. There will be more misery if the momentum continues to go the same way it always has. I think it's time for you people to consider a rightful way to find a drug solution.

"Your trip coming here is very important to open the eyes of the people who deal with your drug problem at home," he continued. "You should invite people who handle the drug policy to come and have a look-see. We will open our doors and windows to those people who are concerned, to have a talk and a rightful solution to the drug problem. In the past, the American policy on drugs is very typical. They always blame the Shan people as the main culprit for the drug problem. The DEA creates a lot of disturbance and gives a lot of trouble to such a miserable people as the Shan."

DEA. Khun Sa pronounced the drug agency "DEE-eeeay," in hurried, slightly irritated fashion. The name of his relentless American hunters was among the few English words he spoke.

"From now on, I think these people should have an open mind," he continued. "The DEA or people from drug-suppression agencies should come here and we'll talk about our differences. There'll be a solution for the rightful way of eradicating opium totally from this Golden Triangle. I have proposed to the U.S. government to eradicate opium, but they never accept. I don't know what is in their minds or what is their objective. It is very exasperating for us.

"I would still extend my help to eradicate poppies totally from Shanland. I hope the rightful persons will join hands with me to eradicate these poppies. There are many methods, you know. Just pruning will make things much more worse. It would escalate the drug problem. But if the people concerned should take my advice or my guidelines, we'll work hand in hand to eradicate opium totally. I shall still extend my invitation to the rightful persons who are concerned to help us to educate our people, to do some crop substitution which is proper for the market, and to find some means of other income for the farmers."

I snuck a glance at my tape recorder. This interview had become a Castro-like monologue, but I was reluctant to cut off a man with a mercurial reputation. Let him talk. I had enough batteries and tapes to let him natter on for hours.

"I am very flabbergasted," Khun Sa said. "I have extended my invitation several times, but the people don't come to me. At the same time these people, they use Khun Sa as a target, as a scapegoat for the drug problem. But if I should die today, the drug problem won't be solved. There's no benefit out of this. To every U.S. administration I have put out my proposals: Carter, Reagan, Bush, and Clinton. I always hope that the U.S. government will send the proper representative to solve the drug problem. But still nobody comes and observes the real situation of what is happening in our Shan land. I have great expectations that they will turn up very soon."

He sat back on the bench, crossed his arms, and regarded his farang visitors. His opium could be a carrot or a cudgel. If, as in the past, there was no official interest in his proposal, Khun Sa would merely shrug. The opium would still flow, southward to Thailand and northward to Yunnan, as sure as the rains of the summer monsoon. In the dry season, the Burmese and the Wa would continue to attack his positions, and to be bloodied. The DEA would make busts, but the Thai would not permit Khun Sa to be driven out of business. Under the guard of hilltop garrisons bristling with machine guns, mortars, and missiles, thousands of MTA recruits would train at Ho Mong's two vast camps, then be deployed throughout Shan State. Khun Sa could wait in the jungle, growing stronger.

"I hope people will read my stories and learn more of the Shan cause for independence," I said.

Sullivan was more effusive: "We will get the word out to America because this is so different from the view that has been seen by the people."

As Sengjoe translated our comments, a vague smile pursed the warlord's rosebud lips. Sengjoe did not have to translate Khun Sa's response.

"Yes," said the General, in English. "Thank you." He stood. The audience was over. He spoke again to Sengjoe in Tai Yai.

"Tomorrow we'll have ample time for a casual interview," our translator related. Khun Sa nodded and an aide, the hong-bao envelope bearer, materialized with a bolt of cloth. It was time to exchange gifts. With a flourish, the warlord unfurled his present, a large tablecloth swimming with silkscreened artwork, atop the teak table. "The General designed it himself," Sengjoe said.

It was unlike any piece of fabric I had ever seen, something I would never find at a Macy's white sale. Made of bleached-white cotton and bordered with white crochet, the tablecloth had a golden Garuda bird in each corner and, across the lengthwise base, a pair of Bengal tigers—the General's personal symbol. Above the tigers were the official flags of the Mong Tai Army and of Shan State. The MTA banner featured a trio of golden mountain peaks, representing the Shan Plateau, and a single, five-pointed white star against a blue field, to indicate one leader, presumably Khun Sa. The Shan standard, three colorful horizontal bars and a white, central disk, resembled the national flag of Laos. The disk was a moon representing "peace and tranquility," Sengjoe explained, while the yellow, green, and red bars symbolized, respectively, Buddhism, the forests, and "blood and guts."

" 'Blood and guts' is our slogan," Sengjoe said. "It's like the British Special Air Service motto: 'Who dares wins.' "

From my knapsack, I produced a navy-blue foulard, a horse-theme 1994 calendar, and a white baseball cap with a red Boston *Herald* logo. Sullivan offered a carton of 555 State Express Filter King cigarettes and a Swiss Army knife equipped with every attachment short of a chainsaw.

"They are not as beautiful as the gifts from the orchard of the Lahu but they are all we have," I said.

Khun Sa chuckled. "Never mind. The most important thing is from the feel of the heart." He thumped his chest for emphasis. "The presentation is from the heart," he added. "It's not the value."

We posed with Khun Sa while Flynn took photographs. The General stood between us, wearing a bland, vaguely preoccupied expression. Sullivan and I sported the grins born of fatigue, elation, and disbelief. The Dragon had one parting word: "Please come back tonight and play tennis. Five o'clock."

I hadn't packed a racquet, or sneakers, or tennis whites. No matter. I happily accepted, although I didn't plan on beating Khun Sa. A hard-court drubbing of this man seemed like a bad career move. We left the Lord of the Golden Triangle, now lost in thought, strolling by his empty, half-finished swimming pool.

14

Opium Tears

The sin does not originate in these mountains; they are merely the latest crucible for an ancient vice. For at least seven thousand years, mankind has relied on the juice of *Papaver somniferum*, the "sleep-bearing" opium poppy, to dull pain, to heal illness, and to lift the despair of unfulfilled dreams. In book 4 of Homer's *Odyssey*, Helen of Troy mixed "mild magic of forgetfulness"—an opium anodyne—into the wine bowl. Hippocrates, the father of Western medicine, wrote of opium's efficacy as a pain reliever, while Assyrian medical texts referred to the narcotic as "lion fat." The plant, which originated in the mountains of the eastern Mediterranean, was carried to Asia after 700 A.D. by Arab traders. By the sixteenth century, opium had become a recreational drug. In the Far East, Dutch traders introduced the practice of smoking opium in a pipe, often mixed with imported tobacco. The British transformed opium into a global commodity during the last half of the eighteenth century. English merchants had wangled a trading concession at the lone open port of Canton (now Guangzhou) on the southern fringes of China's Middle Kingdom, far removed from the Forbidden City. However, the coarse "barbarians" had few desirable goods, aside from fur pelts, tortoiseshell, and *bêche-de-mer*, to barter for Chinese silk, tea, spices, lacquerware, and export porcelain. Instead they paid in silver bullion.

The balance of trade only tilted in favor of the British following the introduction of Bengali opium. Although banned by the Manchu rulers, opium soon became the linchpin of the China trade. In 1773, the British shipped more than one thousand mango-wood chests, each containing seventy kilograms of opium, to Canton; by 1800, Chinese addicts consumed two thousand chests of the drug they called "foreign mud." The opium was delivered by sleek clipper ships to a floating depot anchored off Lintin Island in the Pearl River estuary, then lightered by small craft up the treacherous river passage to Canton, where it was sold with the help of the conniving Co Hong merchants guild and corrupt mandarins all too willing to enslave their own people.

As drug imports exploded, profits poured into British coffers. The opium, cultivated in the Ganges River Valley and refined under a monopoly controlled by the British East India Company, eventually accounted for one-fifth of India's revenues. American firms entered the China trade after the Treaty of Paris was signed in 1784 and prominent East Coast families soon grew rich smuggling the drug. The partners of Boston-based Russell & Company, the largest U.S. opium-trading firm of the "commission house" era, included Warren Delano, Jr., the grandfather of Franklin D. Roosevelt, and Robert Bennet Forbes, the famed Boston sea captain. (In an historical irony, U.S. Senator John Forbes Kerry, the Massachusetts Democrat who chaired the Senate Subcommittee on Narcotics and Terrorism and drew a hard line against heroin kingpins, counts Captain Forbes as an ancestor.)

By 1839, faced with two million addicts, the opium-related deaths of his three eldest sons, and a massive deficit that threatened his nation's economy, Emperor Taukwang finally acted. He appointed a trusted aide, Lin Ze Xu, as imperial commissioner and ordered him to eliminate the opium trade. Lin traveled to Canton and, in a remarkable incident, confiscated more than twenty thousand chests of British and American opium. The one-million-kilo drug haul was dumped, along with salt and lime, into watery pits dug in the banks of the Pearl River. Lin then banished foreign merchants from Canton and Macau. Outraged at the temerity of the Chinese, the British soon dispatched gunboats and sank fleets of outmatched war junks. The Opium War ended in 1842 with the Treaty of Nanking, which forced the humiliated Chinese to pay twenty-one million dollars in damages, to surrender Hong Kong Island to the crown, and to open five ports to British residence and commerce.

Although the Chinese refused to sanction the trade, the opium problem soon worsened. A Second Opium War erupted in 1856 over the Chinese seizure of a British-registered vessel. Only in 1858, with the Treaty of Tientsen, which created ten additional "treaty ports," did the vanquished Chinese legalize opium. Soon, local farmers, especially in the southern uplands of Szechuan and Yunnan Provinces, abandoned cereal crops and planted hundreds of square miles of poppies to feed the insatiable market. Many of the nomadic, persecuted tribes living in these mountains would take their newfound poppy-growing talents southward, to the Shan States of eastern Burma, the Plain of Jars in central Laos, and, by the turn of the century, Chiang Rai and Chiang Mai Provinces of northern Thailand.

But opium abuse was hardly confined to the Far East. Early in the sixteenth century, European chemists dissolved opium in alcohol to create a tincture, dubbed laudanum, that soon became a widely prescribed sedative. In an age of quack cures, laudanum proved genuinely efficacious in treating pain and gastrointestinal illnesses. (Even today, laudanum is prescribed for severe diarrhea, as is paregoric, a tincture of camphorated opium.) Laudanum also proved highly addictive. For decades, Robert Clive, the founder of British India, and William Wilberforce, the British statesman and abolitionist, resorted to opium infusions to treat their digestive complaints. Opium proved irresistible to the Romantics. The English writer Thomas De Quincey described the magic and the horror of "subtle and mighty opium" in his 1821 essay, "Confessions of an English Opium-Eater." An opium anodyne painted the pleasures of Xanadu in Samuel Taylor Coleridge's famous 1797 poem, "Kubla Khan."

In 1805, a German pharmacist, Friedrich W.A. Sertürner, isolated the chief opium alkaloid—$C_{17}H_{19}NO_3$—which he named morphine in honor of Morpheus, the Greek god of dreams. An important anaesthetic, morphine is also habit forming. Addiction rose in the wake of a mid-century American medical breakthrough, the hypodermic syringe. In the 1890s, German scientists looking for a nonaddictive morphine substitute concluded that synthesized diacetylmorphine—produced by boiling morphine and acetic anhydride—was a pain-killing panacea that could treat bronchitis, tuberculosis, and diarrhea. Bayer Company, the German pharmaceutical giant, began producing vast quantities of the drug in 1898. The company also coined a catchy brand name for synthesized diacetylmorphine: heroin. Of noble intentions and market-driven motives was born a global scourge.

Measures to control and contain opiates did not begin until 1906 when the British Parliament, bowing to a long campaign organized by outraged clergymen, agreed to phase out the opium trade to China, which then counted nearly fifteen million addicts. Three years later, United States President Theodore

Roosevelt spearheaded the first International Opium Commission meeting in Shanghai. Acting out of high-minded self-interest, delegates vowed to adopt drastic measures against morphine (which they did not refine or sell), but to take a softer, gradual-suppression stance against opium (which they controlled through profitable state monopolies). At the International Conference on Opium convened at the Hague in 1912, signatory nations agreed to enact national laws controlling the manufacture, sale, and use of opiates, and to treat abuse as a penal offense. Two years later, Congress passed the Harrison Narcotics Act, America's first federal laws against drugs.

Scant drug-control progress occurred in the Orient. When Sun Yat-sen overthrew the Manchu empire in 1911, much of China, including the poppy-growing heartland of Yunnan Province, fell under the domain of warlords. Nearly every colony in Southeast Asia enjoyed a financial bonanza from its state-licensed opium monopolies and smoking dens. In independent Siam, which legalized opium in 1851, opium taxes accounted for 20 percent of revenue by 1905. Although Burma had the region's smallest opium monopoly, the British could never wean the nomadic hilltribes of Shan State, who grew opium as a tributary gift and as a cash crop to exchange for the goods of passing Panthay caravans. The Shan States Opium Act of 1923 did register growers and limit each addict to an annual supply of two visses—about seven pounds—but the writ of law carried little weight in the mountains beyond the Salween River. Not even World War II and the harsh Japanese occupation could break the mountain people from the drug habit. In *The Hill Peoples of Burma*, Frontier Areas director H. N. C. Stevenson noted that opium's high price-to-weight ratio made it an ideal commodity in an undeveloped, underpopulated land: "Opium is one of the few products which has a very high value in relation to its weight and therefore can be exported by pack animals or coolies for great distances without any serious loss of profit."

Still, opium remained a locally consumed vice. It was only with the dawn of the Cold War, which brought the Kuomintang from opium-soaked Yunnan to the Shan hills, that drug production grew to export levels. In the early 1960s, cynical or misguided Burmese policies, such as the trafficking privileges granted to KKY militias, also contributed to the drug explosion. And the ruinous agenda of General Ne Win, the military dictator who pushed Burma along the "Burmese Way to Socialism" after 1962, created an ideal climate for illegal, lucrative activity. Ne Win's decisions to nationalize banks and businesses and to eliminate currency left an economic vacuum in Shan State that was soon occupied by opium. The drug became a cash crop for black-market goods throughout the borderlands. The drug was worth more than even cash—merchants refused to accept near-worthless Burmese kyat notes and took hilltribe opium as payment for rice, salt, and farming tools.

Opium gained another purpose during Ne Win's misguided reign: the funding of ethnic revolutions. In Shan State, the rebel groups that formed in the early 1960s followed the same expedient, if morally dubious, route the KMT had blazed with the blessing of the CIA: drugs for weapons. "In the dragon's-teeth soil of the Shan State," opium expert Albert W. McCoy told me, "where poppy crops beget arms, there cannot be a realistic force without the control of drugs. You just don't have the guns—and you have to have guns."

General Khun Sa had learned the lesson well. He had established control of poppy-growing areas. Their opium had supplied him with thousands of firearms, and the weapons had given him wide-ranging power. When I had gone to see

Donald F. Ferrarone, the director of the DEA in Thailand, he had laid out the scope of Khun Sa's empire. The warlord controlled a swatch of Shan State that stretched nearly 250 miles, from the Sino-Burmese border in the north all the way south to Thailand. Khun Sa's northern command procured raw opium in the poppy-saturated hills northeast of Lashio, then moved seven hundred to one-thousand-kilo shipments south in mule-train caravans under the heavy guard of the Mong Tai Army. In the mountains along the western bank of the Salween River—Ferrarone would not say exactly where—the loads were passed to central command. Security was extremely tight. Even so, the Burmese Army's proxy force, the United Wa State Army, had recently ambushed a Khun Sa opium convoy; it had taken five hundred MTA soldiers to bail out the beleaguered caravan.

After running the lengthy, dangerous gantlet, the caravans arrived at Ho Mong, the southern command. In a "very clearly defined" area straddling the border, charged Ferrarone, the opium was converted to heroin in clandestine refineries controlled by Khun Sa. This precious, near-pure heroin No. 4 was reloaded onto pack mules, then smuggled through the Doi Larng Range and into northern Thailand, to Mae Hong Son, Chiang Mai, and Chiang Rai. Khun Sa's routes through the borderlands were challenged constantly by rival groups such as the Wa, whose own heroin pipeline flowed south along the eastern bank of the Salween and whose gateways to the Thai frontier butted against those controlled by the MTA. There was an old Burmese saying: two buffalo cannot share one wallow. Confrontation was inevitable.

"You think of the United States and the drug violence that goes on," Ferrarone had told me. "Well, that violence starts deep in one of the most xenophobic, unknown places in the world."

Armed with the General's blessing, we left Ho Mong in the early afternoon and drove north, toward the Salween River and the mountains bedecked with poppies. Our struggling Toyota fishtailed through the deep, choking dust blanketing the route that had been hacked from the dry forest. The road so stymied our progress that the driver finally stopped to take on a pair of Shan hitchhikers for ballast; they looked like Dust Bowl farmers, sitting in the rear of the truck bed to give us better traction. Out of the valley and into the hills, we drove for miles with no hint of habitation, save for swidden scars on distant, green mountain slopes. Cirrus clouds drifted on the eastern horizon. The only shaded, comfortable spot in a pickup truck on a logging road in Shan State was the cab, which had become Flynn's domain. Consigned to the back, Sullivan, Sengjoe, and I did the only logical thing to avoid the rough ride and to jump clear in case of a rollover—we stood, clutching the roll bar, jungle cowboys bucking an untamed truck.

I rattled next to Sengjoe, admiring the indigo-colored tattoos, the jumble of cabalistic whorls and curlicues on his straining forearms. Among Shan men, the practice of tattooing was nearly universal. The skin designs weren't for sentimental or aesthetic reasons, as they were in America. They indelibly preserved Shan culture and, more importantly, possessed powerful magic.

"The writing is from the Buddhist scriptures," our guide shouted over the next hill assault. "We have them tattooed on our bodies so we preserve our scriptures and the Shan literature for centuries. Shan people believe some verses bring prosperity; the spirits cannot harm them. The tattoo protects you. It is a superstition." For proof against guns and dah, some Shan elders even sewed talismans and precious stones inside knobs of flesh.

Sengjoe had received his incantation in a painful session while still an adolescent in Keng Tung. He brandished his right arm. "It says, 'The enlightened one. Buddha.' These omens are good scripture that protect me against bad spirits."

Well, I did have a golden tree frog indelibly inked onto my right hip, the legacy of a feature story I had once done on Rhode Island tattoo parlors. Perhaps I carried protection as well, although the Shan considered the frog a lowly creature.

"Does every Shan have tattoos as protection?" I asked.

"The General doesn't believe in tattoos," Sengjoe replied. "His body is unmarked."

With a huge army at his beck and call, Khun Sa could afford to discount the spirits. We passed through a Shan logging hamlet, where unmilled trunks and rough planks of Burmese pine gave the warm air a soft, slightly astringent edge. The wood was bound for Ho Mong, to be sold as fuel or lumber. The teak had already been felled and trucked to Thailand.

"They're not rich. They have only enough to feed their families," Sengjoe said of the woodsmen.

The Shan, despite their natural wealth, seemed doomed to remain destitute victims. It had been that way under the Burmese, then the British, then the Burmese again. "We have a saying: the Burmese cut our teak, the Thai reap the profit, and the poor Shan are forced to replant," Sengjoe sighed. "But they have us in a box. If we don't let the Thai take the teak, they will cut our rations."

Several more brutal miles, until a checkpoint and turnpike blocked our progress. In the shade of a simple log shelter, a sleepy Mong Tai Army soldier fumbled for his AK-47, saw farang, then smiled. No MTA officers, and perhaps even a chance to make a few baht. The guard held up a changeable hawk-eagle (*Spizaetus cirrhatus*) he had shot, a lifeless, magestic mass of golden-brown wings underscored with black- and white-banded feathers.

"The hawks are a big problem for young chickens," Sengjoe said.

"Haa-sip." The guard wanted fifty baht for the raptor. Flynn's mood darkened.

"The General will not be happy when he finds out," he said. "He doesn't like for animals to be killed, or military bullets to be wasted. The bullets are for shooting Burmese, not birds."

Twenty sinuous miles beyond Ho Mong, we let off our human ballast at a fork in the road in the middle of nowhere. The Shan passengers waved their thanks and began strolling north, toward the Salween, still a half day's walk away. We turned eastward, continued climbing through open forest. The undergrowth had been put to the torch, to aid loggers, protect against wildfires, and eliminate ground cover for patrols of enemy scouts.

"Poppies grow best at least one thousand meters above sea level," Sengjoe said. "Along this valley and twenty to thirty miles to the east, it is full of poppy fields. The harvest time here is about December and January. It's too hot now. People have harvested their opium and it's being stocked in the villages. There are a lot of tribal people—Akha, Pa-O, Lahu, Kokang— who are the main producers of opium," he added. "The Shan don't grow opium or know how to refine heroin but we get a bad name. The Shan only tax opium and heroin."

A denuded hill stood in the distance, topped by trenches, bunkers, and hootches. It was another of the MTA outposts equipped with mortars, antiaircraft guns, and surface-to-air missiles that formed a defensive ring around Ho Mong. The General had acquired shoulder-held SAM-7s from the Khmer Rouge and Stingers from the Afghan mujahadeen.

SLORC's limited air force gave Ho Mong airspace a wide berth.

Without warning, our driver made a hard left turn and we tumbled down a track barely worthy of a bullock cart to Mae Ark, a Pa-O village at the heart of the global heroin epidemic. Several dozen raised, thatch-roofed houses straddled a ridge, affording the impoverished people of tiny Mae Ark a spectacular, million-dollar view: a long, forested valley with brown, spent poppy fields carved into the mountain slopes that ran northward as far as the eye could see.

"All their lives they have planted poppies," Sengjoe said of the Pa-O, a Karen subgroup that coaxed a living from the mountains of southwestern Shan State. "They never knew other trades to make a living. For centuries these Pa-O people never possessed flat land or have proper paddy fields. They employ themselves in the slash-and-burn business. It hurts forestry, but having no other means of income they have to cut. They have to rely on poppy growing as well as other edibles, like maize and peanuts. They have relied on opium for many centuries. They are not rich. They have to strive every day just to produce one or two visses of opium for their livelihood."

Papaver somniferum defies agricultural advances. Poppy cultivation remains a time-consuming gamble, opium extraction a tedious, manual exercise. To produce enough opium for just one viss requires the scoring and scraping of three thousand seedpods for their alkaloid-rich opium "tears."

We climbed flimsy stairs to a raised porch built of bamboo joists overlaid with split-bamboo flooring, removed our shoes, dusted as much of the road as possible from our clothes, then ducked beneath the low eaves of the bushy, rice-straw roof. We had crossed the threshold to a world made of opium.

The poppy farmer rose from the groaning floor, a bolus of

betel nut, lime, and tobacco bobbing in his left cheek, and greeted us amiably. Sengjoe relayed the man's pitch:

"Do you want to see the opium?" asked Ar Lain Ta. "Do you wish to buy? We are willing to sell the opium. Do you want to have a look-see?"

"Do they take American Express?" Flynn cracked.

"We just want to take a look," I interjected.

"I'm happy to show you," said the farmer, "but if you want to buy. . . ."

"We'll give a donation," Flynn said, "but no buy."

"Once you see it you'll be very infatuated," warned Ar Lain Ta with a sly smile. "You'll be tempted to buy. Every person who comes to see the opium, they fall in love and just buy it."

"We'll fall in love with it and buy it," chuckled Flynn, "but taking it back to America is the problem."

Ar Lain Ta bade us to sit, then scuttled to a small bedroom separated from the main living area by a wall of teak boards. A half-dozen family members gawked in wonderment at the sweat-stained farang come to see the patriarch's opium. In the dim light, I took inventory of this Pa-O household. A pile of thin rattan sleeping mats and rough woolen blankets. Two large cooking pots. A wooden hearth heaped with cooled ashes. Two large motor-oil jugs salvaged as water containers. Some plastic cups. An oil lantern. A caged warbler.

Ar Lain Ta returned with a folded banana leaf and a carefully wrapped, ivory-colored bundle. The package was a spongy, six-inch cube weighing about three and one-half pounds: one viss of raw opium. Enough weight to fetch the forty-five-year-old poppy farmer three thousand baht, about $120. Enough opium tears to quench thousands of junkie dreams, to foster even more nightmares. The farmer, dressed in a dark blue *longyi*, a Burmese-style sarong, and a soiled white tank top, sat cross-legged on the creaking floor. An indigo god danced on his muscular right bicep; further tattooed script raced down his forearm like a thick, dark vein. Ar Lain Ta wore a cheap plastic digital wristwatch. Why he needed to know the exact time, I could not fathom. The daily schedule in Mae Ark was constant, simple: Sunrise. Work. Eat. Sunset. Sleep.

"We live here since about eight years ago," Ar Lain Ta began. "Before then, we lived on the west bank of the Salween. We come because the oppression of the Burmese force. We had been forced to work as unpaid labor all the time."

The same old, untold story that never made it to the West. The Tatmadaw terrorized the frontier with its "Four Cuts Strategy," denying food, money, intelligence, and recruits to the rebels. There was no policy to win over the hill people, only to seize their property and belongings and to treat them as chattel, to slave as road laborers, army porters, and human mine detectors. In Taunggyi and the surrounding areas of southern Shan State, thousands of men and women had been left destitute by extortion or press-ganged to work on a one-hundred-mile railroad extension from Aung Ban to Loi Kaw. To escape, countless families had fled to Thailand's Mae Hong Son Province or across the Salween River to territory controlled by Khun Sa. This war zone, ironically, was considered safer and saner than the lands under the control of the official SLORC government.

"When the Burmese forced us to work, we did not have time enough to plant our crops," said Ar Lain Ta. "So we come here to the east bank of the Salween and we have ample time to plant for ourselves. We feel more secure here. We have time to cultivate."

Like numerous other ethnic-minority groups, the Pa-O had been at loggerheads with the Burmese for decades. In 1950, the late Pa-O leader, U Hla Pe, had formed a resistance group, the

Pa-O People's Liberation Organization, that battled the government in southern Shan State until a 1989 ceasefire.

From a plastic bag, Ar Lain Ta pulled a small green leaf, a few slices of betel nut, a pouch of slaked lime, and made himself another quid. "Why is opium so troublesome in your country?" he asked.

"They're not open-minded," Flynn said. "If we had you as president, there'd be no problem."

"How long have you grown opium?" I asked.

"My ancestors have taught me only this cultivation," Ar Lain Ta related. "It passes from one generation to another." He paused to part the floor slats and spit the dark juice of his chaw. "This year is freak year. The rain is giving a lot of trouble, so I reap only about five visses for my family. In good weather conditions we can reap about seven to eight visses. This is a bad year."

This farmer was not alone in his misfortune. The U.S. State Department estimated that opium production in Burma had fallen 21 percent from 1993, from the record-setting crop of 2,575 metric tons to 2,030 metric tons. Unfavorable weather conditions, not official antidrug efforts, were responsible for the decline.

"Last year we reaped about four thousand baht per viss, but this year, trade is not so good," Ar Lain Ta said. "The opium is not as good. I get only about three thousand baht per viss. This is the lowest price. It is not enough money to feed my family, so I have to be hired as a farm helper in other seasons."

The grinding poverty, the marginal existence that characterizes the peasant life, always seems to get lost in the grand talk of drug eradication. The conversations always center on putting the powerful druglords out of business, with little concern for weaning the poor farmers off opium and onto other marketable cash crops. Heroin undoubtedly destroys lives, but the Pa-O of Mae Ark would not have even this miserable existence without it.

The Sailor, a steady Boston user, held sympathy, not malice, in his heart for the men and women who nurtured his downfall. "I hear it's pretty rough over there," The Sailor had told me when I met him in a day shelter for addicted U.S. veterans. "Pretty political. People die every day behind all that shit. If you don't do what you're supposed to do exactly right down the line, you get killed. It's a rough situation to be in. I wouldn't want to be there. This country is good. It's free here. You can get drugs, you can get methadone, you can get high for nothing here. Know what I mean?

"The middlemen, people from the processing point to the ones that bring it here, they get rich," The Sailor added. "I don't think the farmers get shit. I think they get nothing. They just make a living. It's just like growing potatoes."

Ar Lain Ta had no concept of heroin, no knowledge of the O.D.s and the criminal acts the drug left in its wake. He knew little of Khun Sa and the Shan cause. He did know that his family was safe from the Burmese and that he had the time to grow opium. And that perhaps a son might someday grow up and even become a soldier, just like the ones at the nearby MTA garrison.

"Poppies are the main crop that we produce," the farmer said. "I don't know about marijuana. I would like to learn how to plant marijuana, but I don't think the authorities would let us grow marijuana. The situation is like this: the MTA organization doesn't like us to plant poppies, but the MTA can't feed us and our families. We are forty-eight families. They can't feed us. So they just turn a blind eye on whatever we do. This is our last resort to make a living. If we had another substantial crop that could feed our families, we would abstain from planting poppies."

"What would you grow?" I asked.

"I don't have any knowledge about what would be the best crop to substitute," Ar Lain Ta replied. "Mainly we plant poppies just to get enough money to buy rice. Our second crop is soybeans and the third crop is corn. But we would be very happy if we knew how to plant other substantial crops that could feed a family."

"Who buys your visses?"

"There are many sorts of traders," Ar Lain Ta replied. "Shan, Chinese. Everybody that comes, we just sell. Simple. When people come, the deal is done right away."

Opium was a godsend to his village. Any other crop meant a long journey down the mountain to a market town, and always a risk of spoilage, of robbery, or of surplus. With opium, there were no such problems. The buyers were happy to come all the way to Mae Ark, to his simple home.

"Do you feel bad that so many heroin addicts result from the poppy you grow?" I asked.

"I never knew that it can be converted into other forms," the farmer responded. "We only knew that it was opium throughout our life. We have never seen heroin in the first place. It is beyond our knowledge. I wish to know because my whole life I have been planting poppies to earn a living. I don't know what effect it is having in the world. I know it is poison to my own people.

"There are no opium addicts in the village," he added quickly. "I plant poppies, but I don't use opium. I never smoke. But for medical purposes I have a little opium. At times we use the opium for a miracle cure. When we have a headache, we just scrape the skull with a knife and patch it up with some opium. When we have a stomachache, we just swallow a ball. It really heals. It works."

He unfolded a banana leaf to reveal a sticky mass of gum,

about one-tenth of a viss, the color of used motor oil, the consistency of tremulous marmalade. Fresh raw opium, direct from his fields.

"If you take a lump of it you'll die right away," he cautioned. "It's very poisonous. But if you take a small amount, it will help cure the aches."

Flynn stuck his little finger in the tar. Ar Lain Ta regarded the dollop on Flynn's finger.

"If you want to have the experience . . ." he shrugged. "It will kick you for twenty-four hours. One full day."

Ah, hell. My bowels were churning with bacteria. My Immodium was back in Ho Mong. I faced a twenty-mile drive, tennis in the evening, a meal of klong chicken or rehydrated beef stew, then another night of screwdrivers and Shan moonshine.

"Shit, I'm going to try some."

I held out my hand and Flynn smeared half of his opium onto my little finger. Ar Lain Ta laughed at us, the two farang who knew nothing of poppies. "If you die," the farmer said, "I won't take any responsibility."

His wife brought out dirty glasses of hot, clouded water. I rubbed the opium onto my teeth and gums, then sipped the foul, scalding liquid. "If you take several times you might get addicted," Ar Lain Ta said.

"I'll be back tomorrow," I replied.

Nothing happened. No blissful jolt. No building waves of euphoria. Just a bitter, rootlike taste. I regarded the viss, oozing sap that would soon stain the paper wrapper the color of khaki.

"In my country, your viss would cost more than one million baht."

Ar Lain Ta thoughtfully chewed betel. "There's one thing I'm wondering," he said. "If you can fetch one million baht out of a viss why don't you people plant it yourselves? I'm willing to give you the seedlings." We all had a good laugh, even Ar Lain Ta. Then the farmer grew serious.

"The American people have a means of living and they are so rich without planting poppies. This is a wonder for me. There must be suitable answer for this."

"I am like a scribe," I said, then made a writing motion. "I tell stories."

"Do you have enough money to raise a family?" he asked. I considered my steep apartment rent, exorbitant car insurance, ludicrous cable-TV bills. All costly, complicated necessities of American life.

"No, not really." Nothing a viss or two of heroin No. 4 couldn't cure. From beneath the bamboo slats, a rooster crowed maniacally. I spilled the steaming contents of my glass through the floorboards and heard indignant clucking. The low roof pressed stale, hot air upon us. The other Pa-O sat and stared. Strange farang—to come so far, then not buy opium. To just talk of opium.

I fumbled in my knapsack, then produced a one hundred baht note. An offering to his family. I also gave Ar Lain Ta a black-ink Bic pen and a pack of Marlboro cigarettes.

"Our poison," I said. "A famous cowboy cigarette."

But Ar Lain Ta was far more interested in the cheap pen. He moved the stylus in tight circles on his arm, creating more dark magic. With seven mouths to feed and only five visses of opium, the poor farmer would need to summon prosperity and many good spirits to survive the year.

The return to Ho Mong: The truck like a sailboat on a wind-tossed sea, rising and dipping on mountain swells and troughs. The unmerciful afternoon sun an interrogator's lamp. Dead teak leaves and pine needles blanketed in dust. My stomach pain . . . gone. Warm, comfortably numb on Pa-O opium. Good medicine. Better than Lomotil or Immodium. Tennis?

Anyone? No tennis. The General called away to a meeting. Straighten up with a Shan shower, the cold water a baptism. Backpacker food for dinner, beef burgundy with near-rancid onion, Ken's Italian dressing, ketchup. Chicken à la klong still better. No electricity tonight, only cheap Chinese candles. No nocturnal shitting. An opium miracle. Warm wax and sharp smoke and powdered Tang everywhere. A few screwdrivers, a shot of Sengjoe's moonshine in the guest-house sitting room, then the bad news. The Salween River too far away, too close to the front lines. Too much danger. The General always said yes. Keeping face. And Sengjoe always at wit's end to stretch the rules. The real, unspoken reason: Saturday was an unlucky day. Bad for travel. Bad for washing hair. Bad for everything. There were just two things to do at night in Ho Mong: get drunk and stay drunk. Another round of screwdrivers, another dead, empty soldier of Absolut. It was a race to see which we would exhaust first: vodka or baht. How long did we wish to stay? There was still plenty to see. Textile factory. Mushroom factory. Gem factory. Soldier factory. We would stay until Sunday, or until the Absolut and the Tang and the money disappeared.

15

A World Made of Thunder

"You'll never learn."

Sullivan stared, dumbfounded, at my Shan breakfast, a steaming plate of khao phat kai fresh from the Ho Mong market. I smiled and liberally dosed the fried chicken and rice with lime juice and nam plaa sauce and sat down to eat in Sengjoe's cafe.

"It beats your beef burgundy, hands down," I countered. "I've got plenty of Cipro. And if things get really bad, we'll just take a road trip to Mae Aw."

Sengjoe joined our table. His wordless, fuming wife, no doubt ready to pay our mulefare back to Thailand, set out cups of hot tea.

"To your health," our guide announced.

We sipped the weak brew, silently regarding the bustling activity of the market. After a few minutes, Sengjoe spoke. "You cannot return to Thailand by mule tomorrow," he said. "The Thai Border Patrol Police have raided a Shan caravan filled with bullets."

The day after our illegal entry, Sengjoe elaborated, the BPP had captured Shan muleteers and ten animals loaded with ammunition on the same trail we had traveled. The General had not wanted to pay a "tax" on the bullets to the Thai and now he had suffered the consequences. The route to Ban Mae Suya was too hot for our return; the BPP knew farang had been seen on the trail. There were even rumors that the farang were being held responsible for the smuggled ammo. If we were caught, the BPP would try to extort money. The solution: an end run around the BPP in this sector of the frontier. We would drive many hours to the east, then sneak into Thailand on another border trail.

"And it'll be safe?" I asked.

"Anything can be accommodated with the application of dollars," Sengjoe said with a shrug. "This business will take two, three days to patch up. Some pocket money and they'll be happy."

My head suddenly felt as if it had been split open with a dah. The BPP was pissed off with the MTA. They had staked out the trail and were spoiling to arrest farang mercenaries. They waited for us. This was a Tylenol moment. I stood and walked out of Sengjoe's house, the top of my skull directly in the way of the rusted metal eaves burning in the sharp sunlight. I realized the overhang too late. Blood from a two-inch gash matted my hair, trickled down my forehead. Flynn jumped to his feet.

"C'mon," he said. "Let's go to the hospital."

Flynn started walking down the road, toward the soldier delirious with blackwater fever, the young boy with meningitis, and the overburdened doctors with dull, unsterile scalpels. I looked toward Sullivan. No way. We dissuaded Flynn from a walk-in visit to Ho Mong General, then returned to the guest house. There the leader of Boy Scout Troop One of Dover, Massachusetts, went to work with his first-aid kit, throwing everything into my cut but a ball of opium. Cotton swabs, a large gauze bandage—the kind for sucking chest wounds—and Q-tips, isopropyl alcohol, iodine, then gobs of Neosporin.

"You'll live," he said, admiring his handiwork, "but you may want to wear a hat for a few days."

"I knew there was a reason I brought you along. I mean, besides as a cook and bartender. You kept me out of that charnel house." I donned my Varig baseball cap. Medicated goo oozed through the plastic head mesh. When we ducked back into Sengjoe's cafe, another Shan, Doctor Sai Yiseng, had joined our table. Like Sengjoe, he hailed from Keng Tung. Educated at Rangoon University, the forty-three-year-old veterinarian had joined the Shan resistance in 1975, fed up with Burmese oppression of the hill people. Because of his command of English, the short, husky man worked as a liaison officer for Khun Sa's organization.

"In the city, I am jungle boy," he said with amusement. "In the jungle, I am city boy."

He returned to his story. He had come to Flynn to appeal the condition of his new house. Khun Sa had ordered that a new, two-story house, with plenty of room for a ground-floor pharmacy business—for humans, not animals—be erected as a gift for Doctor Sai. The jealous builder, perhaps the same incompetent contractor responsible for the gaping sinkhole in the General's lawn, had done a shoddy job. The support columns were not plumb. The ill-fitting planks of pine siding were riddled with knots. The whole thing would blow down during the first monsoon storm. Yet Doctor Sai could not voice his unhappiness to the General, and the builder knew it. Criticism of a gift was tantamount to ingratitude. Worse, it meant a loss of face for the donor. It was unthinkable to complain, given Khun Sa's standing as Supreme Commander of the Mong Tai Army and president of the Shan State Restoration Council, unless one had a rat-pit fetish.

There was only one solution. This afternoon, when we met with Khun Sa, if Mister Barry could casually mention that he had seen Doctor Sai's new house, had been surprised at how poorly built it was. . . .

"Of course," Flynn replied. "Anything for a friend."

Visibly relieved, Doctor Sai stood to leave. "Come by the gem factory later," he said.

Our audience with the General was not until 1:30 p.m., almost six hours away. Not enough time to see the Salween River, even if it had been safe to go. But time enough to see the rest of the big valley. There was more to Shan State than just heroin, Flynn was fond of saying. Now he would show me proof.

Mong Mai, the one-time jungle caravansary and tax station, was about a mile south of Ho Mong. We rode past paddy fields, skirted the giant Bo tree, then wallowed through a foot of fresh dirt. Using bulldozers and graders rented from Thai construction firms, Khun Sa's road crews were laboring to repair the rutted route for a few months of traffic before the summer rains turned the whole valley into swampland.

The gated entrance to Ho Mong displayed an optimistic, English-language sign—LET'S SEE AGAIN—and several concrete deer. Bad lawn art was universal, indigenous even to the jungles of Southeast Asia. A few hundred yards beyond the Buddhist temple and the Shan Human Rights Center, armed soldiers waved us through an MTA checkpoint. A tax station, closed since December because Burmese troops west of the Salween River had blocked the ferry crossings, stood next to the security post. Like countless warlords past and present, Khun Sa extorted a "tax" on any good passing through his territory.

Two months without a caravan to dun, I thought, and the General still enjoyed distributing baht-stuffed red envelopes to every hilltriber who came to pledge his fealty. The man had deep pockets and, as we were to find out, a diversified empire. We soon pulled off the dirt road in front of a long, low building. Beyond the structure, scores of ducks swam in a man-made pond that would soon irrigate another season of rice seedlings. A strange, cracking sound spilled from the open windows.

"The textile factory," Sengjoe said.

When we entered, it took a few moments for our eyes to adjust from the dry-season glare to the unlit interior, to make out the half-dozen floor looms lining the eastern side of the building. The General had purchased one of the simple looms in Thailand, carted it to Mong Mai, and had it reproduced. To instruct his people he then hired a master weaver, an ethnic Mon refugee from Tenasserim Division in the far south of Burma, where the people were also in revolt against the Burmese.

"The Mon are the best with looms," Sengjoe said. "This man brought his whole family from Mae Sot."

Sengjoe fingered the textiles displayed for sale, royal-blue Karen cotton tunics with tassles of pink, yellow, and white, iridescent bolts of silk the color of crimson poppy petals and imperial jade. None of Khun Sa's busily decorated tablecloths were stocked, however. Those were loomed and silk-screened in Thailand.

The new factory employed forty Shan girls, Sengjoe said, who were also provided with housing and bicycles. Many of the women busied themselves winding threads from hundreds of bobbins onto octagonal warp beams nearly six feet in diameter. Others worked the looms, coaxing the bamboo treadles to raise and lower the heavy harnesses and send the weft shuttles sliding through the shed.

ClackClack . . . *ClackClack* . . . *ClackClack* . . . *ClackClack*. . . . Pure rhythm, like the sound of a slow train's wheels on worn steel rails. The textiles would help fund the MTA and help rural women with few marketable skills avoid the temptation of seeking work south of the border—a job hunt that had already ended in misery for tens of thousands of young, illiterate, uneducated women from Burma.

"They can't go to Thailand," Sengjoe explained. "Otherwise they will be lured into the sex industry."

We left the Mong Mai weavers behind and drove several miles south to the grandly titled "MTA Crop Substitution Institute." Deliverance from the Burmese could take many forms, including shiitake mushrooms. The manager of the demonstration farm limped out of his office to greet us. Wounded in combat eight years ago, he was a disabled veteran, as were his forty employees.

"The MTA takes good care of invalids and cripples," Sengjoe said. "We give them double pay and double rations. This is very important for morale of the army."

"The General also makes a marriage arrangement, so they are taken care of for life," Flynn added. "Also good for morale. Normally soldiers are not allowed to be married for five years, unless they can no longer fight. The General had a driver who wanted badly to get married. He couldn't wait five years but he thought he could get an exception, since he was the General's driver. So he got married, he got a wedding gift from the General, and then he got six months in jail. Some honeymoon, huh?"

The farm manager, a tubby man in a loud purple-and-white leopard-skin print shirt, led us inside a musty, tentlike structure covering at least fifteen thousand square feet. The dirt surface held thousands of water-soaked *mai-kaw* logs, which were covered with a small fungi fortune. These mushrooms, he said, would fetch 1,200 baht per kilo, around $48, in Chiang Mai.

"He was sent to Taiwan as a scientist to produce heroin, but he ended up in the mushroom business," Sengjoe said of the farm manager. I hoped our guide was joking.

Cultivation of the firm-fleshed, brown-capped delicacy was a prolonged, labor-intensive business in Shan State. The wood of the mai-kaw, a medium-sized chestnut tree, *Castanopsis argyrophylla*, was cut into yard-long pieces, then seasoned for four months under cover of straw and tarpaulins. Dozens of holes were then bored in the logs, filled with spore emulsions, then sealed with wax, the manager explained. After four months of storage, the logs were soaked, then propped up in serried ranks in the dark, humid, muslin-topped shelter. The mushrooms were then gathered from the logs and cured in a small drying shed. Sengjoe pointed to a small, open hut sheltering a kilnlike contraption. "This is the heroin refinery," he said impishly.

"Last year we produced five thousand kilos," the manager said proudly. "We have three farms. Ninety percent is exported. The King of Thailand has a demonstration project, but the Thai only produce one-fifth of what we produce." The secret, said the manager, was in the mai-kaw tree of Shan State, which gave the mushrooms a strong, distinctive flavor. In Taiwan he had trained on artificial logs, so scant was the mai-kaw supply. And Thailand, well, Thailand had practically razed its forests.

"The taste of mai-kaw is different," the manager said. "The ones cultured in Taiwan are pretty, but the taste is not good. These are the best. With every shipment to Thailand, at each checkpoint they want one kilo of mushrooms."

As tea money went, that was a bargain-basement shakedown. Shan guides were also not immune to the urge to "sample" the merchandise. Sengjoe produced a plastic bag and, with the manager's blessing, lustily scooped one kilo of the precious mushrooms into the sack. Some men brought floral bouquets home to their wives. Sengjoe had a more palatable offering in mind.

Our final scheduled stop was the jewelry factory, a new cinderblock building in Mong Mai, located a few hundred yards west of the main road to Ho Mong. Doctor Sai, the man with the housing headaches, ushered us into the week-old enterprise. Every cement surface—ceiling, walls, and floor—gleamed with fresh white paint. In the rear of the large room, several women sorted piles of rough precious and semiprecious stones. In the center of the expanse, one dozen men and women hunched over screaming lathes and wheels, carefully girdling, bruting, and faceting precious gems tipped on the ends of dopsticks. Khun Sa's portrait and English-language motivational slogans—"Honesty" and "Follow the Order"—hung from the walls. A Muzak version of the Beatles' "Let It Be" poured from the public-address system.

The factory turned out the bounty of Shan State: ruby, sapphire, diamond, topaz, jade, garnet, amethyst, and tourmaline. The stones came from Mogok mine northeast of Mandalay, from Mong Hsu mine in central Shan State, and from mines that geologist Mook Keaw Kam had uncovered near Mong Hsat in southern Shan State, about twenty miles from the Thai border. In Shan State, where jewels seemed to litter the ground, the MTA claimed a cache of ten thousand rubies.

"Just like South Africa holds diamonds," Doctor Sai said. "We don't want to flood the market."

"Don't forget that 43,000-carat ruby," said Flynn. "Big as a basketball. Nine and one-half kilos. I doubt if it's being hoarded. The General's probably using it as a doorstop."

Sengjoe then voiced a decades-old Shan complaint: "The jewels are ours but the Burmese government takes them out. What they sell in Rangoon is all from Shan State—all the rubies, the sapphires, the jade. In Burma proper, they don't have anything, just some rice and ocean products. That's all they have. Shan State is a rich country although people say we have to grow opium. That is not true. If we have peace, we have a lot of things. Now we want the Burmese out. We will stop the opium ourselves if the Burmese leave our territory. So we need sovereignty first. We are the rightful owners."

The fifty factory employees worked for two companies, Shan Jewelry and Mong Tai Jewelry. The latter firm's president was, not surprisingly, Khun Sa. According to Doctor Sai, most of the jewelry workers hailed from Keng Tung and northern Shan State. They were uneducated girls who needed an alternative to the prostitute business of Thailand. "This way," he said, "they won't bring AIDS back to our country."

The jewelry companies provided housing and clothing to the workers; the women wore blue smocks adorned with concentric rings of yellow, green, and red—the colors of the Shan flag—surrounding a brilliant-cut ruby and the initials "MTA." The jewelers first trained on garnets, then graduated to precious stones. Doctor Sai ushered us through the rows of grinding wheels and polishing lathes. The vertically integrated complex contained all the accoutrements of a modern lapidary: a spectroscope to measure gem color, microscopes to check for flaws and imperfections, an electronic scale to accurately weigh stones to one-thousandth of a carat. "All of this equipment comes from GIA, the Gem Institute of America," Doctor Sai proudly announced. There was even a state-of-the-art Euro-therm machine of the kind used to superheat stones to more than two thousand degrees Celsius, nearly the melting point of sapphires and rubies. Such heat conditions affected the internal chemistry of the gemstones and could dramatically improve clarity, color, and profit. The risky process could make a good stone better—or completely worthless.

"The burning technique is very jealously guarded secret," said Doctor Sai. "It is not easy. You must have the feel and know the secret. There are many, many things. Make a mistake and the gem becomes cracked or turns opaque."

"And you know the burning secret?" I asked.

"I learn in Thailand," he replied. "I talk. I peep. I rob."

He nodded toward Flynn and grinned wickedly. "You *know* who is my teacher."

We had a hearty laugh at Flynn's expense. Doctor Sai led us out of the factory and up a short slope to a building that held gem-factory trainees, a jade-cutting complex, and a jewelry showroom. Beside a nearby workers' dormitory, laborers put the finishing touches on a playground and a guard house. The showroom held a trove of eye-popping rocks, enough precious stones to impress even the diamond-encrusted Liz Taylor. There were ivory cigarette holders, intricately carved jade belt buckles, and statuettes of the Buddha.

Doctor Sai held out a large, black lacquerware box. I cautiously opened the slick package. Inside lay a black velvet bag decorated with golden English lettering: "KS Collection." And inside the bag, a pair of white ladies pumps, imported from England. The leather felt soft and light, top quality. But what made the shoes truly sumptuous was the row of rubies arranged in bright, gold settings along each of the toe caps.

"The General design himself," said Doctor Sai. "Only the best rubies, the best shoes. Wholesale, these are five hundred thousand baht a pair. We gave shoes like these as a gift for Lady Brocket. Two pairs. Other shoes we make have jade, sapphires, diamonds. Not only white leather. Black, too."

Khun Sa had decided to leap into the world of haute couture footwear, no matter what marketing and distribution problems a pariah druglord might face in trying to sell twenty-thousand-dollar pairs of ladies' shoes.

"Anything in size eleven wide?" I asked. "Give *me* the ruby slippers."

Doctor Sai smiled. "Only shoes for lady," he said. "And for katoey he-shes."

Flynn gestured toward a half-dozen glass jars filled with jade rings. "Take one," he said. "As a gift."

Doctor Sai glanced around the room. "Be quick!" he whispered.

I selected a ring the hue of a honeydew melon for my wife, while Sullivan took a sample for his teenaged daughter, and Sengjoe for his out-of-sorts spouse. We then walked outside, to a rise just west of the jewelry factory complex. There stood an astounding, incongruous vision, the culmination of a fevered dream as ostentatious as the opera house built by fin-de-siècle Amazon rubber barons in Manaus, Brazil: Brocket Hall East, radiating in the late-morning sun. With its gabled, pantile roof, its white stucco walls, its chimney fashioned from river boulders and mortar, the grand estate easily eclipsed Khun Sa's villa. The General had spared no expense in fashioning his miniature inter-pretation of Lord Brocket's home. Should he deign to visit Shan State, the prominent member of Parliament would certainly feel comfortable. The four-bedroom home featured a marble bath-room, chandeliers, a king-size bed. Outside, impeccable land-scaping—a green, manicured lawn, ornamental shrubs, a cherry tree in blossom—scorned the dry-season weather.

"Nobody can use it until Lord Brocket visits," said Flynn.

We stood in the heat, marveling at the surreal audacity of the villa, the finest house in Burma between the Salween and the Mekong Rivers. A weak breeze carried a low, incessant rumble from the north. *BUMbumbumbum BUMbumbumbum BUMbum-BUMbum BUMbumbumbum* . . .

"Mong Mai Camp," said Doctor Sai. "The recruits are preparing for graduation."

We thanked Doctor Sai for the jade souvenirs, and drove toward the percussive waves, stopping only after we passed through a wooden gate to enter a large MTA training compound. We had no sooner dismounted when we heard chants and shrill whistles cut through the martial thunder. A battalion of MTA recruits swept by, three abreast, their Chinese-made Bren light machine guns and wooden training rifles at the ready, Khun Sa–designed olive-drab fatigues and baseball-style caps resting loosely on their immature bodies. Some in the column marched smartly under the direction of their vigilant drill instructors; others nearly shuffled in their oversized Chinese sneakers. All sang the Shan national anthem, a song written during the Japanese occupation and adopted at the 1947 Panglong Agreement conference, as they headed for a parade ground:

> *The Shan Nation, the nation of the free.*
> *Our flag with three sections of colors,*
> *The moon—symbol of the cosmic sovereign.*
> *We have the inherent might,*
> *We are united in thoughts, words, and deeds,*
> *We are loyal and true.*

The rawest recruits grasped wooden training weapons. As instruction progressed, these new soldiers would have plenty of opportunity to handle real guns. Basic-infantry soldiers drilled for at least six months, while MTA officers received at least one year of training before deployment to existing units in the field. The Noom Suk Harn, the youngest warriors, would train for years. Sullivan marveled at the regimen, which was far more rigorous than the average American G.I. had endured before deployment in Vietnam.

"When I was in the Army, it was eight weeks of basic

infantry training, about six weeks of AIT—advanced infantry training—then on to Vietnam," he related, then surveyed the MTA columns with an officer's discrimination. "A lot of our guys were just eighteen, nineteen years old. Most of these guys are younger, but they train anywhere from five to eight years before active duty. Their experience is significantly more than that of the average American recruit. Very impressive."

The dust kicked up by the riflemen had barely settled when several companies of grenadiers tromped by, three abreast. Each soldier carried a portable, Chinese-made RPG-2 rocket-propelled grenade launcher, or its successor, the RPG-7, on his right shoulder.

"It's an anti-tank, anti–armored personnel carrier weapon," Sengjoe said admiringly. "It's also very good to deploy on bunkers."

Flynn nudged me. A few of the uniforms had Lao lettering. His contribution to the revolution, courtesy of the *Air America* wardrobe department. The parade ground soon bristled with an amalgamation of Soviet, Chinese, German, and American firepower, an armory of bought, bartered, or captured weapons that also included AK-47 rifles, M-16 rifles, G3 rifles, M-79 grenade launchers, 60-mm. M-19 mortars, and 82-mm. Type 65 recoilless cannons. The General's son, Number One, a short, powerfully built man wearing unmarked, olive-drab fatigues, moved among the soldiers, eyeing their uniforms, apprising their weapons knowledge.

"They always say the MTA has only four or five thousand troops total," Sengjoe observed. "We have forty-eight thousand men under arms. In this training camp we have three thousand seven hundred soldiers and one hundred fifty officers."

I couldn't vouch for Khun Sa's total armed strength, but Sengjoe's Mong Mai head count seemed accurate. Thousands of soldiers had assembled on the arid field. Some recruits worked to deploy their rifle bipods and display the weapons in orderly rows. Led by standard-bearers, dozens of MTA companies moved smartly through the dust in close-order drill formation; other columns practiced goose-stepping.

"You've got to be sharp to the command and respond the right away," Sengjoe said.

Right. Hold. Left. Hold. Right legs extended to forty-five-degree angles; left arms perpendicular to ramrod-straight bodies. The soldiers hung in the balance for two, three, four seconds. Everything must be perfect by the end of the month, when the twenty-eighth graduating class of recruits marched past the dignitaries assembled on the teak review stand. The General demanded proper pomp and circumstance. After graduation, these recruits would join MTA outfits along the Salween, where Khun Sa claimed to have stationed ten thousand troops, or be sent to units as far afield as the Wa States in the north or east to Tachilek in the Golden Triangle. The MTA, which operated in a constant state of readiness, was currently on hair-trigger alert. The Shan expected the Burmese to make a move by the end of the month. Perhaps on March 27, Sengjoe ventured, Tatmadaw Day.

"The Burmese Army likes to attack on auspicious days?" I asked.

"Yes," he said. "Especially Martyrs' Day, July 19, when Aung San was assassinated. These attacks usually happen in the north. I don't know if the Burmese have it in mind this year, but we're ready."

We followed the throbbing noise to an assembly hall that could accommodate more than one thousand people. Inside, scores of teenaged boys and girls marched in place, beating on snare, tom-tom, and bass drums. Drumless members of the corps simply beat upon tabletops. Behind the group, a large mural of Khun Sa, at least fifteen feet high and thirty feet wide, dominated the north wall. In the painting, the warlord struck a Resolute Founder pose: he wore an MTA uniform and sat astride a chestnut stallion at the edge of a rocky cliff, over-looking a broad, sunlit Shan valley dominated by a large, bell-shaped stupa.

"He was born to be a leader," said Sengjoe. "He is always attached to our country. His feeling, his mind, is with our people. Whatever he do, the benefit come to our people. He has good decisions for our people. In our hearts and minds he is our leader."

There was no question of who was in charge of Ho Mong, although technically Khun Sa had only recently retaken con-trol. He had stepped down from the Shan State Restora-tion Council in April 1992 and transfered political, military, and economic power to the ineffectual Shan State People's Representatives Committee. But the SSPRC chairman, Bo Deving, a seventy-year-old warlord from northern Shan State whose longstanding hatred of the Burmese had earned him broad support, was considered a figurehead by many foreign observers. In June 1993, Bo Deving had written the United Nations to request admittance of Shan State, then pleaded his case in a six-page follow-up letter to Secretary General Boutros Boutros-Ghali. There had been no reply. Subsequent commu-niqués requesting "the repeal of indictments and warrants for the arrest of our Head of Resistance"—that is, Khun Sa—had also been ignored. Bo Deving stepped down in December when the newly created Shan State National Congress elected Khun Sa, the Lord of the Golden Triangle, to be its first presi-dent. To no one's surprise, the tally had been unanimous. Why anger the mercurial Supreme Commander and spend political exile in a rat pit?

At this very moment, the Shan State National Congress was

meeting in Ho Mong with the MTA field commander, our banquet host Sao Kan Zet, to discuss upcoming military operations against the Burmese. The die were irrevocably cast. The people had been prepared for the coming revolt, the local economy sufficiently diversified, said Sengjoe, and the MTA adequately armed and trained for quick-strike operations.

"We are unlike the Khmer Rouge, the Pathet Lao, the Viet Cong," he elaborated. "They fight first. They didn't prepare the people. Even though they have independence they still have a lot of problems. They haven't solved them yet. We don't want to be like that. We prepare everything first, then we fight."

Khun Sa had been roundly criticized for long ducking a fight with the Burmese Army, but that policy seemed about to change. He had adhered to a carefully formulated order of battle. Fight today's enemies, he counseled. Come to terms with your enemies of tomorrow, and the day after tomorrow. First, he won the opium war. Then, he consolidated control of the Thai borderlands. Finally, he would take on the Burmese in the struggle for Shan independence. In a speech delivered at his December 12, 1993, presidential inauguration, the warlord-cum-nationalist declared as much. The Shan would lay claim to their homeland and cast out the Burmese interlopers, proclaimed Khun Sa, who likened the struggle of the Shan to establish a homeland to the preparation of a garden.

"In order to grow fruit trees in the garden, we first have to remove the grass, the bushes, and the small trees that can hinder our movements," he had said. "Then we can finally tackle the big tree in the field. Now, except for the big tree itself, our field is virtually free of other obstacles." The KMT had gone to Thailand. The Communist Party of Burma had collapsed. Many of the ethnic rebel groups had disbanded or had signed ceasefire agreements with the Rangoon junta. Now, only the

Tatmadaw occupied the field. "The time has now come," concluded Khun Sa, "to deal with the big tree itself. And we will need all the strength, unity, and skill that we can muster."

The drumming intensified, mixed with the rising chants of thousands of soldiers and the cutting whistles of their instructors. The din enveloped the camp. The MTA columns were on the move. More marching. More drilling. A few more weeks and, astrologers permitting, the taste of battle. Uproot the big tree. It was never meant to grow in these hills.

16

The Offer

I had gone over my list of interview questions time and again, tightening transitions, narrowing focus, hoping to avoid another warlord monologue. Now, as we rattled along in the back of another Toyota pickup, I tried to ignore the throbbing pain from my run-in with Sengjoe's roof and to focus on my notes. The relentless sunlight threatened to melt the poultice of antibiotics glistening on my forehead. Sullivan had his wallet out and was absently fingering his prayer card to Saint Jude. Just a sign, that's all he wanted. His lunchtime creation of Spam and stoned-wheat crackers rebelled inside my guts. We had a rendezvous with a druglord.

Instead of traveling along the eastern rim of the valley, to the villa with the zoo, the badminton pavilion, and the unfinished swimming pool, we returned to Mong Mai, to a simple, one-story house nearly in the shadow of Khun Sa's homage to Brocket Hall. A young Shan aide greeted us outside the home and spoke briefly with Sengjoe. The General had a stomach-ache, the aide said, but would meet us shortly. We were to make ourselves comfortable. He gestured toward a sun-splashed veranda that held formal teak chairs set around a large oblong table inlaid with teak marquetry. The house had been constructed on an east-west axis at the advice of Khun Sa's *feng shui* wizards to capture the energy of the dragon current. This columned terrace deliberately faced east, which the geomancers determined to be the most auspicious direction. The veranda certainly afforded a spectacular vista to comfort a wanted man: a long valley filled with factories that brought foreign exchange, fields that yielded rice, training camps that crafted soldiers, and homes that sheltered thousands of true believers.

The veranda itself was decorated casually. I took inventory, curious about the taste of a druglord rumored to be rich as Croesus. An etched Chinese mirror and a buffalo skull hung from the blue-gray wall. An elaborate teak shelving unit, the kind that held home-entertainment centers in thousands of American rec rooms, stood behind the table. The shelves were barren but for a pair of buffalo horns, a box of tissues, several cans of Thai coconut milk, a snarling plastic tiger, and a framed charcoal-and-pencil portrait. The rendering was of Khun Sa and his boon companion, Barry Flynn. The General had commissioned the drawing, a copy of his first photograph taken with Flynn, the kid from New Bedford, Massachusetts, who had somehow become the one farang that the warlord trusted. Of all the big-time celebrities and power brokers whom Flynn had known, this vilified man was the person who treated him with the most respect.

Doctor Sai, who would serve as the General's translator for this meeting, arrived from the gem factory. Making small talk, he pointed to the hazy blue hills across the valley where we had witnessed the Lahu audience. "The General move here a little bit, there a little bit," Doctor Sai said. "He's moving around. Here is one of the places he uses to sleep."

The shell game was a safety precaution, just like the two

pickup trucks bristling with armed bodyguards that always accompanied Khun Sa. Enemies took many forms, appeared in many places. The General, Doctor Sai related, had survived more than forty attempts on his life.

An old woman brought a platter piled with coconut and chocolate cookies, then poured hot tea into delicate, gold-rimmed porcelain cups trimmed with lavender flowers that rested upon matching saucers. The china was part of a "USA Home Set" collection. Our mindful host was trying to make us comfortable.

The parade ground of Mong Mai camp, a fenced all-weather tennis court, a badminton court, and a covered garage area with a matched pair of air-conditioned, four-wheel-drive Toyota war wagons lay below the villa. In the shade of a gazebo near the motor pool, a quartet of guards sat smoking, their beribboned M-16 rifles within easy reach. Near the house sat a pair of white wrought-iron patio chairs, and a purebred German shepherd dozed on the clipped grass. Recently planted saplings of cactus, papaya, Burmese pine, and poinciana, a flame tree the Shan called *alai-apaw*, filled out the lawn.

We were not kept waiting long by Asian standards of protocol. The General appeared, thirty minutes behind schedule, his hair still shower dampened. No entourage, no guards, no factotum accompanied him. Instead of the MTA uniform he favored for formal interviews, he dressed in the same casual outfit he had worn to yesterday's audience with the Lahu: a navy-blue windbreaker, light blue pants, and a white-and-blue checked shirt. Khun Sa looked relaxed and avuncular, an unassuming middle-class businessman in the autumn of his years. For a man who possessed little formal education, whose foreign travel extended only to western Laos and northern Thailand, Khun Sa was completely worldly in matters of image control and public relations.

He nodded toward his charcoal portrait, then rolled his eyes.

"Barry," he sighed in mock exasperation, then sat with his back to the wall. He faced east—the feng shui power seat. Directly behind him, the etched mirror cast back bad energy. Thirty yards away, an armed bodyguard discreetly patroled the villa's perimeter. A warlord did not last long in Shan State without taking all necessary precautions.

I began the interview by thanking Khun Sa for allowing us the key to Ho Mong. Yesterday had been extremely interesting, I added, and informative. He nodded in assent, then spoke in Tai Yai. Doctor Sai translated his remarks.

"I only request that you write what you see."

"I intend to write what I see. Many stories."

"Yes," he said, in English. A thin smile pursed his lips. I slid a guidebook, *Fodor's 1993 Exploring Thailand*, across the table as an icebreaker.

"General, this book says twice that Khun Sa died in 1991. Am I talking to a ghost?"

Khun Sa flipped through the guide's colorful pages as he spoke.

"Somebody comes to Thailand and then says I am a fake? That I am not the genuine Khun Sa?"

"He's an actor I hired from Hollywood," Flynn chimed.

"Is the real Khun Sa still in the shower?" I asked.

The warlord chuckled and sat back. He was Khun Sa, the Prince of Prosperity, the Prince of Death. Look upon his works. I told him I had been impressed with the size and the scope of Ho Mong, with its schools and factories, its hospital and zoo, its dam and temple. The camp did not seem to match the negative image that many people had painted of him. How would he describe himself? Khun Sa launched into a criticism of the Burmese that eventually segued into the politics of opium cultivation in Shan State.

"Our country has been invaded by the Burmese for quite a long time," he said. "The Burmese are so cruel; they are not like the British, who just colonized Shan State. The Burmese act worse than robbers. Once Burma got independence from the British, confusion started. After losing the war in China, the KMT came to Shan State. It was paradise for them. When the Burmese saw this, they brought their army up to Shan State. They said they are coming to fight with the KMT. Actually it was just a pretext to occupy Shan State."

These conditions were a marked departure from the British period, he continued. "Under the British, there was no aggression, no oppression. The jails were big and there were no people in them. Peace was lost when the KMT came in and the Burmese came in. Society changed. The Burmese had to create a jail in every township. People go in jail; every jail is full. Sometimes the jails are overflowing. After the British left, the Shan have been oppressed, have been poor, and have suffered all the time."

The KMT had received financial support from Taiwan and the CIA, the Communist Party of Burma (CPB) was underwritten by neighboring China, and the Burmese government received foreign aid, he complained. But no overseas assistance had ever gone directly to the Shan, a minority people on the periphery of a country nearly as reclusive and unpredictable as North Korea.

"The economic condition of the Shan State is very poor," said Khun Sa. "Because of the poverty and the political instability, the only survival crop for the hill people is opium. In peacetime, our people grew opium only for fun or for traditional medicine. Then, the most production was two hundred tons a year. Nowadays, production is up to almost three thousand tons a year. People who never grew opium in their history, now they grow opium. It is because of Burmese economic and political failure."

Khun Sa then took aim at his American nemeses, accusing the Central Intelligence Agency of covert, illegal actions in Laos during the Vietnam War that created a gigantic heroin problem. "The CIA wanted to use the hilltribes as mercenaries against the Communists. They encouraged these hilltribes to grow opium and then they organized the mercenaries. They had to find a market for the product, so they took the American G.I. If the CIA was not dealing in this opium trade, where did they get the money for themselves and for their mercenaries?"

Although he had reportedly trafficked in opium for more than thirty years, Khun Sa now professed a longstanding disdain for the narcotic. "Since I was a child I realized that opium was not good for humankind," he said. "In 1962, I started rehabilitation treatment. I started eighty schools and clinics to cure people, eighty centers to rehabilitate addicts. From the start, I had the intention to eradicate opium. I wanted to cooperate with the outside world.

"It was the KMT that established a lot of the opium trade and the heroin trade. They have done this for more than forty-six years. They see that only I can go against them and stop them. They don't like me. It was not the Burmese who drove the KMT out of Shan State. It was not the Thai who drove the KMT out of Shan State. It was *me* who drove the KMT out. I drove them out of Shan State in 1986. I have lost thirty years of restoration time just to take them out of my country."

Agitated, he held up the index finger of his right hand. "In 1977, I offered to help the DEA. Your congressman, Lester Woolf [a New York Democrat], sent his representative to my headquarters in Ban Hin Taek. I offered to help. I also said that what the DEA was doing could not stop opium, but my Six-Year Plan could stop opium. I handed over all the details to the American government. I don't understand why your government won't accept my plan, or even answer what I should do."

Shan rebels had advanced drug-control plans for more than twenty years, without success. In 1973, the Shan State Army convinced Lo Hsing-han, then the biggest druglord in northern Shan State, to surrender his crop to American authorities to be burned. In offering the opium, the Shan rebels hoped to achieve positive press and an international forum for their political grievances. Their plan, whatever its merits, was doomed. The United States and the United Nations preferred to address the drug problem via official channels, not through talks with insurgent armies. Worse, the eradication proposal threatened Thai border officials grown accustomed to the tea money paid by smugglers. On July 17, 1973, the very day the Shan proposal was delivered to the U.S. Embassy in Bangkok, Lo Hsing-han was arrested by Thai soldiers in Mae Hong Son Province. Extradited to Burma, Lo was charged with "insurrection against the state" for meeting with the Shan rebels and given a death sentence. (But in the confusing, ever-fluid politics of Burma, he was pardoned in 1980. With the blessing of SLORC, Lo Hsing-han has returned to the drug business, this time with former CPB commanders who lead government-sanctioned militia units and traffic in heroin in the Sino-Burmese borderlands.)

Khun Sa handed me a copy of his Six-Year Plan, which he had first tendered during a secret April 1977 meeting with Joseph L. Nellis, then chief counsel of Woolf's Congressional Select Committee on Narcotics Abuse and Control. Khun Sa's opium-eradication offer was not unlike the Shan State Army's 1973 proposal. For a total payment of $150 million, the bulk of the money pledged to infrastructure development and crop substitution programs, General Khun Sa had promised to wean his people off opium. I leafed through the neatly typed pages of the Six-Year Plan. Year One called for the construction of agricultural associations, teachers' schools, public schools, and a drug-rehab hospital. Further money was earmarked to support former poppy farmers, train a ten-thousand-man self-defense force (presumably Khun Sa's army), and purchase the previous season's poppy harvest and the "old stock" of opium "to prevent from out spread." Year Two called for more farm associations, teachers' schools, public schools, hospitals, farmers' aid, and opium purchases as well as roadway and water-system construction; Year Three also outlined payments for village development programs and for cash crops. Somehow the Shan rebels had heard about the agricultural price-support system manipulated so astutely by North Carolina tobacco farmers and Wisconsin dairy farmers.

The Shan plan requested financial assistance only for the immediate and the medium term. Khun Sa was confident that the abundant natural resources of Shan State would sustain the region over the long term. There was only one difference between his 1977 offer and the Six-Year Plan he now proposed. Adjusted for inflation, the purported cost of eradication had doubled, to $300 million.

No matter the cost—just a fraction of the value of the poppy crop on the streets on America—the plan had no chance of acceptance, I thought. Justice Department officials such as Assistant District Attorney Palmer and influential politicians like Senator Kerry considered Khun Sa a career criminal with absolutely no credibility. Any plan he floated would be indelibly stigmatized, immediately dismissed. Khun Sa aside, there would be diplomatic hell to pay in Rangoon for any outside recognition of, or official contact with, the Shan resistance. Donald F. Ferrarone had explained the political reality to me:

"Say whatever you want about the Burmese—there's not a lot of positive stuff you can say—it still presents an incredibly complicated picture for us to be dumping foreign aid into an insurgent group in someone else's country." William F. Beachner, regional director of the United Nations International Drugs Control Program, had echoed Ferrarone's sentiment. The United Nations, he had told me in Bangkok, could operate in Burma only at the request of SLORC.

"We've been approached by certain ethnic groups for assistance," Beachner had related. "We have to tell them we're willing to work with them, but only if the Burmese government wants us to be involved. We can't operate in anyone's country without their approval."

And the hard-line generals in Rangoon were not about to allow nongovernmental organizations to work with any independent-minded ethnic minority. The situation was depressingly irreconcilable. Without political accommodation between the Burmese government and the major ethnic groups, acknowledged Beachner, there would be no political stability, no economic development, and ultimately no resolution to the problem of opium production and drug trafficking. Burma would be "a very long, difficult task."

According to the warlord sitting across the table from me, the opium problem in Shan State could be solved easily. "It is not difficult," Khun Sa said. "If there is Burmese occupation of Shan State, if the Burmese just go to their territory and the Shan regain their land, I will be the leader. I will tell the public to eliminate every poppy plant from the roots out. In only one day, I can make Shan State free from opium."

The notion seemed an egocentric pipe dream. What about Shan opium merchants, I countered, and heroin refiners? Wouldn't they be unhappy with such an arrangement? How could Khun Sa be sure they would stop?

He waved his right arm dismissively, as if brushing away ants from a banquet table. "The merchants who are staying in Shan State, they always follow my policies and cooperate," he answered. "But the merchants from the outside world are out of my control. I don't care for them. Whether they like it or not, I have to do for my country what I have to do.

"That is why I want you to do some things," he added. "One, let the world know I am ready to cooperate. I am willing to help. Whoever wants to eradicate drugs, come and find me. Another thing: crossing the border. Why do they close the border if they say Khun Sa is a monster? They should open the border and come and see. Prove whether I am a monster or not. By closing the border, somebody is trying to conceal the truth.

"I have offered for nearly twenty years to eradicate drugs but I haven't seen any DEA representative—or any government representative—come to me and talk. The U.N. doesn't come to my people. There is no one who comes and talks to my people. They just go through the Burmese government, they arm the Burmese with weapons. They make the situation worse."

He leaned forward, reiterated his theme. "I want to offer to the world: whoever wants to eradicate drugs, come to me. I am ready to cooperate in everything I can." But there could be no solution to the drug problem, he warned, without his cooperation.

"Without Khun Sa, opium would be more," he reasoned, "because there would be no efficient person to help you with the eradication problem. If Khun Sa is still alive and the justice people come and cooperate, in one day I can make Shan State free from opium."

His empire had been founded on opium. What percentage of his revenue was raised from taxing opium and heroin?

"In the past," he replied, "I make a tax for every caravan. A cow is taxed, smuggling goods are taxed. I take the tax to maintain my troops. In the past, opium is 60 percent of all the taxes."

Who was taxed on opium?

"There are three steps," he explained. "The grower we tax. The buyer also we tax, and the seller also we tax. If they grow opium, we tax 20 percent. If they buy or sell opium, the tax is 40 percent."

With herds of cattle, slabs of jade, and hundreds of tons of opium annually moving on caravan trails through his territory, those taxes amounted to millions of dollars. I asked Khun Sa about a 1991 Reuters story, quoting unidentified sources, that reported he had lost three hundred million dollars when the renegade Bank of Credit and Commerce International had collapsed. Did he bank at BCCI? How much money did he lose? The warlord smiled.

"I don't even know. What is BCCI? Where is this bank? All the time I have stayed with my people and fought in the battlefield. I built my country. I don't have that kind of money because my people always need money. Whatever I have, I work for my people. I don't have that kind of money to put in any bank."

Khun Sa hoped that opium, which funded the bulk of his revolutionary budget, might be the salvation of the Shan. He had often said as much: the destruction of drugs by other people would destroy the Shan; only the destruction of drugs by the Shan would deliver his people.

"This opium is on Shan State," he argued. "Whatever happens with the opium—its conversion, or its destruction, or its eradication—has to be done by the Shan, because it is on our land. The profits have to come to the Shan. That is the nature of the situation."

When I had met with the DEA in Bangkok, Ferrarone had told me that Khun Sa exerted direct control over the heroin refineries along the border, that his organization sold heroin. How did he respond to this charge?

"DEA used the Thai special forces from 1982 to 1987 and they launched attacks against me forty-three times. If I controlled the refineries, they should get some clue, like paperwork and names and bags with heroin. But these forty-three times they never get anything from me. How can they accuse me of control?"

But Khun Sa had repeatedly claimed enough dominance of the drug trade to be able to eradicate opium in Shan State. How much of the trade did he control? Before he could answer the question, a houseboy delivered the General's one-year-old granddaughter to his arms. For several minutes, the DEA, opium eradication, and Burmese outrages were forgotten. The man alleged to be the world's most notorious heroin kingpin chuckled and cuddled the young girl on his lap. Then Khun Sa gently let her down to the floor, where she scampered off toward the house. Had it been a spontaneous moment of affection and reassurance, a young girl's need to see her grandfather, or a cleverly conceived photo opportunity, an old warrior's ploy to seem warm and sympathetic?

Now he wasn't thinking about his opium empire. He was criticizing "Paa Maa"—his diminutive nemesis, Catherine E. Palmer. "I think she is staying abroad and far away," he mused. "She doesn't know this area or this territory. She wants to indict me. She doesn't understand about human life and society. I think she has something wrong with her brain. She understands nothing about justice. She understands nothing about human rights. She just uses her power to indict."

Did he worry he might suffer the fate as Manuel Noriega or Pablo Escobar?

"I think America can do that," he answered quietly. "That's why I am careful for myself, and on guard all the time. Even when you came, I have to be on guard, because I am afraid you will communicate where I am to a satellite. Even if you throw a paper out, I have to check it."

If Sullivan and I had been under constant surveillance during our stay in Ho Mong, I hoped Khun Sa's Shan spies realized our Absolut intake was an anomaly.

Any large-scale American action against Khun Sa would have to be staged from Thailand and would require the cooperation of Thai authorities. Did he consider the Thai his enemy or, as it had been alleged, his business partner?

"They came in as an enemy," said the General, recalling the 1982 battle in Ban Hin Taek. "They used four to eight thousand forces. They used twelve or thirteen helicopters. The fighting was violent. The way they shot, I think they really wanted proof. They wanted heroin or opium from me. But I think they also were afraid because I might die. If I died, there would be no star for them to criticize."

In a perverse way, the Thai, the Burmese, even the DEA, had a use for Khun Sa. The Shan warlord served the Thai by preoccupying the belligerent Burmese military, and by his willingness to trade teak, gems, and opium for weapons. His pariah status obscured the fact that the Burmese generals, who had alliances with more discreet narco-insurgents, were up to their epaulets in the drug trade. For the DEA, he made a perfect villain: a Fu Manchu–like figure who cast the heroin problem in black-and-white terms for American citizens. Although SLORC's low-profile allies, the Wa, the Kokang Chinese, and former CPB commanders such as Lin Ming-shing of the Eastern Shan State Army, probably controlled as much of the drug trade as Khun Sa, they had not received the Justice Department's "kingpin" label.

The DEA considered him a criminal and had said they would never negotiate with him. In the face of such an impasse, I wondered, if Khun Sa considered himself a distraction, a hindrance to the Shan cause, would he step aside? He replied quickly, firmly, his eyes as dark and hard as those of a predator.

"I won't stop."

And did the DEA have the power to stop Khun Sa?

The warlord smiled at the absurdity of the question. The United States had assisted the Burmese Army in its drug-eradication efforts from 1974 until 1988, at a cost of eighty-one million dollars. In that time, Burma's annual opium production had doubled, from six hundred to one thousand two hundred eighty metric tons. Since SLORC's 1988 takeover and the subsequent elimination of U.S. counter-narcotics funding, the opium problem, like a noxious, unclaimed corpse left to bloat in the heat, had swollen to hideous proportions: two thousand three hundred tons by 1992, close to two thousand six hundred tons—more than double the 1988 crop—in 1993. Here was Khun Sa, surrounded by massive, sophisticated defenses, in command of a private army, and conducting lucrative cross-border trade with the Thai, his ostensible captors. A few years ago, Ho Mong was but a few primitive huts. Now, hundreds of houses, a half-dozen schools, and several factories filled the valley floor. The hills had just provided another huge crop of opium.

"The DEA already has tried to stop me, from 1972 up to this day," said Khun Sa, his brow suddenly as furrowed as a freshly tilled field. "What they get are four things," he added, hitting his right fist on the table to enumerate each point. "First, the number of addicts increases every year. Second, the number of merchants and traffickers increases all over the world. Third, the number of people who go to jail increases all the time. And fourth, the problem increases every day. That is what they get from DEA."

Nearby, the principals in a drug enterprise of staggering proportions calmly conducted their livelihood. Ar Lain Ta and other subsistence villagers in the Pa-O village of Mae Ark would soon clear more land to cultivate the poppies that swayed like tempting serpents in the slightest breeze. In surreptitious border refineries, that opium would be transformed into heroin No. 4. Khun Sa sat back in his chair, crossed his arms like a man who held all the trump cards.

Sengjoe gestured at his watch, as if to say my interview was over. I ignored him, nodded toward Sullivan. My companion had come all the way to Burma to ask Khun Sa about the possibility that American prisoners of war might be held in western Laos. Sullivan appealed to the General as one soldier to another: he had made thirteen trips to Southeast Asia in search of POWs; he had come to Shan State because he thought the General might have important information. But Khun Sa had only disappointing news.

"Ever since I started my troops, I have been very friendly with Lao officials," Khun Sa told him. "I sent my representative to the Lao and asked if they had Americans. 'Give me one or two,' I asked. I also sent my own agents to almost every village to search for them, but I cannot find any news. And the Lao government always says they do not have any."

"If, in the future, you were able to negotiate or provide assistance to get live Americans out of Southeast Asia that would do a tremendous amount for public relations and positive feelings from the people of America toward the Shan people," Sullivan said. "It would certainly be something the American people would be grateful for."

"Because I also understand this, I have tried my very best already," Khun Sa replied. "In the future, I also will try my

very best, too. If I know where and I have to use force, I will
do that, too."

Khun Sa stood. Our audience had concluded. He had to get
back to the business of opium and of impending battle. He
gave an order and a uniformed aide materialized with two ceremonial dah for Sullivan and myself. Khun Sa's eyes and ears
were everywhere, reading every scrap of paper, noting every
farang purchase in the bazaar. He had learned that I had bought
a dah. Now I would have the best dah in Shan State. My new
sword was two-and-one-half feet of tempered, deadly beauty.
A work of fatal art, capable of beheading a man with a single
blow. Like the MTA uniforms, the MTA tablecloths, and the
MTA drug program, the weapon had been designed personally
by the General. A decorative sword knot of red-, green-, and
yellow-dyed yarn, the bright colors of Shan nationalism, hung
from a varnished teak scabbard bound with detailed brass
hoops. The intricate metalwork included fine renderings of ivy
vines, flowering poppies, and the Shan and MTA flags; the hilt
pommel bore the snarling head of a tiger, the General's personal symbol. The forte of the slightly curved, razor-sharp steel
blade held an inscription in the banana-leaf lettering of the
Shan language: MONG TAI ARMY.

"You are not afraid of the Thai; you risked your life to come
here," Khun Sa concluded. "I am also very happy and honored
that you come here. In order for the growers not to grow
opium, and the traders not to trade, and the smokers not to
have opium or heroin to smoke, you must let the world know
our offer. Then I have a chance to help with that task. In the
future," pronounced Khun Sa, "if we get our independence
and we have our own Shan State you can use this sword as a
visa. Just enter."

"Anytime I'm in trouble I just show this," said Flynn, flashing a wallet picture of Khun Sa and himself.

We shook hands and posed for a few pictures with the warlord. Then he turned back toward the house to play with his granddaughter and plot the next move in a brilliant, thirty-year career built on opium.

"Bye-bye," said the Prince of Death, in English. And disappeared.

=====

The sun had fallen behind the chaos of dark mountains. The electricity had not yet come on in the guest house, and we changed by candlelight into our last batch of fresh clothes for a final night on the town. There would be no peace in these hills, I thought. The Six-Year Plan would find no takers. The United States found Khun Sa too odious. The United Nations preferred a dialogue with the thugs in Rangoon. And SLORC had determined that Khun Sa had become too political, too dangerous. Their chance for international redemption, for resumption of Western aid, lay in neutering Khun Sa. Everyone was gunning for the warlord, yet his arrest would not affect the supply of heroin. The Wa, the Kokang Chinese, and the old CPB commanders would see to that. Khun Sa's arrest or retirement would not help the Shan. Any ethnic leader, no matter how untainted by drugs, would still be ignored by the intransigent generals, would carry no relevance with the United Nations.

Sullivan was solemn. Khun Sa had not offered him any hope about missing American servicemen.

"I've done my best," my friend said wearily. "I feel very strongly I've done my duty. My moral obligation is complete. May God have mercy on them. They're angels. . . . I told you before we went on this thing that I wanted confirmation one way or another from General Khun Sa. If he had said, 'Yes, definitely they're there,' I'm certain that would have given me hope.

"It's over. I've spent my life savings on this. I've spent my kids' college-education money, which I've somehow got to find a way to get now. This search has cut into my business. In my heart, I still think they're there. But there's nothing else I can do. Nothing. This to me is closing my last chapter of the Vietnam War. I've just had this major-league obligation and I guess I don't know why. Maybe it's because I'm an Eagle Scout . . . I somehow shouldn't give up. I won't give up hope, but I've done everything I can. Now it's time to concentrate on my kids, my family, my girlfriend, my business, and go on with my life."

We walked the darkened, dusty street, following soporific cowboy music to Sengjoe's house. His wife greeted us with a smile: one more besotted night and we would be gone. We sat with Flynn, Doctor Sai, and our guide while she served boiled rice, deep-fried gourd, and a soup with thick Shan noodles, scallions, and sliced shiitake mushrooms. Sullivan begged off—no jungle stomach. As we ate, Sengjoe described the end run we would make to avoid the Thai Border Patrol Police he said were waiting on the mule trail to Ban Mae Suya.

"We will take a four-wheel drive truck tomorrow," our guide explained. "We will drive through Doi Larng. First north, then east, then south, to Nam Kot. It is as far as the truck will go. The driver does not know Thailand. There you walk across the border."

"The walk is only two kilometers," added Flynn. "A truck from Khun Sa's office in Mae Hong Son will meet us in Nam Kot, carry us to the border, and drop us off. We walk from there. That truck goes around through a border checkpoint, picks us up inside Thailand, then drives us all the way back to Chiang Mai."

Just another illegal cross-border scamper. No problem. Sullivan looked at me, dead eyed.

"I'll need vodka," he said.

"It's through rice paddies," Flynn said of the hike. "There's one little hill. We go around one police checkpoint. There'll be border police but they'll be inside their huts."

"The Thai police there know, but they're going to turn a blind eye on you," said Sengjoe. "They have some pocket money."

"They *know* we're coming out?" I asked.

"They know something's happening," said Flynn. "They'll just stay in their huts. They don't know who we are."

A neat border arrangement. Sengjoe poured shots of Shan moonshine into a quintet of old, mismatched tumblers. Mushrooms and jade had earned our guide a special dispensation from his wife.

"*Skol,*" he said and downed his rice whiskey.

His wife placed a small plate of food in front of me.

"What is it?" I inquired.

"Dessert. Just taste it," Flynn urged.

I scrutinized the pale heap on the plate. It resembled a tapioca pudding studded with unpolished kernels of rice. Sengjoe's wife hovered on the periphery of the room, attending to other diners but watching her husband's guests. I had no choice but to sample the dish. I ate a spoonful of the dessert: sour and slightly crunchy. Flynn burst out laughing.

"Do you *know* what you just ate? Tell him, Sengjoe."

"*Khai moat som,*" said our guide. "Egg with red-ant eggs. It is a Shan delicacy."

I could have eaten worse, I suppose. I had been spared Shan delicacies such as *ekok,* a deep-fried beetle larva, and Sullivan staples like freeze-dried beef stew. I tossed back my moonshine, beckoned Sengjoe to pour another shot. Insect eggs would hardly survive repeated 180-proof dosings. There would be one last Cipro moment in Ho Mong.

Our Shan friends wanted to celebrate this final evening, so we headed for the only nightclub in town, a karaoke bar a few doors down from our guest house. The star-strewn night spread above the mountains, gleaming like an intricately beaded *kalaga* tapestry. Pariah dogs bayed in our tipsy wake; we kept a bearing on the garish red and white electric lights burning in the black night: KARAOK. At the door I gave the bored hostess a Purple King to cover admission and we entered the "VIP" club. The empty bar was little more than a glorified shack. Strands of Christmas tree lights and cheaply framed black-and-white posters decorated the pine walls. A mirrored ball hung from a thin ceiling beam. A few slatted wood benches, rattan chairs, and unsteady tables cluttered the bare cement floor. Sengjoe and Doctor Sai, who could not afford the bar on their monthly salaries of five hundred baht, eagerly steered us to a corner table. There we ordered Singha beer and platters of mat-pe nuts and sun-cured Indian beef.

Warlords, ant eggs, moonshine, karaoke. It was shaping up to be a memorable Saturday night in Ho Mong. I had waited more than a week for a moment like this. I pulled a pewter flask from my hip pocket and offered it to Sengjoe: Remy Martin XO, a serious VIP drink. He took a nip and settled in his chair. Life was complete. "Cognac," he mused. Shan rice whiskey would never taste the same.

A plump, limping thirtyish man entered with a quartet of unsavory characters wearing polyester slacks and windbreakers. "That's Mister Lee," said Flynn. "The General's adopted son. Khun Sa found him in the jungle. Carried him around on his back for years. Mister Lee used to manage the teak concession." Now Mister Lee entertained low-class criminals who came to Ho Mong in hopes of buying heroin, who sought to ingratiate themselves with the General's inner circle. The hostess plugged a videotape into a wall-mounted television. Doctor

Sai walked to the front of the room, picked up a microphone, and began singing Paul Anka's treacly 1959 classic, "Put Your Head on My Shoulder." No matter that he sang off-key, or that the words, filtered through reverb, were barely intelligible. Sengjoe felt like dancing. He grabbed the hostess, and led her through a chaste, elegant foxtrot.

"Where the hell did Sengjoe learn to move like that?" Sullivan asked.

"He's the dance instructor," Flynn said. "When the General built Brocket Hall he decided everybody would have to learn how to dance properly. I brought in some dance tapes. Sengjoe knew how to dance from the missionaries. The General made him his personal teacher."

More whiskey. More Singha. More cognac. Irish jokes from Mister Barry. Irish jokes from Mister Jay. A round courtesy of Mister Lee, the former teak tycoon. Tawdry Christmas lights winking. Flynn's turn to sing, improvising: *No more tree, Mister Lee.* Big brass balls. Mister Lee laughing. My turn to sing. "My Way." Mistakes, I'd made a few—backpacker stew and Shan whiskey, for starters. I took the blows for a few more rounds. Then sleep buried me.

17

Getting Out

Corundum is a prosaic mineral, an aluminum oxide with a simple chemical formula and widespread distribution, distinguished solely by its hardness: nine on the Mohs scale, second only to the diamond. Colorless in its pure form, corundum sometimes contains impurities that give it a spectrum of gem-quality hues. Traces of iron and titanium transform the rhombohedral crystals of corundum into bluish sapphires. And on the isolated occasions that the mineral deposit holds traces of chromium, the stones are bathed with red shades ranging from pale rose to cochineal, and carry a magic designation: ruby.

The ancients believed the rare ruby, which appears in limited deposits in South Asia and East Africa, held mysterious and curative powers, could change color to warn an owner of impending harm, and could even lift the vapors of melancholia. The finest of these powerful gems are found in Burma and are called *ma naw ma ya*, a Pali term meaning "wish-fulfilling stones." For more than eight hundred years, the gravel beds of the legendary Mogok Valley have yielded gems blessed with a rich, special fluorescence. Every year, miners at the

high-security site ninety miles north of Mandalay extract millions of dollars worth of rubies for sale at the gem auctions and
jewelry shops of Rangoon. And at least as many gemstones are
spirited away, smuggled through the Shan frontier by mule
caravans to Thailand.

In this way, a fortune in rubies had found its way to Ho
Mong. And so, on my final morning, I did a little gem business
with Sengjoe. I couldn't return from a hazardous, incommuni-
cado trip and present my wife, Maria, with a single band of
jade as a token of my gratitude. Bad marital move. We met
in the front room of the guest house. Through the louvered
windows the town roused itself for Sunday. Sengjoe carefully
unfolded a sheet of white paper. The center crease brimmed
like a deep wound with lustrous cabochon-cut rubies. I
chose four similarly sized stones, all a deep red, but without
the bluish tint of the prized pigeon's-blood stones. Sengjoe
described the color as "rabbit's eye," an unfamiliar shade. I
arranged the stones on the lens of my small, illuminated
flashlight. They held a rich, red fire, the reason that ancient
scholars had classified rubies as "carbuncles," derived from a
Latin term that also described glowing embers. I had neither
scale nor microscope, but these gemstones appeared to be
genuine and of good quality.

"How much, Sengjoe?"

"Ten thousand baht," he replied. "They are excellent
quality. They are the natural color. They have not even been
superheated."

He was almost apologetic about asking for four hundred dollars. I quickly knocked him down to six thousand baht, less
than $250, then pulled a stuff sack from my backpack. I laid out
American clothes for barter: black Levi jeans, a Hard Rock
Cafe T-shirt, a Nike tank top, and a Western shirt in an

astounding purple-and-aqua print, a birthday present from my aunt in Oklahoma City, a shirt I had never screwed up my courage to wear in Boston.

"Cowboy shirt," I declared. "Very popular in America."

Shan State's first fashion victim fingered the garish polyester material approvingly. "How much?" he asked.

"I'll give you 5000 baht," I replied. "And the clothes."

"Fifty-five hundred baht. And the clothes."

"Okay." I peeled off eleven Purple Kings, about $220, and took possession of nearly four carats of Burmese rubies.

I wasn't through paying the bill in Ho Mong. The guest-house proprietress materialized and requested her balance for three rooms for three additional nights: 1,800 baht. Three more Purple Kings, accompanied by a trio of orange 100-baht notes. Our new driver arrived in a white Toyota pickup that would carry us on the long detour to the Thai border. We were going nowhere until he received two thousand baht. Eight more Purple Kings vanished from my wallet. I still had a few notes in reserve, but any large bribes at the border would have to be paid in U.S. currency, American Express traveler's checks, or Burmese rubies.

"We've got to get out of here, Jay," I said. "We're hemorrhaging baht."

The sun had risen above the ridge line in the east; it was already warm enough to guarantee that the heat would soon become uncomfortable. While the truck idled, we quickly loaded our gear into the open bed. Sullivan poured a thermos of hot water left by the maid into two 1.5-liter plastic bottles.

"Think it's enough water?" he asked. "I can get more at the cafe across the street."

"Three liters is more than enough for the ride," I replied. "Barry said we're only walking about two kilometers." Casual acceptance, a by-product of the nascent confidence our stay in Ho Mong had encouraged. We had already been tested, had triumphed. Now, a scenic ride, a short walk, a hotel with hot water awaited. The jungle held powerful truths for such stupid men.

We headed north from Ho Mong, following the same bad path we had taken to the village of the Pa-O poppy farmers. Flynn and Sengjoe crowded into the cab with the driver; Sullivan and I stood in the truck bed clutching the roll bar while five Shan hitchhikers lounged merrily on our packs. The brilliant heat soon made the wondrous scenery an ordeal. We lumbered by Mae Ark, then past a fortified MTA outpost. The rough road gradually arced east and then south. A half hour beyond Mae Ark, we skirted another hilltop MTA garrison. A small settlement had sprouted in the protective shadow of the fire base.

Several hundred yards beyond the hamlet, dull lesions covered the roadside slopes. I pounded on the roof of the truck's cab to get the driver to halt, then Sullivan and I clambered downhill to a recently harvested poppy field. We had missed The Sailor's opium vision by just a few weeks. Now, everything bore the drained, gray-brown colors of death: bulbs, stems, petals. I lay back on the warm, barren earth and shot low-angle photographs of the yard-high plants against the mountains. A hot wind blew from the north and the stiff, dessicated stalks rustled like an organdy skirt. The lifeless plot occupied several acres; a half-dozen other spent fields desecrated nearby hillsides. This one mountain ridge had produced enough opium to put thousands of junkies on the nod. Further poppy-field patchwork spread on the hills across the valley.

"If I didn't have this POW mission, I'd pick up Khun Sa's offer and pursue it," Sullivan said as he surveyed the lethal landscape. "I hate drugs."

Back in the truck and on the move again, he told me one of

the reasons why. "It was around February 1971, a Saturday in base camp in Phan Rang, South Vietnam. Most of the senior officers were out in the field. My buddy, Lieutenant Frank Lorenzo, Jr., the Headquarters Company commander, was in charge; I was the duty officer. We were over at the Officer's Club playing cards when a call came in around nine o'clock: some shooting in the A Company area. We hopped in a Jeep and drove over. About twenty black G.I.s were milling around, most of 'em just regular guys having a few beers. Five or so were really riled up. They were going through the A Company area and the commander, a tough West Point prick, told them to keep it down, then allegedly leveled a weapon at some guy. That's when they all went crazy.

"Frank asked them to break it up. They surrounded him and leveled their weapons at him. I moved in to try and calm the ringleader down. These guys were gone on heroin, higher than kites. Their eyes were totally rolled back, grey and glazed. Heroin was easy to come by and pretty pure. You could get it in town or from the Vietnamese working on base. Half of them were fucking V.C."

I knew the sad, ugly story. By 1971, an estimated 10 to 15 percent of American G.I.s in Vietnam had a serious jones for high-grade heroin. Their downfall, ironically, came courtesy of the very leaders in Laos and South Vietnam they fought to keep in power. General Ouane Rattikone, the victor of the 1967 Opium War, often sent his opium from Ban Houei Sai in northwest Laos to Vientiane, where it was refined into heroin No. 4 by Hong Kong–trained chemists. This China White was then ferried to Saigon aboard South Vietnamese Air Force planes and distributed by Chiu Chao syndicates who paid squeeze to Vietnamese politicians and senior military officers in return for immunity. Hawked from stands near U.S. bases, the heroin could be mainlined or mixed with tobacco and smoked (called "as loud," the mix was less detectable than marijuana). So many strung-out G.I.s had rotated back to the States that the ranks of American junkies had nearly quadrupled between 1965 and 1972, from one hundred fifty thousand to five hundred sixty thousand addicts.

Sullivan paused for a moment as the antique memory of that night in Phan Rang came flooding back.

"I have been rocketed, been mortared, been shot at, but ironically my life was most in danger at that point in time. I had a locked and loaded, safety-off, fully automatic M-16 pointed right at my chest. I thought I could die at that point. We did some fast talking and brought out the ringleader: Dorsey. I'll never forget the name. A poor, dumb, basic kid who never should have been there. We needed to get some independent documentation on his condition so I took him to the battalion surgeon. On the way back from the dispensary, he took off. He ran into a barracks with some buddies and they started beating the shit out of a couple of white G.I.s, shut the place up, began sticking weapons out the windows. It was a hostage situation.

"We were a satellite army unit on an air force base, so Frank called the base commander. The guy went crazy. All he needed was a race riot on his base. The security police showed up, heavily armed and with dogs, and surrounded the place. There was a long stand-off, then they finally agreed to come out if Frank and I brought them out. We went in unarmed, they leveled their weapons again. We finally got 'em out, then took 'em down. When the S.P. searched them, heroin vials were just coming out of their pockets. We released most of them back to their units except for Dorsey and another ringleader. Our colonel came back the next morning and decided to release these two clowns. So they went to the arms sergeant to draw their weapons, which they leveled at the colonel. The colonel doubletalked them, then had 'em locked up. The next day I escorted them down to LBJ, Long Binh Jail, a really scary place north of Saigon. At general court martial, they got ten years hard labor. All because of this. Heroin.

"I hate the thought of this stuff going to the U.S. Maybe someday this will be eradicated. Maybe we'll have had something to do with it."

We continued driving south toward the Thai border, kicking up plumes of dust. The hills grew more unruly, the vegetation more tangled. Forests of teak, then pine. But always the stands of bamboo. Black butterflies with yellow, polka-dotted wings drifted on the breeze. Every few miles, the undergrowth would thin, confessing the presence of woodsmen living in bamboo lean-tos, surrounded by ash heaps and the detritus of subsistence life: rusting cans, sun-faded soft-drink bottles, crinkled plastic bags. The terrain forced us east, the road straining to hold a long, narrow ridge. Flynn leaned his head out the window and shouted above the clatter made by our struggling truck.

"This road is right on the border! The driver said there are sometimes Thai border police here, waiting to surprise trucks!"

On our left, untamed Burma. To our right, an upland Thai valley. Ravines scored the valley's lush slopes like the veins of a green leaf. Strips of raw mountains were stacked in the haze as far as I could see. No huts, no fields, no trails. Only this road, quite literally the borderline, running through the wilderness. Should we encounter a BPP roadblock, we would surely be arrested for unauthorized entry into the kingdom. I could think of only one escape plan: jump out the left-hand side of the truck, land in Burma, and start running. But we cleared this obscure salient of Thailand without incident and turned to the northeast, descending back into Burma, our circuitous route dictated by the arbitrary folds and peaks of the Doi Larng Range.

The trail eventually spilled into a long, narrow valley drained by a broad stream. We drove against the flow of its pristine waters, which raced west to feed the Salween. The driver plunged repeatedly through shallow fords, scattering dark sala-manders sunning on the worn, sun-warm rocks. Two hours beyond Ho Mong, we rounded a bend in the river to encounter a half-dozen men standing waist-deep in the water. They pushed a bamboo raft loaded with sand upstream to a narrow flat at the base of a steep, wooded mountain on the north bank. There, other men and women winnowed and washed the sand with fine-mesh plastic baskets and broad metal pans: gold miners. We forded the river and halted. Our driver alighted, lit a Krong Thip, began speaking with the workers. Rest stop. We dismounted, only too happy to walk solid ground after the long, convulsive ride.

"Basically," shrugged Sullivan, "we're in the middle of con-vulsive absolutely nowhere."

The mining camp, a collection of flimsy lean-tos fashioned from split-bamboo and rough pine planks, reeked of malaria and poverty. These Shan were our driver's people. In the win-ter they cut timber, Sengjoe explained. In the remaining sea-sons they panned for gold. All year was a struggle. The driver, their only lifeline to the relative riches of Ho Mong, carried away timber and gold and prayers. He returned with rice.

"He is very good in business," our guide added. He certainly had an aptitude for it. He made this grueling smuggling run to Nam Kot nearly every day. Each trip meant a new air filter. Every twenty days meant an oil change. Truck maintenance cost 2000 baht a month, and farang fares were extremely rare. We were only the third group of foreigners to enjoy this roundabout route hacked from the forest four years earlier by a Thai timber company.

"General Chavalit, the Thai interior minister, he reap all the wood profits," Sengjoe said. The influential cabinet member and leader of Thailand's New Aspiration Party was a master of playing all the angles. In December 1988, Chavalit Yong-chaiyudh had negotiated timber concessions from the cash-starved Burmese junta, then subject to an international boycott in the wake of its crackdown on the prodemocracy movement. No matter that Chavalit, whose family and close advisers reportedly held interests in Thai logging companies and had previously made lucrative timber deals with Rangoon's arch-nemesis, the Karen rebels. Two months after Chavalit signed the timber agreement, Thailand deported three hundred Burmese student refugees from its borders. Their involuntary repatriation, or *refoulement*, the elegant phrase the United Nations gave to such immoral actions, became the cost of doing business. Government or insurgent, every group in Burma had stands of teak and a critical need for hard currency. General Chavalit seemed only too happy to trade.

"The Shan people have to sell teak to these miserable people," Sengjoe complained. "The Thai cut the wood, and the Thai and the Burmese reap the profit. The Shan have to endure all this."

Our driver flicked his cigarette butt into the river. His people had heard from another passing truck that the journey to Nam Kot was safe today. We took to the road again, bearing east, shadowing the river through thick forest. Then the infernal cry of a band saw and the fresh-cut scent of old leather, a small jungle clearing with stacks of milled teak and a half-dozen Isuzu logging trucks with Thai license plates. Khun Sa's revolt required money; the Thai required teak, even the wood controlled by a hunted man. We rolled through the timber camp, then left the river valley. Once again we inched up interminable corkscrew switchbacks, our Toyota's overtaxed engine summoning cicadas to sing six thousand-rpm harmony.

The ordeal went on for another hour, broken only when we

dropped into a small upland valley holding fallow rice paddies, a company-sized MTA garrison, and the Shan village of Nam Ho. The five hitchhikers exited our truck; a trio of armed MTA soldiers took their place. In these infrequently trafficked mountains, courtesy demanded that every vehicle serve as a jitney. I surveyed the new riders outfitted with swaggering manners, dahs, and AK-47s. We moved our packs forward to allow them plenty of room. One mile and an additional five hundred feet in elevation, the road cut through acres of poppy fields. We had encountered three permanent settlements since departing Ho Mong. In every case, poppy fields and fortified MTA cantonments had also been located nearby. Protection, according to Khun Sa. Extortion, according to his critics.

The road soon turned evil. Eroded earth. Impossible grades. Hairpin turns.

"Be ready, Jay," I cautioned. "Any minute, a logging truck is going to come flying around one of these goddamn curves. It won't be a pretty sight."

"Relax," he replied. "Everybody's got the day off. The only thing keeping us alive is that it's Sunday."

———

We sat in the shade of a roadside stand in Nong Awo, a Pa-O village precisely one half-mile from the end of the earth. The driver had stopped again, to refresh his concentration and rest his overheating truck. Sun-seared hills, cleared for firewood and crops, cut into the sky around us. I drank a Sprite as hot as crankcase oil. Flynn and Sullivan skirmished with Irish jokes.

"What's the difference between an Irish wake and an Irish wedding?" asked Flynn. He waited a beat. "One less drunk."

"What's the worst possible thing on a woman's body?" countered Sullivan. "A drunken Irishman."

The pair laughed maniacally. I mopped my beaded brow,

coughed dusty phlegm, surveyed the village baking in the sun. Thirty households here—one hundred sixty people—and absolutely no prospects.

"The Pa-O people shift," Sengjoe said. "We call them drifters. The slash-and-burn business hurts forestry so much. We try to convince these people to settle down and have a paddy field for themselves. That the water system is better. But these people are so stubborn. They want to live on high ground."

This remote highland village seemed an exhausted, consumptive place. A young Pa-O man, a landless farm laborer, squatted nearby, smoking a cheroot. He wore a dirty blue shirt, soiled gray pants, an expression of dazed fatalism. Sengjoe immediately diagnosed the malady. "He's an opium addict," our guide said. "Look at the way he sits. Look at the eyes. The lips. The black fingers."

The addict managed a sleepy smile. He lived The Sailor's deadly dream. Life was a ceaseless, free fix. He tended poppies for a hilltribe farmer; he was paid in opium. He had become his own slave, had already exhausted his daily ration.

"Give him some pocket money," Sengjoe said. "He needs some more opium balls for tonight. But don't spoil him. Twenty baht is enough."

I gave the man some small Thai coins.

"He will do it morning, noon, night," Sengjoe said. "He's got twenty baht. Tomorrow it's going to be twenty-four hours of opium."

The addict sat at our wobbly table, puffed his cheroot, and tried to focus his opaque eyes on the task he would repeat at least twenty times today and every day: the opium ceremony. He gently laid his instruments on the table. A flimsy bamboo pipe. A scavenged glass jar containing fresh opium. A small wick-lamp filled with tallow. Addicts preferred the fat of buffalo or cow as a fuel over kerosene—better opium flavor. His paraphernalia were cheap, worn. He was a very heavy smoker. "He's very famous," Sengjoe said. Sarcastically. "He's the hero of opium."

The addict worked with the quick, meticulous grace of a craftsman. First he scraped the charred opium dross from his pipe; the residue still contained more than 7 percent morphine. He added the tailings to a tiny ball of *chandoo*—fresh opium that had been boiled with water, then filtered through cloth, dried, and toasted. The mixture was impaled on the end of a stylet, then heated over the wick-lamp. With numb, carbon-dark fingers, he shaped the hot gum into a small, pea-sized ball of roasted opium, then pushed the dose into the pipe bowl. He smiled, satisfied. Ritual completed, he tabled his smoldering cheroot and bent before the flame, clutching his pipe.

The opium sizzled in the greasy fire. The addict rested his head on a filthy rag, gently prodded the contents of his pipe bowl with the stylet, and inhaled deeply, purposefully. Soon he was enveloped by thick fumes that smelled of chocolate. He smiled. The human lungs possess a huge amount of surface area for absorption. The effects of opium are immediate.

"The opium goes into his lungs and he has the feeling he's a millionaire," said Sengjoe. "He loves the feeling. He won't sell this equipment, not for even one hundred dollars."

His name, the addict said, was Agka. It meant "big wise man." He hailed from Paing Pep, nearly a four-day walk away, a village west of the Salween that had the misfortune to be close to a Burmese Army garrison, where soldiers believed it was easier and cheaper to move supplies through the mountains on the backs of Pa-O slaves rather than upon pack mules.

The opium ball fizzled, spent in less than a minute. Agka began scraping the tailings from his pipe to fashion another dose. Soon, his poor Pa-O village would become a clouded memory. He would be far from the Tatmadaw soldiers who had press-ganged him into servitude more than two years before, who drove him like a bullock, who provided only bad water and worse food. They had caused the dysentery he could ease now only with the tears of the poppy.

"From that time under the Burmese, I start to smoke opium," said Agka as he smelted another ball. "I never stop. I like the feeling very much. I enjoy it."

Another young Pa-O man led off two Shan ponies loaded with opium in ivory-colored sacks lashed to an A-frame freight saddle. He was bound for a market town in a distant valley.

"The Shan are forbidden to use opium," Sengjoe said. "The Pa-O people young and old use opium as a tranquilizer and to kill pain. They plant the poppies; they take the poppies themselves. So we have a lot of problems in our society."

Agka shrugged. His eyes filled with something like desire. This was the opium hour. A half-crazed old man, another village addict, crept up to the table, eager to see his first farang. "Opium is very healthy," the old man rhapsodized. "I pray that you have health, wealth, and prosperity!" All the blessings that Agka would never know. Just twenty years old, he was a shambling, slack-jawed corpse, cursed to spend his remaining days drifting between scattered Pa-O villages, searching for poppy farmers who needed extra help and were willing to pay in opium. Agka gently placed another loaded pipe to the oily flame, then put his lips to his ruin.

"I think I'm deeply in the habit," he said.

Feeling faintly light-headed in my downwind seat, I thanked Agka for his time and backed away. I still had miles of bad road to weather and a cross-border walk that would require all of my faculties. Sengjoe also stood, snapped on his bush hat, gave Agka a parting shot.

"I'll see you in a coffin."

═══

We suffered three more hours of pernicious travel in the back of the raging truck. The rutted, broken route was devoid of vehicles or people, save for a lone pickup truck bound for Ho Mong with a squad of MTA soldiers and a few destitute peasants dozing in the tangled roadside undergrowth to escape the midday heat. To the west, mile-high peaks pushed through the blanket of vegetation, announcing the Thai-Burmese border. The air grew thick and moist; the open pine forest gradually deferred to a tangle of teak, ironwood, and creeper. We had left opium country for a malarial river valley. Beneath the jungle canopy, dense sprays of wabomyetsangye and wapyu bamboo cross-hatched the afternoon sunlight. Then the acrid smoke of a forest afire—the scent of habitation—and a blind plunge through the pall created by Shan farmers clearing the hills for *hai*, the fields of dry, upland rice. We emerged, hacking and bleary-eyed, in the hamlet of Nam Kot.

3:30 p.m. It had taken us six hours to drive perhaps fifty tortured miles.

We halted beside a stilted Shan house on the outskirts of the poor village. The border, Sengjoe told us, lay another mile to the south. The only other vehicle in town, a black Toyota pickup, idled in the yard. The truck, which belonged to the Shan State Restoration Council, had been sent from the office in Mae Hong Son. It would take us to Chiang Mai, but only after we negotiated a fare with the driver. I knew immediately that the price would be steep; the driver had brought along his wife for the chance to visit the big city. They would need spending money. The wheelman stepped from his cab, cooly surveyed the battered, dust-caked farang. This was better than hitting the Thai lottery.

"Song-phan-jet-rawy."

Twenty-seven-hundred baht. I shook my head. Nearly $120.

"Tell him too much, Sengjoe. Tell him in November we chartered a minivan from Mae Hong Son all the way to Chiang Mai for only two thousand baht."

Sengjoe relayed my argument. The driver answered animatedly.

"He says he has gotten this price before," Sengjoe related. "So this is the price."

The driver shrugged. Three farang, in Burma illegally, trying to sneak into Thailand, still more than one hundred miles from Chiang Mai? A long, desperate way from home. He had us boxed and he knew it.

"You better decide quickly," Flynn said. "This is the last bus leaving this village today."

Maybe forever. Scrawny chickens pecked the grassless yard. A grazing buffalo moaned contentedly and let loose a stream of dung in the road. From a raised building across the way, two Burmese Army prisoners leaned out a window, gawking at the farang. The Tatmadaw soldiers might be kept forever in this godforsaken hellhole. We, too, could stay indefinitely. Or we could pay. Handsomely. I pulled the remaining barter from my knapsack: a red silk tie, a Nike tank top, flowered running shorts, and two wool blankets pinched from Northwest Airlines.

"Everything here," I said, "plus two thousand baht."

The driver fingered the clothing, then finally nodded. We had a deal. My last four Purple Kings took wing, leaving me with a single 100-baht note. If we made it to Chiang Mai, I thought, this would be the best eighty dollars I ever spent. We quickly transferred our packs to the bed of the new truck. On the hike into Thailand we would carry only essentials in our boogie bags. We cut the luggage and airline tags from our knapsacks, then buried the baggage under an olive-drab tarpaulin. Nothing extraordinary could show when the truck passed through the Thai checkpoint. Camera film, micro-cassette tapes, and videotapes went beneath the driver's seat. Nothing incriminating could be carried should we be stopped on the trail.

"The truck will drop you off near the border," Sengjoe said. "You will go around the checkpoint and meet the driver on the road. No problem. Follow the trail. The guide will show you."

We bade our dignified translator goodbye and climbed into the bed of the new truck. I checked my sweat-misted wrist-watch: 4 p.m. Already *tawn yen*, evening time. A young man from the village joined us; he would lead us on the trail into Thailand. I looked him over as we sped toward the bor-der: Shan, mid thirties, wearing baggy trousers, a dirty T-shirt, dirtier sandals. Why we needed this unkempt man for a two-kilometer hike, a walk that should take us no more than half an hour, was a mystery. I kept my counsel. The guide wanted one hundred baht. I agreed to pay him the last of my money upon our rendezvous with the truck inside Thailand.

The road leveled and widened to the width of two bullock carts; the border had to be near. Huge teak logs lay scattered about a desolate field, awaiting the sawyer. The truck rounded a hill and stopped. The guide gestured toward a footpath that led south into a long, narrow valley of fallow naa wet-rice pad-dies, toward Thailand. We unloaded from the truck, then watched the vehicle fade in a cloud of dust. It's a forlorn feel-ing, watching the hard-won life of your story—notes, film, microcassettes, videotapes—disappear into the unknown. The Shan guide walked rapidly along the worn trail. We scrambled over downed tree trunks and crumbling paddy dikes to keep pace. Within five minutes, we walked gingerly across a log spanning a stream.

4:15 p.m. Thailand.

"The first time I came to Ho Mong with Bo Gritz we went this way," Flynn said. "There was no road then to camp. It took us three days on mules."

A few hundred yards into the kingdom we passed a Border Patrol Police laager site, a simple lean-to shelter of deadwood and split bamboo. Fresh BPP jungle-boot prints scalloped the muck. The guide briefly spoke with two middle-aged women, bent by time and chores, who were scrubbing clothes in the stream.

"Kawn sip naa-thii," said one of the women. Ten minutes before.

"They say the Thai sitting patrol just left to go back to camp," Flynn related. He was starting to breathe heavily in the oppressive heat.

"They are on the trail ahead of us. The next patrol will not be out until after five o'clock."

Take it slow and easy. We didn't want to run up the back of any BPP soldiers, then have to try out our cover story: we were lost trekkers who had found a local Shan kind enough to lead us back to safety. Another half mile along the trail and the odds that the BPP would buy such a story plummeted. We had stumbled upon an active poppy field. Waist-high plants spread across at least an acre of bottomland. It wasn't the ideal site for *Papaver somniferum*, which grew best along mountain slopes at higher altitudes, but the plot was thriving. Some of the plants still held white- or purple-colored petals, but most had shed their tuliplike flowers. Their bare, glaucous-green bulbs bore the fresh, longitudinal scars that were the poppy farmer's harvest hallmark. The field was active, illegal, and completely ignored by the Thai Border Patrol Police. Although the BPP was charged with the interdiction of narcotics, its soldiers passed blindly through this field on a daily basis.

We walked judiciously for another half hour, following bootprints and the stream's meander, then sat and rested on the trunk of a felled, rotting tree. In the leaden, molten heat, our shirts were wet with perspiration, our pants damp and chafing. I made a mental note for my next jungle hike: wear boxer shorts. Flynn had removed his denim shirt, revealing a loud, magenta-colored T-shirt that very nearly matched his complexion.

"A fucking numb nut," Sullivan said to me, shaking his head. "We're trying to sneak into Thailand and he's wearing a pink shirt anyone could spot from ten miles away."

Flynn leaned heavily on a sapling he had snatched for a walking stick, in the throes of an asthma attack. "Ran out . . . medicine," he gasped. "More . . . Chiang Mai."

Sullivan handed him a half-empty water bottle. Flynn gulped lustily.

"Just a few sips, Barry. It's all we have. Then it's this klong of a creek."

"We've been on this trail nearly an hour," I moaned. "This is the longest two-kilometer hike in history."

"Halfway . . . one more hill," Flynn answered.

We resumed walking; we needed to make the rendezvous with our truck before sundown. The hike grew more difficult—sucking paddy muck, clutching thickets, harassing mosquitoes. On a slippery tree-trunk bridge six feet above the rocky stream, Flynn's heavy glasses slipped from his sweating temples. We dropped into the creek bed and studied the frames, now irreparably broken in two. Our man in Thailand, wheezing as if he had a sucking chest wound, was now nearly blind. We muddled on for another quarter hour to reach Flynn's "hill"—a daunting ridge rising into the sky. A secondary path forked from the valley trail; we left the stream and began a steep, steady ascent with empty canteens. Some choice, no water or bad water, since Sullivan's filter was inside his backpack on the truck. We looked at each other, silently cursing our carelessness for not bringing more water.

As we had done on our foray into Burma, we allowed our Shan guide to walk the point, some fifteen yards ahead of us, in hopes of flushing out any BPP. Ever solicitous of his florid-faced, jungle-challenged farang customers, our pathfinder frequently turned to check our progress. He then waited until we caught up with him before resuming the walk. We would smile, slow our pace, and drop back again. Fifteen, twenty paces further along the mountain, the guide again stopped, and we had to replay the Alphonse-and-Gaston routine. In this manner, we spent nearly an hour tackling the thirty-degree incline, urging and cajoling our asthmatic, myopic, thirsty, loudly dressed friend. The banana trees and bamboo thickets of the bottomland gave way to swidden clearings choked by elephant grass and dry scrub. The slopes of the nearest mountain also bore the brown patches of hilltribe slash-and-burn cultivation, but the successive, stepped peaks still held virgin forest. In a year or two, when the soil that we walked was exhausted, the distant hills would be put to the torch.

We had climbed at least one thousand feet above the stream when we passed through a jawlike wooden gate of a hilltribe settlement of two dozen huts. The ground-level structures were fashioned of bamboo poles that held basket-weave siding of flattened split bamboo and low, rice-straw roofs with overhanging eaves.

"Akha," the guide said.

Usually the villages of this nomadic Tibeto-Burman people, who arrived in Thailand only in 1903, appeared further east, in Chiang Rai Province. But this parched, forlorn spot had somehow passed the egg-drop test. Their lives would always be a rootless, marginal struggle. The Akha, who were animists, gave water spirits a wide berth, so every day the women were forced to trek downhill to the stream, then hump heavy, brimming bamboo ewers back to the village for cooking and drinking water. Looking at the dirty children playing between fire-scorched stumps, I knew that such a precious commodity was rarely used for bathing.

The women wore silver headdresses and jackets and leggings of faded indigo and busied themselves with the recent grain harvest, flailing sheaves of mountain rice against downed logs to thresh the kernel-packed panicles. The entire village wore a fine, willow-green down of pulverized rice hulls. Sallow pigs roamed underfoot, foraging. The men were in the forest, setting controlled fires for new fields of rice, maize, and poppy. Had we been earlier, I would have insisted on halting in this village for a few hours, if only to meet the *aw shaw*; the middle-aged widower who instructed eligible girls in the art of love-making, and his female counterpart, the *mida*, a widow who revealed the mysteries of love to adolescent boys. It was impolite to pass through an Akha village without stopping, but the first blush of sunset already smeared the evening sky. There was no time to enjoy such Akha delicacies as dog soup or roasted mouse.

We struggled uphill for another half mile, skirting untethered cattle and smoldering forest until the trail finally leveled. The guide turned, smiled. The road. Even better, the truck. Best of all, the driver waving a one-liter bottle of water. We hurried, delirious with thirst and relief, to the vehicle. I pulled a sweat-sodden one-hundred-baht note from my fanny pack for the guide. I was officially broke. Flynn tipped him an extra, equally soggy, one hundred baht.

"Good," gasped Flynn, patting our pathfinder on the shoulder. "Good."

After two hours of anxiety, our relief was palpable. We had

avoided the Border Patrol Police. Our gear had escaped search and seizure. Low on water, we had hiked six miles in brutal heat and humidity, climbing nearly fifteen hundred feet. But we had made it.

Sullivan and I flopped into the bed of the truck. Our tarpaulin-covered backpacks felt as luxuriously soft as a down-filled comforter. Flynn slumped into the two-seat cab; the driver's dutiful wife joined us in the back. No time to tarry, in case a BPP vehicle patrolled this single-lane dirt road. The iron-legged guide waved, then slipped back into the forest, bound for Nam Kot. The driver gunned the Toyota's engine and we launched in a cloud of warm dust toward Chiang Mai.

The western sky held thick brushstrokes of claret, rose, and titian. Pillars of karst erupted out of the valleys, casting long shadows. Swells of sea-green jungle blazed in the luminous, vanishing light. Danger had painted the Doi Larng landscape with beauty. The aubergine-colored dusk came within minutes, and horseshoe bats wheeled from hidden mountain caves to feed on insects. Night had fallen when we stopped a few miles later to pick up two monks walking along the road. We made room in the back and the saffron-robed holy men rode silent and erect, perched on the tarpaulin until we reached the Shan village of Ban Mae La Na. When they alighted, Sullivan handed the elder sangha one of his last 100-baht notes. Money for the monk's temple; merit for us. This trip had already consumed our good fortune.

Soon the tire-crunch of dirt and pebbles vanished, replaced by the warm hum of rubber against macadam. We had arrived at Highway 1226, the outer limits of civilized transportation. A few dark, narrow miles, then the junction with Highway 1095, the main northern artery between Mae Hong Son and Chiang Mai. Remarkably, the Shan mule camp at Ban Mae Suya, the terminus we had avoided through this eight-hour ordeal by truck and foot, lay less than fifteen miles to the west. We turned east, to face a four-hour drive on devious mountain roads. With sundown, the air had grown cold. The driver's wife donned a quilted windbreaker, a red scarf, and a black woolen stocking cap and huddled in the lee against the back of the truck cab. Wearing nothing warmer than T-shirts and thin, long-sleeved shirts, Sullivan and I wedged our backpacks against the rear of the truck bed, then squirmed beneath the mildewed tarp to break the wind. Oncoming trucks became irrelevant; we had worried enough for today. No more notes, no interviews, no pictures. Only sleep . . .

An unseen hand ripped back the tarp, a faceless soldier leaned above me. A few yards away, the harsh illumination of a BPP checkpoint.

"Where you from?" the shadow asked.

"America."

"No. Last night. Where from?"

"Mae Hong Son," I lied.

"Where you go?"

"Chiang Mai."

He spoke with several BPP soldiers sitting by the small checkpoint building, smoking. We were still in the mountains, somewhere beyond Pai. "Farang, song farang."

The other soldiers laughed. Two crazy trekkers, too old to be hippies. Riding around in the back of a truck like kariang, like hilltribe bumpkins.

"Okay," our interrogator said. "Bye-bye."

We continued into the hazy night. I had expected the sky to be clear and the stars crisp at this altitude. Instead, smoke billowed from a thousand springtime swidden fires, blotting the heavens. In the distance, the hillsides glowed like embers. Highway 1095 became a hellish passage: soot and ash on the macadam, flames licking at the crumbled shoulder, thick, roiling smoke cutting visibility to near zero. For meager hilltribe plots of cabbage and corn, the borderlands would end in fire.

The harsh, cool fumes finally dissipated and the night grew balmy, scented with the sweet, loamy perfume of orchids and fresh-tilled earth. We had survived the mountains, descended into the Ping River Valley. Soon, the chainsaw whine of a tuk-tuk cut through the darkness. Chiang Mai was close. At Mae Taeng, we swung south on Highway 107, and soon found ourselves in Bangkok-style traffic, a churning mess of song thaews and cement trucks, buses and motorcycles. A congested Thai road never smelled or sounded so good.

It was after 11 p.m. when Flynn dropped us at one of the best hotels in town, a high-rise Westin so new that only a few dozen tourists occupied rooms. We shook hands with our contact, the kid from New Bedford who had delivered such improbable Asian adventure. Then Flynn went home to his wife and young children. Sore, filthy, utterly defeated, Sullivan and I stumbled into the lobby that still smelled of new furniture and fresh carpeting. The night clerk looked dubious until Sullivan rolled out the heavy artillery: his American Express platinum card. Then we were no longer dirty trekkers, merely eccentric tourists. Doors opened, porters appeared. We were whisked to a sixth-floor room fit for a pasha: fresh-cut flowers, international direct-dial telephones, a stocked minibar, showers pulsing endless streams of hot water. When we had scrubbed the sweat and dirt and grime from our bodies and donned our least-soiled clothing, we presented ourselves in the deserted dining room. The restaurant, to my dismay, could not prepare khai moat som. I ordered chicken satay; Sullivan opted for meatless spaghetti. And drinks, many drinks. Cold Singha for me, vodka with orange juice—no ice—for my relieved side-kick. We hoisted our first civilized beverages in nearly a week. A toast was in order.

"To my good buddy, Saint Jude," Sullivan proposed.

"To Absolut," I replied, clinking his glass. "And Cipro."

We had made it back from Burma, from the moon, from the dragon's lair. I had my story. Sullivan had his answer. I slept heavily that night, without the burden of dreams.

EPILOGUE

In early 1995, I flew to the Land of the Big Tree, SLORC-controlled Burma. After the unfiltered, amphetamine bustle of Bangkok, Rangoon seemed nearly comatose, too listless to erect a single high-rise building or scheme of impossible traffic. Polite black marketeers and a pervasive torpor awaited beyond bored bureaucrats at Mingaladon Airport. This is monsoon country, a land of two seasons: dry and hot, and wet and hot. The alleged "cool season"—also dry and hot—is a cruel rumor fed to gullible Westerners. So, too, is the advice of the guidebooks to the country: bring duty-free Scotch (preferably Johnny Walker Red Label) and cigarettes (always 555 State Express Filter Kings) to exchange for kyat. My plane was filled with the duty-free bags of tourists who had heeded this counsel. They imagined windfall profits in Rangoon. They were rudely disappointed. Burma's black marketeers had a surfeit of Scotch and cigarettes. Crafty traders, they knew the prices of duty-free items in the few foreign cities with air service to Burma, and underbid accordingly. Tourists who paid eleven dollars for a liter of Johnny Walker Red in Dhaka, Bangladesh, walked away with one thousand kyat, the equivalent of ten dollars in Rangoon. I kept my bottle of Famous Grouse for social tippling, my carton of 555s for small bribes and favors.

Fern-fingered rain trees, buckled sidewalks, and shabby colonial-era buildings line the route into the city, an aging dowager that clings to its fading beauty and lost promise. Only the towering, gilded spire of Shwedagon Pagoda, blinding in the afternoon light, breaks the horizon. Before World War II, Burma had been the pearl of the Orient, the world's leading rice exporter and a regional center for business that overshadowed Singapore and Bangkok. But that had been before General Ne Win's mad reign.

A Burmese acquaintance of mine cited a parable taught by U Uttara, a dissident Buddhist monk now living in England, to explain his tragic country. In Benares, India, went the tale, there had once been a very devout man cursed with a scoundrel for a son. When the old man died, so great was his merit that he went to heaven and became king of the angels. The son soon dissipated his inheritance, lavishing money on women, drink, and games of chance. The old man felt sorry for his destitute son and came down from heaven to give him an *atesah thah ya-owe*—a magic pot for all wishes. But the young man would not change his dissolute ways. He would drink, then toss the pot to the sky, catch it, then cavalierly toss it again. Life was all a great game. The old man warned his son, but the talk fell on deaf ears. The son continued to drink, then toss the pot until finally, inevitably, the pot was dashed to pieces.

Wasn't Burma like the magic pot? Ne Win had squandered his nation's riches, toyed with a great treasure. Burma was at its breaking point. Power was in the wrong hands, in the clutch of thieves. Infrastructure—railroads, highways, schools, clinics—went neglected as the military consumed at least one third of the annual budget. Fisheries, forests, fields, all were plundered to underwrite the swelling martial force, the largest standing army in Southeast Asia, that propped up a brutal kleptocracy.

"In engineering we learn that 'k' equals constant," a sad, university-educated man told me in Burma. Desperation and disillusion led him to talk to strangers; fear of government retribution will leave him anonymous. "SLORC would like to be 'k'—to be the constant. They have sampled the tastes and the flavors of the entire country. They know what tastes good and what tastes bad. They go to inspect the gem mines at Mogok. . . ." His voice trailed into disdain. He opened his palm. "Tea money is not enough for them."

In 1934, George Orwell had set *Burmese Days*, his early, anticolonial novel, in this resplendent jewel of the British Raj. Sixty years on, Burma is an oppressive, joyless place, an appropriate setting for Orwell's grim, final novel, *1984*. The very name of the ruling junta—the State Law and Order Restoration Council—reeks of Newspeak. And SLORC invites the Big Brother comparisions. To gather information on its own citizens, the generals created a pervasive internal security apparatus, the dreaded Directorate of Defense Services Intelligence. The state-owned English-language newspaper, *The New Light of Myanmar*, plays stories in inverse proportion to their news value. On the day I arrived, the entire front page of *The New Light* was devoted to the urgent news that SLORC chairman Than Shwe had played in the Tatmadaw golf tournament. Major international stories, except for those about the civil war in Yugoslavia, were buried in the back pages. As a lesson against federalism, the paper prominently features stories about the Balkan conflict, intimating that any accommodation of Burma's ethnic minorities would lay the groundwork for similar strife.

Throughout the country, hectoring SLORC billboards, such as the sign hung between the ionic columns of the Information and Public Relations Department, constantly reminded the people of the junta's selfless altruism:

NON-DISINTEGRATION OF THE UNION OUR CAUSE!
NON-DISINTEGRATION OF NATIONAL SOLIDARITY
   OUR CAUSE!
CONSOLIDATION OF NATIONAL SOVEREIGNTY OUR
   CAUSE!

The fading sun bathed the ancient stone façades an ochre
hue and gave curbside pools of betel juice the color of kiln-
fired bricks. On the ground-floor galleries, book vendors
packed their stocks of Burmese comics, already wrinkled in
the humidity, their moldy, fifty-year-old British pamphlets,
and their mint-condition stacks of post-coup apologia. Despite
their voracious reading habits—the high literacy rate had
very nearly cost Burma its United Nations–designated "least-
developed nation" status—no Burman seemed moved to buy
toadying books such as Naing-Ngan's *The Conspiracy of Treason-
ous Minions Within Myanmar and Traitorous Cohorts Abroad*. Free-
lance guides and moneychangers hovered outside the Strand
Hotel, armed with letters of recommendation and damp wads
of kyat in bewildering denominations.

Visitors saw the renovated, three-hundred-dollar-a-night
Strand, the sedans purring along the wide boulevards, the new
stores stocked with Japanese electronics as proof of SLORC's
market reforms, but blood money also fuels Burma's modest
economic growth. According to human-rights activists, SLORC
commanders extort immense sums from rural villages, then launder the cash through the Union of Myanmar Economic Holding
Co., an army-owned firm with huge farming and financial interests, or through family members in Rangoon who invest the
lucre in small businesses. Without SLORC connections and
access to hard currency, life in Burma is a constant struggle
against pervasive repression and mounting inflation.

In the wide, empty street fronting the Myanmar Port

Authority, a restaurateur arranged the low tables and wooden stools of his temporary, nocturnal cafe. Soon the warm river air carried the fragrance of tea, cheroots, and candles, the low talk of serious, disillusioned men forced to mark time and play checkers with worn bottle caps.

=====

Jet lag and campylobacter, a gastrointestinal bacteria I blamed on a meal of curried mutton and pickled mango, laid me low the next morning. I didn't have Sullivan along to hound me about my gone-native diet, and I paid dearly. For the rest of my two-week stay in Burma I suffered recurrent nausea, chills, and diarrhea amid some of the most wondrous scenery on earth. I gobbled multivitamins, Lomotil, Cipro, to no avail. And so I drifted through Burma, condemned to feverish dreams.

To see the country, I fled the capital. The night train to Mandalay eased from Rangoon Station at precisely 5 p.m.; for all of its considerable faults, SLORC—like Mussolini in Italy—made the railways run on time. The departure offered no grand views of Rangoon, only the backsides of shabby suburbs and impoverished satellite towns where men lounged in the portals of salvaged-wood shanties and women wrung *longyis* in brown, putrid tidal creeks. The living conditions had been better in Khun Sa's remote jungle bastion. On lots strewn with corn husks and banana leaves, spirited children played *chinlon*, using elegant kicks and delicate head taps to keep aloft a small rattan ball. Then the slums gave way to fallow rice fields where gaunt cattle foraged on rice stalks beneath the gaze of racket-tailed treepies clinging to power lines, their long, flared tails like oars dipped in dark oil.

Roving vendors squeezed between the lower-class passengers crowded on the floor of the upper-class car, selling beer, paperback novels, and fried sparrows—high-fat, no-merit birds. After a riotous sunset daubed the rising moon the color of copper ore, the train ate up the dark, empty fields for hours. Its slow, rhythmic progress was broken by whistlestops in darkened towns that harkened Burma's storied past. Pegu, the thirteenth-century capital of Lower Burma and site of Shwe-mawdaw Pagoda, a golden *chedi* to rival Shwedagon. Toungoo, the cornerstone of the Second Burmese Empire that overran Southeast Asia during the sixteenth century. Pyinmana, where a dispute over a shipment of teak had escalated into the Third Anglo-Burmese War, a succinct 1885 campaign that brought all of Upper Burma, including Shan State, into the British fold.

Mandalay. The name conjured the romance and nostalgia of the East and of empire but delivered only heat, dust, and the distinctive aromas of a police state: gasoline and fresh paint from a sprawling Tatmadaw motor pool, old leather from flat-cars piled with newly felled teak, fresh excrement and cold ashes from neighborhoods of the disenfranchised. Once, in the time before the British, Mandalay had been the center of a small, arrogant universe ruled by the Arbiter of Existence. The symbol of that faded glory, and of the cruelty that haunted the national character, was Mandalay Palace. In 1857, King Mindon ordered a new capital on a sun-fried plain east of the Irrawaddy River. Within two years, thousands of slaves fulfilled his decree, building a moated citadel of four square kilometers. As further protection, Mindon's astrologers ordered that fifty-two people be buried alive beneath the massive brick battlements. The spirits of these *myosade* could not prevent the inner complex of teak reception halls, throne rooms, and consort apartments from going up in flames in March 1945 during fighting between the Japanese and advancing Allied forces.

After decades of standing empty, SLORC had decided to rebuild and beautify the palace in time for 1996, which had been designated "Visit Myanmar Year." The eastern and southern stretches of the moat had already been dredged of nearly 140 years of detritus and refilled. The fortress walls were decorated with gigantic SLORC banners:

TATMADAW AND THE PEOPLE, COOPERATE AND CRUSH ALL THOSE HARMING THE UNION
THE TATMADAW SHALL NEVER BETRAY THE NATIONAL CAUSE

Careful replicas of the corkscrewed watchtower and the throne hall, with its gabled, seven-tiered *thuyma* roof, now vaulted toward the cloudless sky. Along the western wall, beneath crenalated ramparts and wooden pavilions, hundreds of workers repointed the stone-and-concrete revetment and scooped muck out of the drained moat. My guide said that "murderers and thieves" performed the stoop work. If he spoke the truth, Mandalay had an astounding crime rate. Closer scrutiny revealed a motley work crew: uniformed soldiers, prisoners wearing white, jailhouse-issue shirts, and ordinary civilians clad in longyis and dirty T-shirts who had "volunteered" as corvées. The alternative to this unpaid labor, from which military families were exempt, was a fine of two hundred kyats—the equivalent of two black-market dollars and well more than the official daily working wage.

Many of the prisoners had been jailed and convicted of petty crimes, such as violating curfew or, if they came from out of town, failing to register with local authorities, an irate local told me over dinner. Each domicile, he explained, carried a document that listed the names of all household occupants, their distinguishing physical characteristics, and their national registration certificate numbers. The specialty of the local police was late-night head counts.

"And if there are discrepancies?" I asked.

"Six months in jail and a three-thousand-kyat fine," he replied.

I wondered how he felt about foreigners coming to such a country on holiday.

"It is good," he said, "and bad. Tourists who bother to look and speak get to know the situation from the Burmese people. The bad thing is that not much money goes to the people. It all goes to the government and the military." He paused to spit a crimson gob of betel juice into a cup. "They don't care if you come or not. They're doing the drug trade with the Chinese and the Thai. They have very good money. All the drugs to New York City are coming from Burma."

Laundered through a camouflage of real-estate and business ventures, the drug money has reshaped Mandalay into the southernmost city of Yunnan Province. In the urban area south of Mandalay Palace, new Chinese enterprises line 80th Street. The latest edition to the cityscape, four-story Zego Market, which boasts the only escalator in Upper Burma, is stuffed with cheap Chinese goods, from clothing and cosmetics to bicycles and motor scooters. The food stalls are piled high with Chinese produce.

"We used to export to China: watermelons, apples, mangoes," the Burman told me. "Now we import from China: watermelons, apples, mangoes. The Chinese are the cause of the trouble. Very soon, Burma will be swallowed by the Chinese."

Chinese commercial domination had bred local resentment. In September 1993, a minor traffic accident in Mandalay had sparked a huge riot after the perpetrator, an ethnic Kokang Chinese, tried to use his SLORC connections to intimidate his Burmese victim.

"Development is all drug-related," the man continued. "The Burmese want to know why the authorities aren't catching and arresting the Chinese. They arrest us for petty crimes—staying out after ten o'clock, not reporting visitors—while the Chinese are dealing drugs. It is a joint-venture scandal between the army and the Chinese."

The chaw of betel had ceased to bob in his cheek. He grew quiet.

"We're in the middle of nowhere. This is a Buddhist country. We don't believe in killing. Not killing humans, not animals, not even an ant. Yet SLORC shoots people like dogs. We are living hand-to-mouth. There are no jobs. We can't overthrow the army. They are too powerful. We have no arms, no ammunition. We can't fight against guns. We die in despair."

The thousands of temples, monuments, and shrines that crowd Pagan went up in a two-century spasm of piety, atonement, and masonry that began in the mid eleventh century during the reign of Anawrahta, founder of the First Burmese Empire. None of these ancient edifices haunts the soul like the modest Manuha Temple and its "jailed" Buddhas. Temple construction began about 1059, underwritten not by Anawrahta, but by his royal prisoner, Manuha. Once the ruler of Thaton, a Mon kingdom along the Andaman Sea, Manuha had unwisely rebuffed a request by Anawrahta, a fresh convert to Buddhism, for a copy of the holy *Tripitaka* scriptures. Enraged by Manuha's refusal, Anawrahta had marched his army several hundred miles south to Thaton and laid siege until Manuha surrendered his capital. Anawrahta took possession of the holy books and the entire population of Thaton, who were herded back to Pagan to fulfill his vision of a new center of Thereveda Buddhism.

Amid a grove of jacaranda trees and coconut palms in the

small lacquerware village of Myinkaba, Manuha built the temple that became a metaphor for his miserable exile: a trio of huge Buddha images, uncomfortably constrained in small rooms by massive, whitewashed walls. Two of the somber figures held sitting positions, a pose the Burmese called *Tinmyinkwe*, accentuating the protruding torsos meant to express Manuha's heartache. The third statue took the uncommon *Shinbinthalyaung*, or "witnessing the earth," form of the reclining Buddha. The Buddha figure stretched more than fifty feet, his red, giant lips pursed in a beatific smile as he entered Nirvana. All life was suffering; only death brought cessation from pain, escape from incarceration.

After sundown had bathed the brickwork of Pagan, foreigners gathered at the bar of the lone tourist-class facility in the archeological zone to discuss temples: the terra-cotta tilework of Mingalazedi, the masterful masonry of Dhammayangyi, the view of sunset from atop the fifth terrace of Shwesandaw.

"Hellohello."

A bar girl's greeting, but for the childish voice. A Burmese girl, no older than ten, hovered below the raised deck of the bar and practiced her new skill—begging—on the tourists. It might have been the only talent she knew: one third of Burma's children do not attend school; one half of those who do attend never finish primary grades. Poverty, the cost of books, the demands of farming, the threat of war, all encourage truancy.

"Present," the girl whispered shyly, standing on tiptoe to extend a jasmine bud and a small block of thanaka through the balustrade of the deck. "Present."

I reluctantly accepted the sweet flower and the chalky cosmetic. The girl smiled and held out her hand.

"Present," she demanded.

I rummaged through my knapsack, gave her a red-ink Bic

pen. She accepted, although clearly disappointed. She wanted a worthwhile trinket or money, even kyats.

"Mother," she said. "Come see mother."

"No."

"Come," she persisted, pointing toward a dark bank of acacias. "Five minute. Walk. Bring T-shirt. Stay with mother."

"No," I said, offering a black-ink pen. "No stay with mother."

But she was already gone, clutching another flower and walking in the deck's shadows toward another tourist. I left the hotel by foot, bound for Ananda Temple, where Buddhist pilgrims were in the midst of a three-week festival. The road through the ruins was cloaked in eerie, empty silence, save for the clopping footfalls of distant horse-drawn carts. The construction of Pagan's fired-brick temples nearly a millennium earlier had denuded the countryside and permanently altered the regional climate. The arid earth now nurtured little more than acacia trees, brambles, and sandburs. Gawdawpalin Temple rose from the spare, sandy landscape, black and ominous in the moonlight. I swept my flashlight in half-arcs ahead of my route, looking for snakes that might be basking upon the still-warm pavement. A dark car traveling in my direction slowed beside me.

"Where you go?" the driver asked.

"Ananda."

"We go the same way. Please."

A back door opened. Two shadows in the front seats.

I entered the vehicle, gripping the Swiss Army knife in my pocket.

"Don't be afraid," the driver said. "We are honest Burmese."

They let me off a mile later, just beyond Sarabha Gateway. The place buzzed with the chatter of food vendors and dry-goods merchants, the discordant tones of a *pwe* musical. Behind the temporary encampment stood serene, nine-hundred-year-old Ananda Temple, its whitewashed walls and gilded, one-hundred-sixty-foot-tall banana-bud spire flickering in the festival lighting. Ananda's patron, King Kyanzittha, a son of Anawrahta, had been so impressed with the design and crafts-manship of the low, elegant structure that he ordered the ritual execution of its architect upon the temple's dedication in 1090. Royalty knew no higher compliment. The usual contingent of reliquary merchants, florists, and men with cheeping cages of merit-making sparrows sat on the periphery, taking stock of the day's business.

I soon tired of the pwe and wandered through a bazaar bursting with Chinese-made cookware, bolts of cotton fabric, toys, tools, and cheap baseball caps carrying American iconography: Camaro Z28, Navy SEALS, Chicago Bulls. I bought a bundle of fifty cheroots for twenty-two kyats, just twenty cents, and headed for an outdoor restaurant across the road to enjoy a green cigar and a lukewarm Tiger Beer. The courteous driver who had delivered me to Ananda sat alone at a table beneath the sulphur-yellow trunk of an acacia tree, smoking. He saw me, motioned me over. I sat and ordered two Singaporean beers. Although Mandalay had a brewery, it was impossible to find a restaurant that stocked anything but imported beer.

"Have you enjoyed the temples?" he asked.

"Amazing," I replied. "In Europe, you see maybe one or two cathedrals in a city. In Pagan, it's like having hundreds of cathedrals together."

"From the eleventh century to thirteenth century, Pagan was a Golden Age," he said. "Sixty thousand people. Today, it is like a Stone Age."

We sat silently for a while, drinking beer. He leaned forward, grabbed my forearm, whispered conspiratorally. "We are waiting for a new government." He surveyed the customers at other tables, then spoke again. "We are all hiding behind something."

His dark eyes seemed clouded with regret and alcohol. Without prompting, he recited his army serial number, told me he once worked for SLORC. "You have to understand what I was," he said firmly. "I would like to talk to you later. There are many spies here."

I paid the tab and we walked out to Sarabha Gateway to stand under the whitewashed trunks of a stand of neem trees. Beyond the portal guarded by a pair of nat spirits, Lord of the Great Mountain and his sister, Lady Golden-Face, had stood Old Pagan, a home to nearly five thousand people until 1990.

"I was born in this village," said the driver. He gestured toward the empty, sandy stretch of ground. "They moved us for nothing. We lost everything."

In a decision that pleased only archeologists, SLORC had razed Old Pagan, a thriving village of tourist-oriented shops, restaurants, and guest houses that had grown amid the ruins. More than one thousand families were relocated three miles away to New Pagan, to scratch out a living from small, barren plots of a former peanut field far from the tourist trade. The driver turned away. In the moonlight, I could see the tracks of the tears streaming down his dusty cheeks.

"You must understand what I was," he repeated.

It was nearly ten o'clock, a late night by Burmese standards. The pwe had concluded, and festival merchants were covering their stalls. A few bird men were preparing to sleep under the stars. If I wanted to build some last-minute merit, I could turn loose a caged sparrow for the cost of a few kyats. There was no act of charity to set free a people imprisoned by their own government. I returned to Ananda and dickered with a *trishaw* driver. We settled on the exhorbitant sum of thirty kyats, then rode through the gloom toward Sarabha Gateway. The distraught veteran suddenly appeared on the roadside, walking towards us. He extended a moonlit arm; I shook his hand as my driver pedaled past. It was a proper introduction and a sad farewell to a guilty, bitter man.

That night, the fever taunted my dreams. The beautiful, dessicated blonde of my Ho Mong visions lay upon a bed. Another woman sat on the edge of the mattress, administering a heroin injection with a gesture that seemed almost a caress. I leaned forward, intent on begging her to stop feeding her fatal habit. Instead, I kissed her lips.

═════

The road to Taunggyi, the capital of Shan State, rose beyond the rail-junction town of Thazi, following the kinking folds of Highway 4 up a narrow river valley, hemmed by ever-lusher, ever-darkening jungle. The air cooled and freshened, and Burmese pines and Chinese-made army transport trucks appeared in profusion. The smells and sights of Indian country. The road leveled and straightened beyond the old hill-station of Kalaw, and the terrain held the character of the myelat, the "middle land" of rolling downs that extended toward the Salween River more than one hundred miles to the east.

This road was passable until the great river, my betel-chewing driver said, then turned bad—very bad. In the early 1980s, he had spent four years coaxing trucks through the mountains from Taunggyi to Tachilek, four hundred miles to the southeast. A one-way trip was a five-day ordeal along bad tarmac and impossible grades. Trucks always rode in armed convoys of several dozen vehicles, a necessary precaution against the bandits and warlords who roamed the mountains. The land and its proud people did not embrace the Burmese.

"They believe they are living in Shan country, not Burma," a Burman had told me. "They call it Shan *pyi*. Shan land. They are very proud to say they lived under the saophas."

The deeper the passage into this restive region, the more plentiful became the SLORC billboards that warned against any notions of a separate Shan State:

ANYONE WHO TRIES TO BREAK THE UNION IS OUR ENEMY. WE WILL STRIVE FOR PERPETUITY OF THE UNION

NEVER HESITATING, ALWAYS READY TO SACRIFICE BLOOD AND SWEAT, IS THE TATMADAW

ONLY WHEN THERE IS DISCIPLINE WILL THERE BE PROGRESS

Not unlike Mae Hong Son, Taunggyi was the official end of the line for outsiders. The ridges to the east held dacoits, rebel armies, Tatmadaw press-gangs. The eastern military region of the Tatmadaw was headquartered here, but the lowland Burmese were in the minority, outnumbered by the Shan, the Intha who lived on nearby Inle Lake, and the Pa-O and Palaung tribesman settled in the surrounding tumble of purplish mountains. In the swirl of the talaat, sun-darkened faces bore a patina of suspicion that came with decades of Burmese occupation. Old men still wore baggy gon trousers, not the wraparound Burmese longyi, and defiant turbans.

This land once belonged to the saopha of Yaunghwe, who ruled from a town along the north shore of Inle Lake for more than six centuries. The prince's teak palace now stood empty. The last Sunset King, Sao Shwe Thaik, died in military custody in 1962. The Ministry of Culture owned the property, now called the Nyaung Shwe Haw Museum, and operated the eighty-year-old building with the neglect and penury that had characterized Burmese treatment of the Shan. I found the palace in a forlorn state, its foundation riddled with cracks and fissures, its galleries slumping in terminal fatigue. Its rare, seven-tiered thuyma roof, a design found only atop royal buildings and the holiest of temples, was a rusted shambles.

The curator of this crumbling cenotaph materialized to open the padlocked palace door only after a lengthy search. Inside, coils of barbed wire were strewn across the floor of a large reception hall. A water-stained painting, depicting a Shan royal barge on Inle Lake, leaned against a massive teak pillar decorated with the antlers of a deer. The creaking stairs led to a room that held a few puckered photographs of Sao Shwe Thaik and a selection of ancestral chairs, howdahs, and litters. The assembly hall, the throne room, and the levee hall were silent and barren, alive only in fading photos and in the wrinkled memories of old men in baggy pants. The Burmanization of Shan State would come like the ocean tide, slowly, inexorably.

In the evening I ate dinner with a Burman in a near-empty Chinese restaurant overlooking a foul-smelling canal that drained into Inle Lake. Out on the water, the fishermen rowed home in unique fashion, standing in flat-bottom boats, using their arms as fulcrums and pushing long, single oars with sweeping leg strokes through clumps of water hyacinth. Swallows skimmed the dead-calm surface, feeding on insects. Our dinner conversation eventually turned to the forbidden subject of Burmese politics, as it often did when there was plenty of Chinese beer and few eavesdroppers.

"SLORC does not hold to Buddhist doctrine," my companion said in a low voice. "Abstain from evil, do good works, purify the mind. SLORC does what is good for them. They are not truly Buddhist people. In 1988, they violated the sanctity of life. SLORC should understand who is telling lies. They promised to hand over the power when there is peace, but it is difficult to hope. It is as if you are sitting in a very comfortable chair. You don't want to get up. SLORC is sitting in such a chair."

The chair was a palanquin, borne on the shoulders of a gentle people burdened with spiraling inflation, benumbed by constant oppression. The devoutly Buddhist Burmese looked to the next life for salvation, making merit to improve their destiny, earning a few black-market dollars from tourists, then purchasing gold leaf for a temple or buying a sparrow's freedom.

"We have to close up our mouths, our ears, our eyes," my dinner companion continued. "We have to wait for one day." He smiled thinly. "According to Buddhist doctrine, nothing is permanent. Everything is subject to decay. Even SLORC."

I said nothing. What could I tell him of America's commitment to Burma? Most Americans couldn't locate Burma on a world map, let alone speak of the country's complicated history or of the plight of The Lady. Would I tell him that his country was of almost no concern to U.S. policymakers? That even if there was a groundswell of American support for the democracy movement, that Washington was loathe to become involved in another quagmire in Southeast Asia? I only nodded my assent. Perhaps SLORC, corrupt and sated, would finally alienate the Burmese, a people with a famously high tolerance for dictatorial rule.

"I have a question for you," the Burman said.

"Fire away," I replied. After two weeks in the country, I felt comfortable articulating my impressions about Burma. Ne Win, SLORC, or Daw Aung San Suu Kyi, I was ready to provide an American perspective. The man leaned across the dining table.

"There is one thing I would like you to tell me. Michael Jackson—he or she?"

Close to a year later came Khun Sa's stunning news: the warlord had stepped down from the Shan State Restoration Council, crafted an amnesty deal with the Burmese, and retired from drug trafficking and ethnic revolution. The development took all but Khun Sa's closest confidants by surprise. Through the spring and early summer of 1994, his Mong Tai Army had fought the Burmese to a virtual standstill in Shan State. In May, his forces had blown up a reservoir dike outside of Tachilek, severing the Golden Triangle town's water supply. SLORC retaliated with air strikes on MTA positions in the area, causing refugees to flee into Thailand. Although casualties to both parties reached into the hundreds, there was little notice of the battles, beyond brief wire-service reports, in the Western press. In a departure from past doctrine, Khun Sa began far-reaching mobile guerrilla operations the following year. In March 1995, the MTA destroyed Tatmadaw installations in Tachilek, then melted across the Sai River into Thailand. The following month, MTA saboteurs staged a late-night raid on a lumber mill south of Mandalay. Hoping that the projection of force would impress SLORC, he threatened further urban attacks if the Burmese Army, which was preparing to launch a post-monsoon assault on Ho Mong, threatened his headquarters.

The decisive blow against Khun Sa, however, came from within his own ranks. During the summer rains of 1995, hundreds of soldiers of the MTA 16th Brigade based in northern Shan State broke with him. The mutineers complained that the Shan struggle for independence had been overshadowed by Khun Sa's preoccupation with drug trafficking and his promotion of ethnic Chinese to key organizational positions. The breakaway force renounced the MTA and adopted a new name, the Shan State National Army, and took a new leader, Major Karn Yod, a Khun Sa protege and one of the movement's best political organizers and tacticians. The MTA field commander, Sao Kan Zet, was dispatched across the Salween to persuade Karnyod to return. Instead, hundreds of troops in Sao Kan Zet's escort deserted to the breakaway faction. In Ho Mong, the Shan intellectuals and armchair revolutionaries who had long questioned Khun Sa's ethnic credentials became openly critical of their half-Shan, half-Chinese commander. They lobbied for a realignment of power. They wanted collective governance, not a supreme leader. Khun Sa should remain in the background, but still underwrite the Shan movement.

On November 22, on the tenth and final day of a merit-making festival to celebrate the completion of a new pagoda in Mong Mai, Khun Sa formally announced his retirement from the Shan State Restoration Council. The MTA defections and his subsequent failure to generate political credibility and support among Shan nationalists had been too great a loss of face. "It is as painful to me as if somebody was cutting out my heart," Khun Sa said. "But the time has come for me to finish." He would become a humble farmer, he told associates, and spend his retirement raising livestock and growing vegetables.

It was expected that Khun Sa would continue to wield power from behind the scenes, as he had after relinquishing political control of the Shan independence movement to his critics in 1992 and 1993. But the old warlord sensed the walls closing in around him. His tax revenues had declined as an increasing percentage of the heroin trade was smuggled through China via territory controlled by warlords with SLORC cease-fire agreements. The Tatmadaw and the Wa were preparing for a massive, two-front assault on MTA positions. At the urging of the DEA, the Thai had decided to step up border security, making it more difficult and expensive to resupply Ho Mong. And the Shan patriots had forced him from power. Khun Sa's hurt was immense: he had built Ho Mong from nothing, had made a name for Shan State in the press, then had been cast aside. The fight of the Shan would no longer be his fight. He would make a separate peace with the Burmese. He revealed himself to be, ultimately, a survivor.

After more than a month of secret, back-channel negotiations conducted by his uncle, Khun Saeng, with top Burmese leaders, SLORC battalions entered Ho Mong in early January 1996 without a shot being fired in anger. Khun Sa and senior SLORC commanders signed a peace agreement, then raised glasses of whiskey in a toast. Giving up was painful, he reasoned, but the only other course would have been further bloodshed. "Now it is up to the Shan people to determine if what I did was right or wrong," he said in a statement.

Once again, Khun Sa had demonstrated a capacity to confound: he would become a private, wealthy, legitimate businessman. The warlord undoubtedly had some guarantee of government amnesty, for the Burmese Army would never have taken Ho Mong without heavy fighting. Sources close to the General said he would be allowed to keep his city-state, to take commissions on timber and mining agreements in southern Shan State, and to retain seventy-five hundred soldiers. The MTA would become a government-sanctioned militia in the fight against the new opium villains, the Wa. Ho Mong would become a district of Loi Kaw Province, administered by SLORC and MTA officials.

The surprise agreement allowed SLORC to claim it had driven the world's most notorious druglord from the business on the eve of "Visit Myanmar Year." The foreign community would howl in indignation, but it was unlikely that Khun Sa would be sent abroad for the druglord trial of the century, United States of America v. Chang Chi-fu. For one thing, Burma had no extradition treaty with the United States. For another, Khun Sa had too much damning information about too many of SLORC's top leaders. It was to their advantage to keep him in Burma, despite a two-million-dollar bounty offered by American authorities. Khun Sa was said to be particularly close to Lieutenant–General Maung Aye, the Burmese Army Commander in Chief who also headed the eastern military region. While the MTA skirmished with the Tatmadaw, Khun Sa had paid Maung Aye five thousand dollars a month since 1992, according to MTA officers.

In early March, Khun Sa took a villa near Ne Win on Inya Lake, Rangoon's most fashionable suburb, and began organizing gem factories in the capital and developing trading centers in Tachilek. If I knew how I would have been treated by the Burmese, he jokingly told Flynn, I would have given up a long time ago. While Khun Sa shuttled between Rangoon and Ho Mong by helicopter, the Shan nationalists were forced to flee into hiding or to Thailand. They angrily fingered Khun Sa for the stunning collapse of their movement. But these overconfident patriots, who had chased Khun Sa from power in the belief that they could sustain the fight, also had themselves to blame. Some view Khun Sa's abdication as an opportunity to rebuild the Shan movement anew—without the taint of drugs or the force of Khun Sa's personality. Karn Yod merged his Shan State National Army with another former MTA group, the Shan State Army, to create a force of eight thousand men. They will carry the SSA banner, for the time being.

Khun Sa's "capture" briefly disrupted the drug trade until the Wa boosted production at their heroin refineries along the Thai border. After the weather-weakened harvest of 1994, the poppy fields yielded a near-record crop in 1995. The latest U.S. State Department report paints a grim picture of Burma. The few drug seizures by Burmese police target low-level dealers; the heroin warlords, legitimized by SLORC as "leaders of national races," enjoy "complete autonomy" in their private fiefdoms. "The drug trade in Shan State continues virtually unchecked," according to the State Department.

———

Sengjoe plans to retire to Thailand and open a tour company specializing in day-trip tours of Ho Mong, "the last rebel outpost" of Shan State. If any Shan gets the tour concession, it will be Sengjoe, whose surviving daughter from his first marriage is now married to Number One. Doctor Sai Yiseng, the veterinarian, moved to Rangoon with the General to oversee the gem business.

Lord and Lady Brocket will never spend a night in the costly Shan replica of their English manor. The couple divorced acrimoniously in December 1994. Two months later, Lord Brocket was arrested on a fraudulent, £4.5-million claim he made on four classic cars he said had been stolen from his Hertfordshire estate in the spring of 1991. The investigation had been assisted by Barry Flynn, who said he contacted English authorities when he learned that his cousin, Rick Furtado, and Lord Brocket were trying to use his contacts to sell the cars in the Far East. In December 1995, Lord Brocket pleaded guilty to insurance fraud; he is currently serving a five-year prison sentence. The M.P.'s empty Shan villa became a showroom for the General's haute couture shoe enterprise and a house for visiting VIPs.

Au Cheng has tried to put his mercenary ways behind him. He sings American country-and-western music in Chiang Mai restaurants, and polishes jade in Khun Sa's Chiang Mai gem factory. Monsoon rains flooded northern Thailand in 1994 and 1995, but Keutsada "Noi" Panyatipaya has rebuilt his restaurant along the banks of the Ping River. His fried cashews remain exquisite. Mook Keaw Kam and his wife live in Chiang Mai with their daughter, born in December 1994, one year after their marriage. With no external-relations department to represent, Khernsai Jaiyen resigned from the MTA and moved to northern Thailand, where he works for a Shan human-rights group. The fate of Sai Ching and other young recruits of the Noom Suk Harn is unclear. Hundreds of the boy soldiers were reportedly left homeless in the wake of Khun Sa's brokered peace with Rangoon.

Somwang Oonman, the head of the Shan State Restoration Council's office in Mae Hong Son, was arrested in November 1994 during Operation Tiger Trap, a roundup that coincided with the Bangkok visit of DEA chief Thomas Constantine. The agency termed Somwang a senior lieutenant in Khun Sa's drug-trafficking organization and requested his extradition to the United States. Senior Thai officials, however, characterize Somwang as "little known."

With his ever-fluctuating status in Thailand, Flynn moved his wife and children to New Bedford, Massachusetts, in the fall of 1994. He continues to split his time between the United States, Shan State, and northern Thailand, selling Mogok rubies and Kachin jade and trying to interest investors in the wondrous natural resources of Shan State.

In the unlikely event that the "Prince of Death" is to be brought to American justice, it will not be by Catherine E. Palmer. The Dragon Lady left the D.A.'s office in 1994 and returned to her old corporate-law firm, Mudge Rose Guthrie Alexander & Ferdon, as a partner. In September 1995, Palmer joined the powerhouse firm of Latham & Watkins, where she specializes in intellectual-property litigation. In May 1995,

Donald F. Ferrarone forsook the migraines of Southeast Asian counter-narcotics work to head the DEA's Houston division. It is a prestigious domestic posting; only New York and Miami have larger staffs among the DEA's nineteen U.S. divisions. William F. Beachner retired from the United Nations in 1994. At last report, he worked as a consultant for ASEAN, the Southeast Asia regional economic cooperation alliance.

Retired Army Lieutenant Colonel James G. "Bo" Gritz has a variety of lucrative, ultraconservative interests. In addition to developing Almost Heaven, a survivalist-oriented real-estate venture in Idaho, he hosts "Freedom Call," a nationally syndicated radio talk show, and travels the country with David Scott Weekly teaching combat, first-aid, and personal-security skills to the public at SPIKE (Specially Prepared Individuals for Key Events) seminars. Lance E. Trimmer remains a Montana P.I. Vinnie Arnone moved home to Massachusetts from Thailand in 1994 and edits a weekly newspaper in suburban Boston.

Jon Stuen-Parker has taken his needle-exchange program to Thailand, Burma, Vietnam, and Singapore. Tom "The Sailor" Williams' guardian angel has worked overtime. After receiving several thousand dollars from a car-accident insurance settlement, The Sailor tried to go straight. He bought a truck, which he promptly rolled over on the Maine Turnpike in a spectacular accident. After a hospital stay and detox, The Sailor bought a motorcycle, which he soon wrecked in another, near-fatal crash. When he got out of the hospital in late 1994, he moved to California. His current whereabouts are unknown.

The potency of The Sailor's drug of choice is undiminished, according to the Domestic Monitor Program, the DEA's street-buy survey. Average retail-level purity climbed to 40 percent by the spring of 1995. Purity levels in Philadelphia (74 percent), Boston (73 percent), and New York City (69 percent) were even higher. Intravenous drug use remains a major vector in the spread of AIDS in the United States and in Southeast Asia. Burma has the world's highest rates of infection among IV-drug users, nearly 75 percent, according to the U.N. International Drug Control Program.

Gracious Thailand continues its headlong plunge towards public-health disaster. By 1995, the kingdom had almost eight hundred thousand HIV cases; more than 40 percent of its AIDS-related deaths occurred in the northern provinces of Chiang Rai and Phayao. At an international AIDS conference held last September in Chiang Mai, speakers warned that the epicenter of the epidemic had shifted inexorably from sub-Saharan Africa to Asia.

"We are losing the fight," said John Dwyer, president of the AIDS Society for Asia and the Pacific. "Things are going to get worse, not better, unless we do things smartly." According to projections, Thailand will have more than four million HIV-positive citizens by the end of the century, and upwards of one hundred thousand orphaned children whose parents will have succumbed to AIDS. But in Bangkok, the farang bars along Patpong and Soi Cowboy continue to rollick, all except for Lucy's Tiger Den, which has been sold and renamed Demoiselle. Phoumano Nosavan still resides in Bangkok, still dreaming of liberating Laos, still swindling Americans with bogus information about alleged American POWs.

Thailand's relations with the United States have cooled since the July 1995 inauguration of prime minister Banharn Silpa-archa. Two of Banharn's key supporters, power brokers Narong Wongwan and Vatana Asavahame, have been denied U.S. visas because of suspected links to drug trafficking. Under Banharn's shaky coalition government, slippery General Chavalit Yongchaiyudh added a new title to his resume: Defense Minister.

Thailand's relations with Burma remain frayed. In early

1995 the Burmese Army and another of its proxy forces, the Democratic Karen Buddhist Army (DKBA), a disgruntled faction of the Christian-led Karen National Union, overran the last KNU border strongholds at Manerplaw and Kawmoorah. Thousands of ethnic refugees fled across the Moei River to Thailand. Disdaining Thai sovereignty, DKBA and Burmese troops crossed into Mae Hong Son and Tak Provinces to attack villages, loot refugee camps, and kidnap Karen leaders. That July, Burma closed the border for eight months after four Burmese were killed at sea by Thai fishermen. In early 1996, Tatmadaw offensives chased thousands of refugees from Karenni State into Mae Hong Son Province and routed the Karenni Army.

The SLORC rules Burma with a heavy, arrogant hand. The Lady, Daw Aung San Suu Kyi, was discharged from house arrest in July 1995, but SLORC has blocked her from leading the political party she helped to establish and continues to detain and harass her supporters.

"I have been released, that is all," said The Lady, who urged foreign nations to withhold investment until democracy has been restored.

Under President Clinton, the United States initiated a confusing two-track position on Burma, condemning SLORC for human-rights violations but supporting the military regime's counter-narcotics efforts. The conflicting goals of the State Department, which has pushed democracy and human rights, and the DEA, which believes SLORC has not gotten credit for its counter-narcotics work, have created a nasty interagency feud. When DEA special agent Richard A. Horn was recalled from Burma, he took the unusual step of filing a civil suit against the top American diplomat in Burma, *chargé d'affaires* Franklin P. Huddle, Jr., for harassment—including the tapping of his telephone—stemming from policy disputes. All documents filed in the suit are under seal in U.S. District Court in Washington, D.C.

Jay F. Sullivan never did give up his search for American prisoners of war in Southeast Asia. Despite General Khun Sa's discouraging news about POWs, Sullivan's foray into Shan State had given him a taste to which his man in Bangkok, Phoumano Nosavan, could not cater. Sullivan had to see the black hole of Laos for himself. In November 1994, I found myself once again on a Bangkok-bound flight, riding shotgun alongside my obsessed friend. After Ho Mong, I figured I owed it to him. With the same freeze-dried stores of beef stew and twice the amount of Absolut vodka, we four-wheeled down the Ho Chi Minh Trail to become the first American civilians to reach Attapu Province in extreme southeastern Laos in a quarter century. Sullivan has since returned to the far reaches of the Laotian panhandle nine times.

My four-day series on Khun Sa, Shan State, and the resurgent heroin epidemic began in the Boston *Sunday Herald* on June 12, 1994. Two days later, the double murders of Nicole Brown Simpson and Ronald Goldman dominated the front page; "Mainline: The Heroin Trail" was brushed aside in the frenzy over O. J. Simpson. It was a valuable journalistic lesson: no matter how much planning, risk, and effort went into an exclusive story about a timely topic, a celebrity murder case always got bigger play. And about the same time that O. J. was dominating the headlines, my wife Maria accidentally threw away a small paper packet containing the rubies I had bought her. Their current whereabouts are unknown.

A year to the day I returned home from Shan State, Maria gave birth to our first child, Timothy Otis. March 9, 1995. A day divisible by three. A very auspicious day, according to the Burmese.

ACKNOWLEDGMENTS

Many of the people I met in the course of my rambles through Southeast Asia are included in this narrative; their contributions are obvious, but other valuable people and institutions are not mentioned and I would be remiss if I did not cite their assistance.

First and foremost, I owe my wife, Maria, and my young son, Timothy, a debt that can never be paid off in rubies, jade, or even shiitake mushrooms. They allowed me the countless hours away from home that were required to complete this project. My gratitude also goes out to my parents, Gerald and Nancy Cox, my mother-in-law, Doracy Bahia Cahill, and her niece, Maria Norman Velasquez, who all picked up my domestic slack as deadlines loomed.

Although their assistance is apparent throughout this book, I must convey my deep thanks to Barry Flynn and Jay F. Sullivan. It would have been impossible to enter Ho Mong without Flynn's help; that he got us in and out of Shan State safely is to his everlasting credit. Sullivan's optimism kept me going on the numerous occasions when it seemed I would never get beyond the "border problems." Selfless, experienced, cool headed, Jay was a terrific traveling companion. I am lucky to count him as a friend.

Kevin R. Convey, the Boston *Herald*'s managing editor for features, shaped and edited this material into its original newspaper form and vetted early chapters of my manuscript.

Publisher Patrick J. Purcell, editor Andrew F. Costello, Jr., and his predecessor, Kenneth A. Chandler, planted the seed for this project by sending me on assignment to Southeast Asia on two different occasions, a major commitment for a tabloid newspaper whose mission has always been local news.

The *Herald*'s information technology genius, Emmanuel "Manny" Korkodilos, worked Macintosh magic throughout this project, while national/foreign editor Christy George kept me abreast of wire-service reports related to the Far East. *Herald* reporters were never less than encouraging about my outside work, but special mention must be made of my overworked features coworkers, past and present—Dana Bisbee, Matthew Diebel, Jane Dornbusch, M. A. J. McKenna, Jill Radsken, Eleanor Roberts, Stephanie Schorow, Beth Teitell, Linda Tischler, and Sonia Turek.

This trip might never have become a book had Douglas Preston, an author whose talent is exceeded only by his generosity to near strangers, not introduced me to his agent, Thomas Wallace, who was willing to take a chance on an unknown writer with a half-formed plan. I also owe an enormous debt to Marian Wood, my editor at Henry Holt, for her gimlet-eyed work on this project. As a first-time author, I am extremely fortunate to have someone of her caliber and experience.

Two travel agents, Nancy Storer of American Express Travel in Boston and Kate Maxwell of Absolute Asia in New York, took it as personal challenges to book me on obscure planes, trains, and steamers throughout the Far East. Avenue Victor Hugo Book Store, the Boston Public Library, the Bostonian Society, the New England Historic Genealogical Society, the Peabody Essex Museum, and the Widener Library at Harvard University were invaluable scholarly resources.

At the United States State Department, Thailand and Burma Affairs desk officers John Lyle and David Young generously provided information, as did Lynne G. Platt, Olga McGrath, and Lynette Williams of the Bureau of International Narcotics Matters. So, too, did William Hass of the United Nations International Drugs Control Program in New York. I must also acknowledge the assistance of several Drug Enforcement Administration officials: in Boston, Michael A. Cuniff, Michelle Dello Iacono, and Jack Kelly; in Houston, Robert Paez; in New York, Nicholas J. Caruso and John M. Tully; in Washington, Donald Joseph and William Ruzzamenti.

I am grateful for the advice of retired United States Army Major Mark Smith, an old Bangkok hand, as well as the assistance of Rotjana Phraesrithong of the Duang Prateep Foundation, who kindly helped me negotiate the mazes of Klong Toey. Professor Mya Maung of Boston College, Simon Billenness of the Massachusetts Burma Roundtable, Kevin Heppner of the Karen Human Rights Group, and Harn Yaunghwe, the publisher of *Burma Alert*, provided information and answers to my many arcane questions about Burmese and Shan matters. Harvard graduate student Linda Yueh took time out of her hectic schedule to fill me in on Chinese symbolism.

Finally, I would like to express my thanks to the men and women of Burma who, at great personal risk, allowed me a glimpse behind the lacquer curtain. Their names will stay with me, close to my memories of their tragic, golden land.